WORKING LIKE A HOMOSEXUAL

Edited by Michèle Aina Barale,

Jonathan Goldberg, Michael Moon, and

Eve Kosofsky Sedgwick

WORKING

LIKE A HOMOSEXUAL

✄ CAMP, CAPITAL, CINEMA ✄

MATTHEW TINKCOM

DUKE UNIVERSITY PRESS

Durham and London

2002

© 2002 Duke University Press

All rights reserved

Printed in the United States of America on

acid-free paper ♾ Designed by Amy Ruth Buchanan

Typeset in Bembo by Tseng Information Systems, Inc.

Library of Congress Cataloging-in-Publication Data

appear on the last printed page of this book.

Warhol Images, Copyright 2001

The Andy Warhol Museum, Pittsburgh, PA,

A Museum of the Carnegie Institute.

THE DISTRIBUTION OF THIS BOOK

IS SUPPORTED BY A GENEROUS GRANT

FROM THE GILL FOUNDATION.

Man's heart is a
wonderful thing, especially
when carried in the purse.

KARL MARX

CONTENTS

ACKNOWLEDGMENTS

Despite our best intentions, we claim the name of author when we know how much work and affection such a nomination covers over. This book is no exception. So many people were involved in the research and thought in this volume that another might be written to honor their support and companionship, and chances are that I might omit the name of someone whose goodwill made this book possible. The thought pains me, and I hope no kindness is forgotten.

I am indebted to several friends for their love and companionship. Amy Villarejo, Barbara White, Sally Meckling, Madhava Prasad, Joy Van Fuqua, and Elayne Tobin were among the best teachers I had in graduate school, and my teachers in graduate school were more than that; they were intellectual models who made this work a pleasure: Jane Feuer, Janet Staiger, Eric Clarke, Lucy Fischer, and, finally, a scholar who offers new forms of exciting intellectual work and makes them a joy that I carry with me, Marcia Landy. Many people were kind to me at moments when it wasn't clear whether this project was viable and I needed some guidance and cheer: Steven Cohan, Ina Hark, Douglas Crimp, Colin MacCabe, Eric Smoodin, Caren Kaplan, Jonathan Arac, Carol Kay, Paul Bové, Eve Sedgwick, Paul Smith, Carol Stabile, John Groch, and Allen Larson. Timothy Credle, Stewart Waller, Alison Hoff, Patrick Clark, Jamie Poster, Anna McCarthy, and Tara McPherson are the best of friends. Diana Reed and Barbara Fine bought me dinners and told me I could finish this work. My colleagues at Georgetown, Pamela Fox, Kim Hall, Ed Ingebretsen, Colleen Cotter, Christine So, and Anne Cubilie made my entry to faculty life an immense pleasure; Michael Ragussis showed me how to write a book. Ken Wissoker not only is the editor who asked me to keep working on this project and waited patiently for it but also extended love and friendship. Cathy Davidson single-handedly reminds me that intellectuals can and should work to remake the world, and I send her a big valentine.

Ned Comstock at the archives at the University of Southern California and Barbara Johnson at the Margaret Herrick Library of the Motion Picture Academy of Arts and Sciences are astonishing resources, and the Minnelli chapter could not have been done without their help. Peter Haldeman and Peter Jones in Los Angeles were sweet to a stranger in a strange place, and George Feltenstein at MGM told me I was right to keep working. Matt Wrbican, John Smith, Margery King, and Greg Pierce at the Andy Warhol Museum, Callie Angell at the Whitney Museum of American Art, and Neil Prinz at the Andy Warhol Foundation were wonderfully generous and made possible much of the work on Warhol and Anger. John Waters let me ask my questions and answered them with patience and good humor. Ryan Cook kindly helped with the illustrations; Heather Kerst and Mary Madden helped to complete the final manuscript.

The Lambda Foundation of Pittsburgh took a risk early in this project and provided the funds for research in Los Angeles for the Minnelli chapter; an Andrew Mellon Doctoral Fellowship at the University of Pittsburgh allowed me to complete a first draft of this research. Summer research grants and a Junior Sabbatical from Georgetown College and the Graduate School allowed me the chance to rethink the entire project once more, and I am grateful to Leona Fisher, Joseph Sitterson, Martin Irvine, and Gerald Mara for making that possible. I thank the anonymous readers of the book manuscript.

James and Alberta Tinkcom, and my siblings, Mary Tinkcom, Martha Brisky, Margaret Listopad, and Michael Tinkcom, are the best of families. Matthew Veltkamp sees the goodness and the camp in the world every day, and for that and for everything else, I say again: all my love.

INTRODUCTION

The plural of demoniacal texture which opposes text to work can
bring with it fundamental changes in reading, and precisely in areas
where monologism appears to be the Law: certain of the "texts" of
Holy Scripture traditionally recuperated by theological monism
(historical and analogical) will perhaps offer themselves to a
diffraction of meanings (finally, that is to say, to a materialist
reading), while the Marxist interpretation of works, so far resolutely
monistic, will be able to materialize itself more by pluralizing itself
(if, however, the Marxist "institutions" allow it).
— *Roland Barthes*

You better work.
— *Rupaul*

This book begins by admitting to a sin, or at the very least, to an act of
intellectual bad taste: It takes camp seriously. Even more appalling, it
begins with the assertion that the history of the now world-engulfing
experience called modernity needs to attend to a variety of critical responses beyond those called Marxism, and that camp can be understood
as one such response. Compounding its offense is this book's driving
impulse to see camp as a philosophy of modernity that illuminates capital in the past five decades in ways that the "institutions of Marxism,"
as Roland Barthes calls them, frequently do not. Indeed, as Barthes suggests, capital's widening effects need to be seen as multiple and dif-
fracted, not solely because there are a multitude of intellectual responses
that can be understood as engaged forms of critique of the dynamics

of modernity (and modernization and modernisms), but because to become aware of them, we need to understand how such engagements
with the effects of the political economies of profit may and may not
coincide. This book situates two philosophical practices of modernity,
Marxism and camp, as they each can offer assessments of capital's contradictory tendencies to enforce its defining logics of contemporary culture and political economy, and thus decides to sustain its bad taste by
continually considering camp as something more than the seemingly
lightweight pleasures of consumption to which it has been relegated in
most of the literature on the subject.[1] In this regard, this book extracts
from Barthes's comment the sense of "work" as both the open-ended
object to be given to a variety of readings and work as labor—in this
case, the sense of camp as a form of queer labor that has shaped a way
of knowing capital in its lived dimensions within production by queer
male intellectuals. In taking camp seriously, we should be clear at the
beginning of this book that the legacy of Karl Marx's critique of capital
and the camp intellectual work of queer men in the Western metropolis
perhaps seem to have little in common, and in point of fact it may be a
camp act on my part to attempt to put them together. In the former, we
rediscover the somber-faced legacy of the German philosophical tradition, the heir of Kant and Hegel, going about his work of turning the
world on its head and dreaming of a human society freed from the constraints of routinized labor and necessity; while the latter summons the
vision of some queer men finding, in the slightest slouch of a movie
heroine's hip and the snort of smoke from her flared nostril, a utopian
world of plenitude and the fun to be had with the most debased of cultural forms.

Against such apparent failures of Marxism and camp to concur in
their critical dimensions, *Working Like a Homosexual* proposes that Marxist and camp intellectual practices derive their energies from similar but
hardly identical interests in upending, in their disparate ways, the world
that capital has brought about and, further, wonders how shared features
of these two ways of producing critical knowledges of modernity can be
understood in relation to each other. Taking Barthes's prompt that the
interpretation of contemporary culture simultaneously be grounded in
the realities of life under capitalism (his insistence to become, ultimately,
materialist) and be aware of the subtle and playful movements of the
sign in which being materialist does not mean being vulgarly materalist,
in this book I align particular features of Marxist critique with the cine-

matic visions of four queer men to suggest that both Marxist interrogations of the unstable behaviors of value *and* camp intellectual practices
are occupied with similar features of modernity and capitalism. This
conjoining of Marxist critical thought and camp is perhaps a heuristic
device that yields an absurdity in seeing the enterprises of Marxist critique and camp play in conjunction; it remains for the reader to decide
if the strategies of this book can offer a new way of thinking about what
it means for scholars of Marx and for practitioners of camp (who are
not solely queer men) to work alongside one another in their attempts
to make sense of a world defined by profit and its value codings as they
are reigned over by capital. Although I would want to trace a longer
history of camp beginning in the nineteenth century with the appearance of Oscar Wilde and his philosophy of surfaces in that moment
of industrialization (and extending to a number of figures on different
national stages and in various moments—Marcel Proust, Sergei Eisenstein, Jean Cocteau, James Whale, Rainer Fassbinder, Pedro Almodovar), for the scope of this project, I limit my investigations to a handful
of post–World War II American filmmakers, specifically Vincente Minnelli, Andy Warhol, Kenneth Anger, and John Waters. Through their
work I hope to demonstrate the continuities between Marxist critique
and camp sensibilities and to suggest further ways in which the problem of value has been a long-standing challenge for many intellectuals,
camp ones among them.

It should be clear from the outset that this is *not* a Marxist treatment
of camp, in which I frame the camp object of scrutiny within a Marxist
critical legacy. I avoid speaking of Marxism as the lens through which to
make sense of the camp text but want to play Marx's writings and camp
intellectual production (including film) one off the other to illuminate
the contours of these two philosophical enterprises; in this sense, the
book at hand is not an anthropology of camp beheld by a Marxist critic
so much as a way of taking camp's intellectual work seriously through
what we can know of capital through Marx's critique. My hope here
is not simply to prioritize one form of knowledge production, either
Marxism or camp, over the other, in that there are numerous hazards
for deciding that the instances of camp cultural production that this
book examines might be made sense of through the language of Marxist knowledge production; most significant among those pitfalls is that
camp could only appear as a form of accommodation for the queer men
whom I discuss. In this regard, were they situated in a more typical

Marxist ideological analysis, Minnelli, Warhol, Anger, and Waters might seem only to have offered visions of how the subjects of capital might temporarily evade capital's most deleterious effects by ironizing and dismissing the force of capital's value coding in its exploitation of human labor and the maximizing of profit. Rather than deciding in advance on this argument, which approximates a version of false consciousness (where more orthodox Marxist assessments deem such endeavors as, at best, distraction and, at worst, capitulation), I want to explore camp as a philosophy in its own right, one that offers explanations of how the relation between labor and the commodity is lived in the day-to-day by dissident sexual subjects who arrive at their own strategies for critique *and* pleasure.

It is true to say that the critical strategies contained here in the name of Marxism contain a perhaps more "rigorous" (i.e., internally coherent) program for examining the ways that language and representation are themselves caught in the value codings of capitalist cultures. It is equally important, though, to understand the tactics through which queer men of a particular historical epoch have made sense of their frequent omission from representation and sought to invent their own language to appear, in a particular critical fashion, in those complicated moments of exchange under capital. While these tactics, gathered in this book under the name of camp, are less about a larger strategy for the subversion and supersession of capital in the name of a socialist future, they reveal what it is that the camp intellectual can know about capital that a reader of Marx might not (such as the pleasures of the discarded commodity, the efforts to recuperate it and make sense of it, the kinds of historical knowledge about capital that such a commodity might reveal). Further, my examination of camp emerges less from a concern with a "progressive" narrative of gay identity of which camp seems not to have been a part, and more from the ways that camp forms a philosophy of how one can and cannot (or must and must not) participate in the labor of humans to produce the world for themselves, famously, under conditions not of their own making. This book attempts to pervert Marx (in the sense of overturning his writings in order to renew them again) through camp; the world of capitalism as Marx grasped it seems sometimes unconcerned with the ways that some subjects of capital forge their own compelling understanding of themselves within it. Simultaneously, none of the queer male figures whose works I discuss might be summoned as revolutionary figures seeking social change based on questions of social and economic justice, and the fact that many members of contemporary human societies invent representational sleights of hand to signify their social presence would, in many Marxist accounts, simply point to how we may have made the dismal truths of life under capital into something tolerable. That these subjects so seldom invoke discourses of struggle, revolution, and liberation perhaps only serves to compound matters, and it should be clear that the task of this book is not to reclaim camp simplistically as a revolutionary practice. So naive a pronouncement would only make foolish the work of camp, and the intent here is in fact to argue that the already seeming foolishness of camp—its apparent critical weightlessness, its seeming unconcern with the problems of finance capital and the subsequent international divisions of labor, in short camp's frequent refusal to be taken seriously— allows for a critical stance to arise *because* one might never expect such an outlook to appear where it does in the queer male subcultures of the postwar United States.

Despite the apparent distance between the sober, critical assessments of more orthodox Marxist pronouncements and the playful, inconsistent strategies of camp, I would argue, we can understand camp as a tendency, indeed an insistence on, continually examining the contradictions that capital gives rise to on a daily basis, specifically through the ruptures and fluctuations of monetary and cultural value; and I would heuristically define camp as an alibi for queer men to labor within those contradictions, when paradoxically it would seem that no subject is ever prohibited from exerting him- or herself on capital's behalf. Camp functions as an alibi (in the sense of being elsewhere) because the men whose productions this book addresses found themselves caught in a specific historical bind of entering capitalist approximations of labor's contribution to value, and they did so during some of the most virulently homophobic periods in American history. The bind of this position may to some seem poignant and curiously outdated, while others (queers among, but they are not alone in this predicament) will see homologies with their own situations: while one is seldom prohibited from offering his or her energies to capital, the historical emergence of the category of the "homosexual" and the firm, violent strictures on claiming that social nomination as anything but a form of pathology has meant that the efforts of queer subjects *to labor, to engage in the spheres of production,* allow us to (re)discover two countervailing tendencies at work. First, the capacity to labor on the material world is the modernist predication of every subject's social worth. Second, within the domain of production, the impulse to ensure that one's habits of desire fail to signify is the only way of surviving within the censorious regulation of sexuality that is not determined by, but too often coincides with, capital's social regulation.

"Never pay more than a dollar for anything, otherwise you just don't get as much": Value and Its Fascinations

The cumbersome name of Marxism might be too large an enterprise to distill in relation to camp, and in this book the particular insights of Marx into the unstable and dynamic fluctuations of value are the specific enterprise that I invoke in writing about Marx's legacy.[2] The now lengthy history of the many intellectuals who have struggled to remake the world with Marx's critique in mind challenges this project at its inception; is this the same Marxism of the revolutionary struggles of workers, the same Marxism reviled by a host of conservatizing practices around the world in different spaces at different historical moments? In short, no. Those vital legacies of Marx are not encompassed here, but this Marx is the writer who offered a knowledge that not only does capital reorganize human societies around the worth of labor in the production of commodities but its ensuing crises of value will themselves simultaneously defy explanation all the while that such explanations themselves become more necessary and more strange and bewildering. (These last we more customarily call "ideology.") The camp visions made available through the cinematic work I discuss, in point of fact, demonstrate how at odds many queer intellectuals have felt to the very revolutionary movements that would want to seize the historical stage for the emergence of a different set of social relations.[3]

I refrain here from rehearsing at length Marx's critical analysis of the workings of capital (value, both in terms of use and exchange, money, profit, labor, and exploitation) but instead move to his comments that are motivating for this particular theory of camp. In his critical provocations of the *Grundrisse,* Marx asserts that the political economy of capitalism is most forcefully conceived through the category of production; he then distinguishes each feature of economy (distribution, exchange, consumption) as a moment of production in order to illuminate how humans under capital are producing themselves and commodities. Working on the problem of whether exchange value could be in fact not solely an innovation of capitalism but a historically long-standing feature of human life that capitalism has seized on in the expansion of value, he remarks that "exchange value leads an antediluvian existence," which is not to say that it is positively true of pre- and noncapitalist societies, but that it could reside for the philosopher and the historian as a coincidental hallmark of those societies. In a remarkable passage about the status of exchange value, where he moves to include intellectual work as one of these forms of production, he writes that

> the consciousness for which comprehending thought is most real in man, for which the world is only real when comprehended (and philosophical consciousness is of this nature), mistakes the movement of categories for the real act of production (which unfortunately receives only its impetus from outside), whose result is the world; that is true—here we have, however, again a tautology—in so far as the concrete aggregate, as a thought aggregate, the concrete subject of our thought, is in fact a product of thought, of comprehension; not, however, in the sense of a product of a self-emanating conception which works outside of and stands above observation and imagination, but of a conceptual working-over of observation and imagination.[4]

Consciousness produces the world through its own categories but can only produce the world of which human labor and imagination (critical imagination included) are capable. Marx carefully insists on the power of his own particularly weighted category (production) and yet also gestures to other habits of thought that might themselves *produce* knowledge that is not necessarily mystification. Of interest for my argument is Marx's allowance that any particular abstraction (production, value, exchange) needs continually to be pressed to answer what feature of the material world it describes. This notoriously challenging question, of the relation of the world to a language that might represent it, is one that Marx takes up in the name of the appearances of value, and virtually all of the ensuing project of *Capital* can be read as the struggle to find a *universal* language of representation. Marx speaks of money's function to "supply commodities with the material for the expression of their values, or to represent their values as magnitudes of the same denomination, qualitatively equal, and quantitatively comparable . . . it thus serves as a *universal measure of value*" (italics mine), and here he is inadvertently encompassed by his own philosophical category, giving his project over to what Barthes calls the "monologism of the Law," where the singularity of the category bars any perverse, aberrant, playful reading (Barthes's "diffraction").[5]

This is no small thing, for although labor in Marx's work remains relatively "simple," to use his word, throughout his critical elaborations value evades the conception of which he writes in the foregoing quotation, and indeed, to my mind, demands a "working-over of observation and imagination" on which he could only begin to speculate. Marx manages to stabilize value for his analysis by making it a function of money, in which the equivalences among commodities (where a linen coat is said to be worth a measure of wheat or iron) are measured through the seemingly universal form of money; and when money and commodities are circulating, money manages, according to Marx, to "represent only different modes of existence of value itself, the money its general mode, and the commodity its particular, or, so to say, disguised mode."[6] This is a startling turnabout, because here Marx argues that the commodity in fact seems to conceal something about itself, something it had not needed or managed to disguise prior to its expression as an equivalent to money.

It is tempting to say that the commodity is failing to disclose its status as an object of use, but Marx's nostalgia for precapitalist forms of value notwithstanding, we might wonder if in fact what is concealed is the particular human exertion demanded for its making, which elsewhere Marx suggests is rendered abstract through capital's demand for "labor-power," that is, the demand that human exertion become interchangeable and equivalent. One might read the history of capital as, in fact, the overpowering insistence that all humans make themselves adequate for their abstraction and insertion into the processes of production. Arguing in a contrary direction, I wonder if the commodity's status as an object with some undisclosed feature of its historical moment of production that might be revealed in its movement through exchange might not be, at least sometimes, the fact of its having been shaped by some anomalous labor and laborer, and at this point camp emerges as an expression of such concealed efforts.

The unstable status of value, famously dissatisfying for its being corralled into "use" and "exchange" and through which Marx can note the discrepancies that money itself conceals (i.e., the difference between money as form of exchange and money as profit), is probably the place where we begin to notice the long-standing fascination of queer intellectuals with the commodity. Were it to move with relative ease through the processes of production and consumption in some stable register of value, there might be little interest, but in fact those processes break down both in the surfeit of sheer amount of things produced (i.e., the volume of commodities that capital is capable of putting into distribution) and in their stubborn refusal to be consumed in their totality and somehow returned to an allegedly organic form of decomposition. Instead, the value of the commodity persists to the degree that it rapidly becomes devalued, or put another way, the problem of the value of the commodity becomes more apparent when, after its initial immersion in the cycles of consumption called "fashion" (or even more temporally constrained, "fad"), it disproves a model of full and adequate consumption. This is where camp's critical energies become engaged with the commodity form, but rather than situate camp as a form of engagement appearing at the moment in which the commodity languishes after its tour through the industrial cycle described by Marx, I want to insist that camp can also be detected in the very forms of mass culture that call attention to their own tendency to become unfashionable. In short, what if certain commodities betrayed the knowledge that they were destined to become "useless"? Is this not potentially a critical knowledge that demands that the recipient acknowledge both his or her affection for that moment after the commodity's apparent terminus in the cycle of consumption and the wonderment that the thing embraced has been manufactured in order to arrive at this moment?

In making this claim, I have simultaneously to suggest that critical knowledge can appear in a variety of unexpected places, not least in the things of mass culture themselves, and we can thus think of the commodity (say, the film musical or the "trash" cult film) as, in a certain manner, "in drag," as it coyly gives up some secrets about its production while withholding other knowledge from unsuspecting viewers. While there has been an emphasis on rediscovering the political dimensions of the historical avant-garde in its relation to mass-cultural forms, we should equally be at pains to discover the political dimensions of camp in the popular form as a knowledge of, and delight in, the apparent uselessness that travels with the commodity in its trajectory toward the moment after its seeming consumption.[7] That camp's knowledges do not emerge easily for all spectators will frustrate some readers, not least those taught to universalize themselves insistently (i.e., like most liberal subjects, to see themselves as capable of all forms of knowing); I would argue that this is all the more tribute to camp's tactics of dissemblance, but it also allows us to remember that not all camp intellectuals are determined solely by sex/gender difference around the particular axis of male queerness.

Marx helps us to understand these figurations of value's wild fluctuations in camp productions because while we remain mindful of the long-standing confusion over the specific historical agent of camp (usually queer men, but as I discuss below, also women, teenagers, blacks), we should also keep in mind the force of production under capital, particularly in terms of how capital seeks to treat all labor as undifferentiable, even when the regimentations of industrial production demand the increased specificity of each task within the processes of production. Marx called this tendency, from the perspective of wealth, the abstraction of labor within the industrial mode:

> Indifference towards specific labours corresponds to a form of society in which individuals can with ease transfer from one labour to another, and where the specific kind is a matter for chance for them, hence of indifference. Not only has the category, labour, but labour in reality has here become the means of creating wealth in general, and has ceased to be organically linked with particular individuals in any specific form.[8]

Underlying Marx's stress on the apparent indifference toward the specificity of labor by those who profit from it is the sense that all tasks seem commensurate when performed for wages. The labor of queers within the alibi of camp, though, suggests that perhaps only the particular sensibility under scrutiny here could have had a hand in producing the films that I discuss. Homophobic social attitudes work in concert with the abstraction of labor to suppress homosexual camp style *and* specific kinds of work that are enabled by the camp emphasis on stylistic commodity differentiation, differentiation known quite often as fashion.

By theorizing camp as the result of labor by queers, this book displaces camp from being solely a hallmark of consumption to being more vitally situated in relation to the creation of profit. In this respect, I am treating camp as a strategy for being able to labor and simultaneously providing the opportunity for queers to use their labor to mark the product in ways unanticipated by Marx's account. The argument that camp emerges as a concealed knowledge that travels with some commodities begs another question about how the labor—specifically as Marx understood that category—that "congeals" within the commodity might also be accompanied by another form of human enterprise that cannot always be directly expressed (or made tangible) through its exchange for money; in short, the nexus of labor-commodity-money-value has another feature of queer subject's life that accompanies it—that of the frivolousness, the lack of apparent seriousness, that which we might call play and which Hannah Arendt called "work."

Labor and Work-as-Play

In her discussion of the category of labor in *The Human Condition*, Hannah Arendt corrects what she sees to be a key shortcoming in Marx's analysis: Marx, according to Arendt, fails to attend to the consequential distinction between labor and work. Ever the careful philologist, Marx seems to ignore the abiding presence (in most European languages and in the classical Hellenic philosophy to which he refers) between these two names of different human activities. Arendt insists that this omission of such a significant category signals Marx's resistance to encompassing theoretically those endeavors that stand alongside labor, which she labels "work." Whereas waged *labor* sponsors the production of commodities and subjects, according to Arendt, the efforts entailed by *work* are given to the production of something else, and the distinction would seem to function thus: labor is characterized as the ongoing, repetitive, dull task of scratching out a life from the world, but work appears in the acts by which humans create for themselves something recognizably outside of themselves by which they can know their relation to labor—in short, work seems something hidden from the forms of tacit and explicit compulsion to labor implied in the notion of subjectivity. Most subjects of capital are bound to capital through the regimentation of labor and the institutions of the family and school, implying that only a few can know work and its rewards. Further complicating matters is the fact that the division of labor between laborers and workers is not simply one of class but of access to forms of human endeavor (and work and its pleasures) made possible by the subjection of *others* to labor; Arendt tells us that the slaves of classical Mediterranean cultures could not *work* because their efforts secured something much more intangible, not least the apparent freedom of their overseers. She suggests that for slaves, "what they left behind them was their master's freedom," a freedom, paradoxically, to work. Summarily, the necessity of labor for some subjects allows for the luxury of work for others.

Despite the impulse to see work in itself as a utopian activity, whereby communist revolution might be seen to present an alternative world of fulfilled workers, Arendt suggests that

> all serious activities, irrespective of their fruits, are called labor, and every activity which is not necessary either for the life of the individual or for the life process of society is subsumed under playfulness. In these theories, which by echoing the current estimate of a laboring society on the theoretical level sharpen it and drive it into its inherent extreme, not even the "work" of the artist is left; it is dissolved into play and has lost its worldly meaning.[9]

Camp draws attention to the kinds of human activity of work that "loses its worldly meaning," in which some queer subjects fashion themselves neither to produce in wholesale the things for consumption—although queers too must labor—nor in fact even to appear as social beings who contribute enthusiastically to the "life processes of society." Because the prohibitions against the appearance of a language through which same-sex desire can be made to signify, camp stages the moments in which dissident same-sex subjects draw attention to the very labor (used specifically in Arendt's terms here) required to conceal themselves, the labor to produce themselves, and the work of camp.

Arendt offers that "play" (the negation of all profit-generating labor under the auspices of capital) becomes a deceptive category of human endeavor aside from labor, in that play is perhaps more akin to the classical conception of work. The realm of work-as-play is where subjects may glimpse another kind of exertion of themselves toward the material world that labor does not and cannot encompass. Vexing to our understanding of the imbrication of labor and work-as-play as activities undertaken under capital is that they move alongside each other and—like another of Marx's most famous concept-categories that deserves to be pulled critically asunder, that of money—they can appear to be the same thing. How, then, are we to know when we witness the *work* of camp as the labors of queer subjects are exerted in the production of the commodities of entertainment? Although queer men are largely not exempt from the conditions of labor, this book argues that their work is often disguised as precisely through what Arendt calls its "playfulness" and through other forms of negation to labor—laziness, lack of seriousness, indifference to the formal logics of the popular commodity of the motion picture. It is tempting to label camp, then, as an exemplary form of work undertaken by queers as they sometimes distance themselves from the commodity—through the camp derision for distinctions of good and bad taste and its enactments of parody of the mass form (drag, for example)—and were this book to emphasize solely the aspects of camp that seem to dwell in the sphere of leisure and consumption, the additive function of Arendt's notion of work would seem adequate. The problem of situating camp in relation to production, then, means combatting the confusion of labor and work—and we might most often decide that since the examples of these chapters take aim at cinema, we would continually discover the labor of queers that covers over the work of consumption. There is a further pitfall, to the degree that the emphasis on the "play" of work in Arendt's scheme tempts one to ignore the strictures under which labor is undertaken: as mentioned previously, strictures not only on the queer laborer that are similar to those on all who labor but also on their ability to name themselves as queer. With this in mind, in this book I designate the camp valences of these texts, as they are *produced* as camp, as the marks of queer labor that allow for visions of work to emerge, if you will, in moments where these films emphasize the utopian and dystopian possibilities that can appear in relation to mass generic forms. It then becomes less coincidental that camp becomes a designation of the pleasures unleashed in the sphere of consumption of popular culture that seem unwarranted by it; camp reading practices, so amply treated in the accounts of Susan Sontag and Andrew Ross, detect the work that underpins the labor of queer intellectuals who produce the camp object.

Despite the shift in emphasis from consumption to production that this theory of camp insists on, there are several key distinctions between Marxist critique and camp play that it is helpful to identify; I would in summary fashion name a few as such:

Marx	*Camp*
value	cheapness
labor	work-as-play
exploitation	performance
use	misuse
history	nostalgia

If the (conventional) Marxist account of the world of capital organizes its critique through the sense that labor is the predication of value, and most labor is extended through the political economy via the use of one human by another—hence, exploitation—then the function of historical consciousness is to discover the forms of social differentiation from one form of human economic life to another, leading eventually to the eradication of class-based difference. Yet through the categories of negation beheld in camp intellectual work, we discover another version of value's derivation: not solely through labor but through the disguised work-as-play into which queer subjects enfold labor and through which they discover that not only is exploitation the rule of their labor and work-as-play but performance itself—an enactment of a social self that engages with restrictions about the queer laborer naming himself or, more importantly, his efforts as queer—is demanded before such efforts enter the domains of production. Last, the camp forms of historical consciousness that recuperate prior moments are nostalgic ones, but nostalgia understood (as its etymology reminds us) as the pain of the past, the remembrance not of history as an act of fidelity (i.e., history as realist text) but of history as the past now situated in camp stylistics. For example, when in *Scorpio Rising* Kenneth Anger cuts footage from a historical epic about the life of Jesus into images of the biker orgy, the queer features of the life of Christ become apparent not so much as a fact of historical veracity as they do about the meanings of those popular cinematic images for contemporary erotic imaginings.

Kitsch versus Camp, or The Discovery of the Queer Agent of Bad Taste

Anger's dynamic cutting in *Scorpio Rising* from biker boy imagery to Christian figurations has been an important avant-garde landmark, but the images he handles—the pop-pietà stylings of the Jesus footage, the already frayed comics page from the newspaper, a scorpion-in-glass paperweight souvenir—could also enjoy nomination as conspicuous pieces of kitsch. Indeed, the crises that emerge around forms of social distinction that adhere to the commodity, particularly in its moment of having become passé, have vexed left intellectuals for quite some time, and while the effects of montage in this example ultimately serve to situate so much cultural debris within a larger dialectic of production and memory, there remains perhaps the sense that the flotsam of consumerism might always carry with it a taint so powerful that it cannot be overcome. Kitsch was an important problem of cultural politics for the critical projects of Marxism to the degree that its historical sponsors could hardly be identified through the logics of class difference; in 1964, Susan Sontag nominated homosexuals as kitsch's intellectual agents and camp as its subcultural manifestation, effectively removing kitsch (through its renomination) to the sphere of consumption. Although kitsch and camp share a fascination with the bad object of consumption, they can hardly be considered identical, to the degree that camp stages the kitsch object in order to understand its conditions for coming into being alongside the domain of bourgeois good taste.

In their essay "Enlightenment as Mass Deception," Max Horkheimer and Theodor Adorno invoke the commercialization of culture as the dying gasp of the romantic individual, for the oppressive stylization of the culture industry, its apparent but nonexistent variation of the product, seeks to banish consciousness to the realm of consumption through repetition. "The need which might resist central control has already been suppressed by the control of the individual consciousness," and

> that factor in a work of art which enables it to transcend reality certainly cannot be detached from style; but it does not consist of the harmony actually realized, of any doubtful unity of form and content, within and without, of individual and society; it is to be found in those features in which discrepancy appears: *in the necessary failure of the passionate striving for identity* [italics mine].[10]

The advent of an administered culture from above creates for itself the perfectly adequate recipients of that culture who, despite the incommensurate relation between form and content of mass culture, are said to offer little resistance. The discrepancies of the mass culture object, however, the tension between its style and its evaporating content and between its steamrolling forms of address that really seem to address no one specifically at all, are where Horkheimer and Adorno detect the possibility for the viewer who might, for other reasons, not answer the call of the culture industries. Their frustration, though, in locating the subject for whom such an object might be of intellectual interest emerges when we consider how little the queer agents of camp were invested in a form of identity they describe; in short, we might through camp reformulate their assessment as the passionate failure to strive for a compulsory identity.

In a curious diversion, Horkheimer and Adorno subsequently discuss the phenomenon of what they term "light art." Light art is unlike mass-cultural forms in that it cannot solely be construed as ideological; it does not answer the claims on the everyday in the way that realist codes might, and it fails to ascend into the realm of bourgeois representation, but not for reasons that we might expect. The failure of light art is that its mimicry of high art carries with it the bad faith of the corporatizing spirit, the knowledge that indeed there remain subjects largely exiled from the leisure to consume the pieties of the mass form. "Serious art has been withheld from those for whom the hardship and oppression of life make a mockery of seriousness, and who must be glad if they can use time not spent at the production line just to keep going," suggest Horkheimer and Adorno.

> Light art has been the shadow of autonomous art. It is the social bad conscience of serious art. The truth which the latter necessarily lacked because of its social premises gives the other the semblance of legitimacy. The division itself is the truth: it does at least express the negativity of the culture which the different spheres constitute. Least of all can the antithesis be reconciled by absorbing light into serious art, or vice versa. But that is what the culture industry attempts.[11]

Attempts, but does not necessarily succeed at. The negation of high art, light art and its other nominations such as "amusement" or "distraction" give truth to the lie that all of mass culture's consumers can accommodate themselves to its various operations. And notwithstanding the writers' claims that such important deficiencies as are implied in light art become irrelevant because of the "totality of the culture industry," their invocation of an aspect of cultural production or consumption (it remains unclear in their account) that is in excess of high art and mass culture tells us that even their analysis had to sustain a category for alternative visions.

Without any particular examples of light art that Horkheimer or Adorno might have offered, we can only speculate that they are invoking precapitalist forms of pleasure. ("Amusement and all the elements of the culture industry existed long before the latter came into existence.")[12] There remains the possibility of distractions that pertain to pleasures not to be had within mass-cultural consumption, not simply prelapsarian but forged and vitalized in the prosaic now. Distraction might not only take the form of diversion of attention from the drudgery of work and domesticity, but distraction from the very forms of mass culture itself when it fails to complete its address to its working-class viewers. In short, there is the possibility for some form of response not implied by mass culture, and here we discover Horkheimer and Adorno allowing for a greater latitude in kind of both production and reception of the mass form than even subsequent New Left critics such as Clement Greenberg or Dwight MacDonald would seem to have tolerated.

Indeed, subsequent revisions on Horkheimer's and Adorno's insights have detected this possibility and been quick to fend it off, for the pleasures of forging one's own reading might endanger the totality of the culture industry *and* its critiques from various quarters. Even as they argued that a more complex and complete integration of high art and mass culture was taking place (obviously, in the latter's interests), critics such as Greenberg and MacDonald forestalled alternative relations to mass culture even as they argued that varieties of reception were the hallmark of a high art, which mass forms mimic in the name of product differentiation. "Where there is an avant-garde, generally we also find a rear-garde," wrote Greenberg in the late 1930s, and his horror at the prospects of a mass culture that imitated high culture gave rise to Greenberg's formulations about kitsch.[13] Kitsch, according to Greenberg, formed a product of industrialization that circulated widely and offered its consumers the feeling that they were participating in new democratic forms of high art. Imbedded in the marketplace and seeking, in the end, only returns on its investments, kitsch heralded a fake universalizing of cultural consumption in the name of increased wages and the expansion of leisure among the working classes. (Worth noting is that Greenberg saw both American mass culture and Soviet socialist realism as falling into the same trap, watering down the innovations of technique in avant-garde painting, music, and film, and all of this executed in such a way that recently arrived proletarians might find themselves included in "classless" nationalist discourses.) Apart from its status as a debasement of avant-garde innovations for either entertainment or propaganda, for Greenberg the primary problem with kitsch was that it contained its own aesthetic response, and yet its productive historical agent was difficult to identify without resorting to estimations of false consciousness.

The legacy of Horkheimer and Adorno's assessments, felt most extensively in the American setting in the hostile stance of most intellectuals toward popular forms until the 1960s, meant that the very complexity of response that serves as an index of high culture had to be withheld from discussions of popular forms; the net effect of this is that no ironizing or playful engagement could be entertained, and here camp, even as a negative effect, seems a remote possibility. Exemplary in this regard are the variety of sociological approaches to matters of taste witnessed in the work of Herbert J. Gans in the United States and Pierre Bourdieu in France, where the solemn tone of the critical enterprise in Gans's and Bourdieu's writings betrays a horror at the prospect of so many football fans hoisting drinks in a dim sports bar while the masterpieces of Western art go, it would seem, largely unappreciated.[14]

While literary and cinematic critics have more recently theorized the possibility of differential readings, and Greenberg's analysis of kitsch may strike us fifty years hence as somewhat dogmatic in its flattening of the aesthetic response, the implications of the various analyses of taste witnessed in Greenberg, MacDonald, Gans, and Bourdieu remain symptomatic of the status of kitsch and camp for several reasons.[15] First, their analyses obliquely pose the question of what *kinds* of recipients the kitsch object might and might not be able to summon to the "imbedded" kitsch response, and second, this particular strain of Marxist analysis has sustained critical responses to mass culture in the present moment that neglect the possibility of a productive agent for kitsch— someone who might be a counterpart for the queer male responsible for camp intellectual production.

Camp and kitsch have so often been seen as tantamount expressions of a particular debased version of modernist aesthetics that given my argument about the relations among camp, queer intellectuals, and the exigencies of value's representations, there appears a question about what the name of kitsch means and, more interestingly, for whom. Greenberg comments in 1939 that "it appears to me that it is necessary to examine more closely and with more originality than hitherto the relationship *between aesthetic experience as met by the specific—not the generalized—individual,* and the social and historical contexts in which that experience takes place [italics mine]."[16] Striking is Greenberg's omission of the specific individual whose aesthetic experience of kitsch should be taken seriously, and here we discover that it would take another twenty-five years for Sontag, in "Notes on 'Camp,'" to finally disclose an agent who might be named for kitsch's sins; so powerful was such a naming that the critical commentary on kitsch virtually disappears after the 1960s as the topic of camp, conjoined to gay male identity politics, would now take on a political and aesthetic urgency that continues into the present moment.[17] The kind of distress expressed by Greenberg and others around the specter of kitsch emerged from its inability to identify the unstated political actor who translated kitsch into the intellectual strategies of camp. Before Sontag's "Notes," kitsch could be named as a general cultural phenomenon; inadvertently, the shift from kitsch to camp as the name of a self-conscious fascination with capital's troubled value codings made the queer man into a new political figure, one who was despoiling high culture with his failed seriousness. Vivian Gornick saw a conspiracy at work by gays interested in derailing the value of a straight mass culture. Whereas Sontag might argue that "homosexuals have pinned their integration into society on promoting the aesthetic sense," Gornick panicked at a darker tendency that she saw taking shape.[18] Gornick, in a 1966 *Village Voice* article titled "It's a Queer Hand That Stokes the Campfire," outlines camp both as the unwillingness of the male homosexual to integrate into the fabric of American life and simultaneously as his revenge on bourgeois straightness for excluding him. She proffered that

> popular culture is now in the hands of the homosexuals. It is homosexual taste that determines largely style, story, statement in painting, literature, dance amusements, and acquisitions for a goodly portion of the intellectual middle class. It is the texture, the atmosphere, the ideals, the notion of "camp" (a term, from its beginnings, the private property of American and English homosexuals) which currently determines middle-class taste, directs its signs, and seems to nourish its simple-minded eagerness to grind the idea of "alienation" into yet another hopelessly ironic cliché.[19]

Even within its paranoid dimensions, Gornick's account has the merit of allowing for camp as a force of production at work in the moment in which she writes. Placed alongside Sontag's depiction of camp as an outdated and antiquarian pursuit, "It's a Queer Hand" situates camp, primarily via pop art, as a key element of the cultural politics of the mid-1960s. Despite Gornick's trafficking in gross stereotypes of "the homosexual," which means the "pathetic," dyed, mincing effeminate homosexual man, and despite the unnoticed contradiction surrounding camp as being both the cause and effect of the alienation of the homosexual from an integrative American society, Gornick does suggest that camp is not simply a feature of "small urban cliques" but is more coextensive with metropolitan culture.

We might now understand the topic of kitsch as the expression of the revulsion of left mid-twentieth-century intellectuals at the fact that their specific array of taste choices (their habitus) was, like all such choices within the cultural landscape, specific to them as a material class formation and one in competition with the taste formations of the burgeoning working class or, even worse, with queer men. More to the point, the sense that the avant-garde was defined by the *choice* of certain paintings, sculptures, literary and musical works, and a few popular forms (some cinema, for example), for their internal complexity, their personalized languages, and their sense of the historical past, meant that other cultural forms such as kitsch were somehow more the result of a form of coercion. Sontag's "Notes" counters this sense of aesthetic domination within kitsch by arguing that in the act of disregarding distinctions of high and low culture and good and bad taste, new possibilities, both political and exclusive at once, emerge in the landscape of commodities. Further, her assertion that "one feels that if homosexuals hadn't more or less invented Camp, someone else would" located these possibilities in the world of queer male subcultures, quite a distance from the *Partisan Review* editorial board.[20]

The reader attuned to the varieties of political namings around sex/gender difference in the present moment will notice that I adhere to the term "queer" when discussing the subjects of this book. I do so to historicize the moments that the book addresses, moments before the post-Stonewall identity politics that claimed the name of "gay" for the strategies of altering the social landscape through which dissident sexualities and genders have been addressed politically. Recalling these men as queer restores in some measure, I hope, the sense of their difference not only from the normative and regulatory strictures of their own historical periods but also from what we too often conceive as the present sense of what constitutes a "gay man." The fact that Vincente Minnelli was married and enjoyed a happy family life in Hollywood, or that Andy Warhol seems to have dispensed in later life with most forms of genital sexuality in favor of the scopophilic pleasures of watching and photographing men *and* women, suggests that the complicated entanglements of erotic desires and practices are neglected by the now too cumbersome and too narrow forms of same-sex male sexuality as they are named by the term "gay." Alexander Doty argues that "queer" is a more productive term for understanding these entanglements of desire and cultural production by reminding us that "queer" appears as a term of negation and through its negative capacities might disclose where same-sex-desiring men have not and are not allowed to appear on the sexual and cultural landscape, not least in situations where "gay" might be the term of preference.

The tension between these two nominations, "queer" and "gay," has other implications as well for this theory of camp, not least in that there are multitudes of queer men and queer women, adolescents, nonwhite subjects, and others who can be conceived as having their own forms of camp that this book fails to address. In historicizing the men whose work I address, I have had to sacrifice these other possibilities for conceiving of lesbian camp, feminist camp, black camp, Latino camp, and riot-grrrl camp, to name a few such practices, as these social actors theorize and produce their own accounts of life under capital. As Paula Graham has written about feminist lesbian camp, "this means . . . that instead of tearing up porno mags in Soho in confrontation with dominant constructs of 'woman' as sexual object, lesbians play with and redo the heteropatriarchal language of sex in their own sweet way,"[21] and while her account largely dwells on the possibility of female viewers interpreting dominant images of women through their forms of excess (i.e., camp as reception), Graham's work (as well as that of other feminist writers) directs us to the possibility of thinking of about how different kinds of cultural production by blacks, women, Latinos, teenagers, and others might bear the name of camp.[22]

Here it is worth recalling that the men whose works I discuss enjoyed forms of privilege, by virtue of being men and being white, not accorded to others, and the ability to smuggle camp into the production of cinema, especially Hollywood cinema, was brought about by their capacity to pass in ways that all too many other subjects cannot. Despite the weak pleadings of the current film industry, in both its more corporate and "independent" aspects, that there is greater commitment to including others in addition to white heterosexual men, we have yet to see what would seem to be camp visions (or, for that matter, any other visions) by the various groups long excluded by the industry. However, the few more recent instances available, such as Isaac Julien's *Looking for Langston* (produced at quite a distance from Hollywood), would indicate that the longer history of such intellectual work by other than white men could be considered to be a form of camp. There is the possibility, for example, of reading much of the 'zine writings by female adolescents as a kind of "teen camp" that comments acerbically on the homogenized and antiwoman imagery available in mass-market magazines, television, and cinema—even in using the curtailed name " 'zine," such writings tamper with the sense of what constitutes a "magazine" for younger female readers.

Inside Labor, outside Labor: Camp Consciousness and Cinema's Attractions

In a history of Southern California domestic architecture in the decades following World War II, architect John Chase provides us with a sense of how the film industry can be studied for its impact on habits of everyday life beyond the space of cinema's screenings, and his account leads us to wonder about how the labor of queer men allowed them to inscribe their own relation to labor and to history in such a way as to protect them from censure. In *Exterior Decoration: Hollywood's Inside-Out Houses,* Chase describes the transformation of private houses in West Hollywood in the 1950s and 1960s as the movement of Hollywood cinematic style from the back lot to the front porch.[23] During the expansion of what the author calls the practice of "exterior decoration," home owners rebuilt the facades of 1920s small-scale houses by installing Doric columns, classical urns, dummy windows, and clipped topiary. Perhaps not coincidental was the fact that a large number of the renovators were queer men, many of them in the employ of the film studios and their related industries of glamour and publicity, employees skilled at the production of short-term spectacle for the mass-distributed entertainment commodity. These employees in their leisure time took matters of domestic design into their own hands by effectively making the enterprise of home improvement one that announced on the outside of their houses that a certain variety of camp consciousness had arrived in these neighborhoods. Despite the more customary association of homosexuality with the spaces of interiority, spaces associated with privacy, intimacy, and the nurturing of undisclosed social alliances, these exterior decorators inverted the concepts of inside and outside by effectively making the house into a showcase of the owner's personal aspirations for a new kind of domestic vernacular architectural language and the display of a privatized language of camp.[24]

The capacity to envision home renovation as the site on which to build such fantastic recollections of film style might seem an unlikely place for the extension of camp labor outside the realm of industrial production, but this rendering of private spectacle into public space provides a felicitous moment in which to wonder at the labor that capital's queer subject undertakes in his quest to mark himself as what Marx called "an animal which can individuate itself only in the midst of society." Marx, worrying over the homogenization of labor at the behest of industrialization, is by rights speaking largely of the sphere of production as it unleashes new forms of value, and yet his sense that labor abides as that effort whereby humans produce their livelihoods and the wealth of societies is not blind to the fact that labor might also be the activity whereby humans produce themselves and their forms of consciousness and by so doing call attention to their forms of difference from one another, even in such cases, as with camp, when such attentions are fraught with potential forms of attack.

The movement of film style from soundstage to stucco-clad bungalow is one trace of camp's subtle capacity to allow its practitioners to inform the world of their ability to produce themselves as different within the socius, and here I want to play on this labor of the private subject (i.e., the subject at pains to disclose something about himself) as it becomes, in the example at hand, literally exteriorized. Given that industrialized labor is regimented in such a way as often to neglect the talents of the individual who is required to perform it—Marx calls this the "indifference" of capital to those strive on its behalf—can the subject not only attempt to mark the commodity to make it apparent that he is, even despite himself, differentiated if not individuated, but can he perform such forms of labor and work, to recall Arendt, as the disguise for such difference? In this regard, I think that here we discover that labor has different roles for its practitioners, an interiority and exteriority to it that provide both a kind of privatized reward and the more customary form of sustenance to be gained in the form of wages and so forth. Camp's relation to the cinema, as I will discuss, has an especially pointed trajectory in its capacity to designate the movement of the interiority of labor (what might also be called the subject's consciousness of his efforts) to an external manifestation; while serving to remind of the more general energies required to perform labor, camp tells of a concealed, specific condition for labor and work-as-play that may not be apparent to all who embrace the camp film. Indeed, by installing the general (i.e., unmarked, unqueer) form of labor before the commodity's recipient, camp serves as an instance in which to wonder at the multitude of languages whereby the many different subjects of capital describe and theorize their experiences. Marx and the institutionalized readings of his theoretical enterprise have not always been helpful in recognizing these languages, given the historical vision of class difference as the sustaining force of history. Although he is hardly at fault for not anticipating the important advent of gender and sexuality for the industrial societies of capital, it does seem remarkable that Marx discounts the specificity of how subjects come to have consciousness of the conditions of their labor, and in this regard camp provides a form of knowledge production by queer subjects and others to wonder how they *live* inside their labor.

Writing in the *Economic and Philosophic Manuscripts of 1844* (like *The Grundrisse* of 1857–1858, an unpublished theoretical attempt at a critique of capital), Marx speculates on how consciousness is predicated on alienation from the material world that humans shape. This is not identical to the specific form of alienation that he will attribute to the force of capital on human consciousness, but a kind of estrangement built on the sense of making something apart from himself that reminds the human laborer of his own being even as he discovers the thing he makes to be not himself but an object that takes on a kind of social life apart from that of the producer. In Marx's account, humans only come to know of themselves in the world to the degree that they understand themselves as capable of producing such objects (in the specific case of capital, commodities), which they then see apart from their mental and corporeal selves. Marx calls this the "alienation of self-consciousness" and writes that "this externalization of self-consciouness has not merely a *negative* but a *positive* significance," to the degree that it is grounded in the material sense of the subject discovering his capacity as an actor in history and in politics.[25] Repeatedly in this account in the 1844 writings, Marx invokes self-consciousness as corporeal and sensuous and writes that such consciousness, bound up with the objects produced outside himself, is characterized by a relation in which "to be sensuous is to suffer." Here Marx's use of "sensuousness" carries with it an older form of the word, meaning that which is known of the world with the organs of physical discernment. However, I want to diverge from an impulse for historical adherence and wonder at how he might equally now be reread to encompass a more contemporary notion of sensuousness and corporeality, as sustained by erotics, and I dwell on his account to tease out its implications for the twining together of a sensuousness born of same-sex erotics and the particular functions of labor mandated under capital. Marx's recognition of human self-consciousness as "other" to itself is fundamental to his account, and it is not, as he suggests, an otherness steeped only in negation; otherness from the physical world as a thinking creature and from the social subjects who surround us has its own rewards of knowledge, and camp is one such reward, often delivered through the cinema.

In this regard, the discovery by subjects that the irregular dispersal of value under capital not only entails knowing where capital's cultural logics are fraught with incoherence but provides the opportunity for such subjects (in this specific case, queer men in the American metropolis) to offer their own visions of how even the most homogenized of expressions, such as the Hollywood film, might be tampered with. Gayatri Spivak writes of this in her reading of Marx as "the possibility of an indeterminacy rather than only a contradiction" in the procession in Marx's account from value to money to capital (and back through that chain).[26] These indeterminacies are precisely where camp's work, both in its similarity with labor in the processes of production (not least, of cinema) and in its critical attentions more customarily noted as forms of playful reception, find their motivation, for while there are necessary contradictions that must abide within the insistence that capital's adjudications of value (say, of "good" cinema and its bad-taste cousins) are somehow reasonable, what can so often not be determined is who might be responsible for seizing on them for a variety of productive capacities. Spivak, commenting in that writing on the problem of such failure to draw attention to those who are subjected to regimes of value within canon formation, thus proposes the question: "What subject-effects were systematically effaced and trained to efface themselves so that a canonic form might emerge?" By locating the question of value as not solely a monetary one but a monetary one that coincides with cultural value, she offers in that phrase "subject-effects" the sense that the shadow of the subject who produces lingers over the commodity, and his or her efforts might more helpfully be discussed not as the "positive" form of a socially necessary labor but within the category of *affectively* necessary labor.

Chaining affect and labor together allows us to understand how the range of responses often made visible (and audible) in camp texts unleashes forms of disgust, laughter, nausea, delight, and the general sense that what is being displayed is, at the very least, not in the best of possible taste; and it is precisely at those sites of indeterminacy in Marx's analysis that Spivak identifies where the occurrence of such responses seems so often to be likely. Such inappropriate emotions, which themselves have strong homologies with the status given to homosexuality within normative imaginations, are the camp expression, through its labor and its work-as-play, of how queer subjects are made to endure those reactions by others. In this regard, queer male camp is the consciousness, expressed through the terms of value in its multiple registers and fluxes (i.e., in the terms of the political economy that Marx identifies), of not only how queer men labor within the world but how they labor affectively to ward off the homophobic stances that they encounter on all too common a basis and, through their labor on the commodity, stage in deflected fashion such forms of affect again in the world.

To be conscious of this labor as that which gives rise to consciousness itself makes each human a philosopher of his or her own conditions, but such a recognition also forces us to extend Marx's critique of our political and economic conditions for life to the spheres in which we exert ourselves for something besides money. In this regard, it is worth recalling from the example of the exterior decorators of Los Angeles that their enterprises were undertaken largely within the realm of leisure and for what ends we can hardly know; even if their nonwaged efforts eventually gave rise to improved resale profit, a scheme that would make them in some Marxist visions simply petit bourgeois strivers, they could hardly know that the extravagant display of their stylistic talents would lend itself to the value codings of profit. I would propose that such camp displays allow queer laborers to recognize themselves in exteriority, to play on Marx's sense of self-consciousness, but in many instances the conditions for this recognition arise not solely in the more customarily identified sphere of production. Marx himself was never vulgarly Marxist and continually emphasized throughout his writings that consciousness itself was what he intended to apprehend. In this spirit, this project focuses on the labor of its queer subjects (Minnelli, Warhol, Anger, Waters) as their efforts often inhabited the more properly understood notions of industrial production but sometimes corrupted that distinction, in the designations of "underground" and "trash" cinema, for example, which seem to undo or at least fail to obey the strictures of routinized, serialized production as classical Marxism would insist on that concept.

The chapters that follow are thus an attempt to demonstrate how some queer subjects have lived within their labor through camp. The density of labor demanded in the production of cinema, most usually concentrated in the form of industrial organization and divisions of the efforts demanded in scriptwriting, cinematography, lighting, acting, direction, has produced the historical phenomenon of the bulk of feature films being given over to the narrative form. This has important implications for camp's attractions to the value codings of the film form as a relatively standardized commodity, not least because of camp's displaced relation to dissident sexualities (queer male, but also female sexualities too), but also because so many of the camp examples offered in the following chapters devote considerable energies to film's nonnarrative components, even when a given film seems largely organized through narrative. The most prominent of these nonnarrative features is that of film spectacle: the film image parsed, however momentarily, from its situation within a larger diegetic world of events, temporality, and causation.

Worth considering in the most general sense is why camp intellectuals have historically been drawn to the cinema; although a myriad of popular forms (comic books, pulp fiction, street fashion, pop music) have maintained their appeals to the camp imagination, cinema holds a particular form of appeal for camp intellectuals. This can be explained by recourse to the sense of cinema's capacity as the medium, par exellence, that visualizes—renders onto a visual register—the indeterminacies and contradictions of capital and the effects of modernity. In its dynamics and movement, cinema attempts to make value's abstractions materialize, and perhaps more than any mass medium, the cinema has lent itself to the fascination of intellectuals, camp and otherwise, who strive to make sense of the representations to which the specific political economy of capital gives rise.

Part of the concealed labor of camp on the commodity form of cinema resides in the efforts to make a film's images and sounds as something added to the recognizable conventions of narrative. Although there are instances of camp narratives, as discussed in the movement of camp melodrama into the more mainstream product of John Waters's films, camp's traces are, to my mind, most productively discovered by wondering at those moments where narrative fails as an explanation of how a given text is formally and aesthetically conceived. In this regard, the affectively necessary labor of camp resides in the occasions where one senses that the film image has diverged from *narrative* expectations, but in ways such as the visual excess of an early Minnelli musical number or the playful corporeality (all the eating and fondling in Warhol's or Waters's films) that might easily be dismissed by even the most engaged of viewers as so much "fluff" or "bad taste." The fact that one sometimes feels about a camp text that one cannot quite locate its aberrance tells us that camp's work-as-play succinctly mimics the labor in a film's production; camp efforts accompany labor on the path of a film's production. Therefore, one way of locating camp in the sphere of production is by finding the repeated incidents of narrative filmmaking that seem to depart from the more usual expectations of visual and acoustic form. In short, we discover ourselves thinking about film genres.

Two genres in particular lend themselves to the kinds of examinations I have in mind, the film musical and the melodrama, and in each we can access forms of visual and affective extravagance. In both of these generic forms of film narrative, perhaps not coincidentally, the story revolves around the crises of heterosexuality within the constraints of capital's social formations, in the case of the musical, around romantic bonding of men and women, and in the instance of the melodrama around the ensuing familial discord produced in the wake of such pairings. In the chapters on the Freed musicals of Vincente Minnelli and the film melodramas of John Waters, I treat each of these genres at greater length, and in the chapter on Andy Warhol's films, I consider the eventual movement of Warhol's films toward (considerably loosely formed) narratives.

The production of narrative film bears scrutiny as the endeavors that Arendt considers to be labor, while the extra-added exertions, say, in the excessive forms of performance, lighting, mise-en-scène, more fruitfully inhabit her category of work-as-play. Like the houses of Chase's West Hollywood renovators, the structure of the commodity remains relatively intact, but many of its outward stylistic flourishes offer a clue to the additional efforts of camp as work-as-play. In this regard, camp reveals itself as a luxuriance in the inefficiencies of capital's modes of production, because despite the insistence (one that occurs often in Marx's theorizations as much as anywhere) that capital is a wholly more streamlined way to organize human labor, within the lacunae of its modes of production, camp filmmakers find the opportunities to press the cinematic commodity into a new form of service that expresses their presence within the domain of production.

That some camp intellectuals should be drawn to the cinema reveals something of the peculiarity of that specific industrial form for allowing the work of camp to reside on the film form and, more importantly for theories of contemporary culture, to be disseminated to new and unexpected venues. Recalling Marx's compulsion to see the appearance of the commodity as multiple instances of its production, named as distribution and consumption outside the more proper sphere of production as such, the camp valences of the studio and avant-garde film travel to unanticipated arenas whereby camp might be produced, *within the sphere of consumption,* by audiences. Camp, as theorized in the present account as a knowledge about capital's changeable and volatile attributions of value, can and does migrate to recipients outside the sphere of its production. This helps to explain the intense affiliation between camp and the notion of cult-viewing formations, to the degree that when recipients of the camp film discover its alternative visions of the modern world, they attach themselves to it with a devotion not typical of the usual cinematic fare (i.e., a film's reception shares affective homologies with its production). They subsequently move that way of knowing and thinking about capital to other cultural productions, so that even when we acknowledge that a particular form — say teen pics or slasher films — seems not to have a discernible camp intellectual responsible for its making, the recipients of camp remobilize camp's attentions anew.

Given these possibilities for ascertaining how film narrative forms a site for interrogation around the questions this book asks about camp, there is another strategy, employed at greater length in my considerations of the earlier works of Andy Warhol and Kenneth Anger, for considering how other meanings are forged in the editing of film images together, a kind of camp consciousness made available through film montage. If narrative is a comparatively demanding formal structure for organizing the cinematic moving image — demanding from the viewpoint that divergences from its modes of representation always beg explanations as to their motivation (artistic license, costs in production, sloppiness) — then montage must certainly be one of the least expensive (both for capital investment and for labor) techniques for mobilizing cinema against itself, and the relation between film montage and camp is worth dwelling on as a circumstance for realizing how intellectually productive capital's indeterminacies and internal contradictions become when rendered on the visual plane. Perhaps an anecdote will help here, one offered from my experiences as a teacher. In the instances where I have taught montage as an expression of modernist politics (in the socialist visions of Sergei Eisenstein or in the droll antibourgeois and anticlerical visions of Luis Buñuel), the reaction produced among students is one of pleasure, expressed as outbursts of uncontainable laughter about the movement across the edit from image to image. For a teacher of spectators schooled primarily at the hands of film continuity as the singular formal device for making sense of the reproduced moving image, this comes as a surprise, inasmuch as the bulk of contemporary television advertising is delivered within the sensibilities of montage; yet as one of my students once commented, "The ads are about the commodities, but the movies [Eisenstein et al.] are about the societies that make them." Having such socialized forms of contradiction staged before them comes as revelation, and I dwell on this moment in the work I do with students to make sense of our wonderment at how *easily* montage helps to vivify the contrary tendencies of our own lives. This "ease" of montage derives from the sense that one does not necessarily have to worry about the ordering of images as an irreducible logic, in the way that film narrative so often seems to dictate; with montage, cinema can be made to disclose with relative quickness and inventiveness — in short, *playfully* — its own conditions for being.

Metropolitan Life: Camp and Film Form

While camp forms a philosophy of modernity produced through an ongoing attention to the crises of value coding under capital, part of its labor can be ascertained as the efforts to produce commodities, notably those of the cinema. In this regard, camp is complicated by the sense that it both responds to the things of mass culture (camp as the habits of ironic reception attended to by Sontag, Ross, et al.) and simultaneously underpins forms of industrial production. This counters the more usual sense of the relation between the intellectual labor of critique and the labor demanded in industrial production, to the degree that most critical responses to capital's effects are beheld as those offered by intellectuals remote from arenas of commodity production. In the chapters that follow, I argue that camp informed the making of films, some distributed widely (i.e., Hollywood) and others more restricted in the kinds of exhibition provided for them (underground and trash). Here I will outline briefly a conceptual framework for the book's chapters, seeing the examples that follow as part of how a larger dialectic of camp and production, of critique and commodity, inform each other through medium-specific qualities of cinema that this book's sites of inquiry discuss; but it is also worth mentioning that the examples in this book form only a fragment of a larger intellectual and cultural genealogy in the study of sexualities, critical thought, and modernity, what we can call metropolitan life. In the case of this book, the constellation of filmmakers is organized between two poles of American film culture, New York and Los Angeles. If we situate the camp instances of this book in relation to these two cities, we can discern them as part of an organizing tension between, in the case of the first, live performance, high art, and the ideations of effete intellectual life, and in the case of the second, the industries of popular culture and the rhetoric of mass address to the nebulous social category of "America." Vincente Minnelli, trained in the organization of stage performances in Chicago and Manhattan, marks the movement of "eastern" metropolitan culture into the Hollywood soundstage, but numerous other men shared in this migration, among them the musicians, dancers, choreographers, set designers, and cinematographers who translated the styles and performances of the live stage to studio film. In this regard, Minnelli figures as part of one generation of camp intellectuals at the twilight of the studio system; no small irony is contained, then, in the fact of Kenneth Anger's upbringing in Southern California in the 1940s and 1950s, for Anger marks a counter-direction of an experimental film practice that moved from Los Angeles to New York. Anger's fascination with film emerges in having been raised within the social world of the studio system, and his intellectual energies were devoted to producing a countercinema to Hollywood that appealed more often to New York's underground audiences of the 1960s than to those of the studios.

If New York and Los Angeles form one axis for understanding the queer cinematic tradition offered in this book, then Pittsburgh and Baltimore form satellites to that larger field between the East and West coasts. These "other" American cities, where Andy Warhol and John Waters were born and raised, tell of the fascination for queer men of the metropolis as a space of escape, and a significant part of the life of American sexual subcultures is of course played out in the movement to the anonymity of cities such as New York and Los Angeles, where queers could not only discover larger social networks of like-minded subjects but, equally for the sake of this book, put themselves more centrally in the space of capital's dynamic movement. While the migration to the city of queer men and women is so familiar a narrative (both fictive and historical) about the liberatory possibilities contained in metropolitan life, equally significant is the chance given to queer men and women *to labor as queers*. This is not to discount queer labors undertaken in non-urban settings (they too might take the name of camp as it is understood here) but to suggest that the particular figures discussed in this book are seized on at the heart of urban modernity, in both its New York and its Los Angeles variations, as each of the figures examined in this book—Minnelli, Warhol, Anger, and Waters—marks the insistence of the camp intellectual on inserting himself into the matrices of cultural production in their most powerful venues. In this light, the metropolitan lives of these men delimit what I am calling camp, and the astute reader might conjure other spaces, other moments, other media, in which to judge whether the theoretical claims of the book are constrained by the specificity of its examples.

In chapter 1, the early film musicals directed by Vincente Minnelli are examined in regard to Minnelli's widely noted talents as a director given to the making of powerful film imagery in the context of film narrative. The fact of the Hollywood product's having historically been organized formally through the conventions of its own strong languages of film narrative can too often occlude our sense of the more general fact that cinema is, first, a visual medium, and the Minnelli Freed films often, as discussed, seem to overwhelm their narratives with a chromatically saturated and kinetic mise-en-scène.

Given that the historical scope of this book extends from the late 1940s to the present moment, across the immensely important period in which a more public acknowledgment of queer sexualities has emerged, it is worth considering how the examples of camp discussed in chapter 1 differ from succeeding examples in the ways that they exemplify camp intellectual work. While most of the films discussed elsewhere in this book, even those such as Kenneth Anger's earliest works, were part of a larger phenomenon related to the (relatively) increased accessibility of images and acoustic and written culture devoted to same-sex erotics, the Freed musicals of Minnelli's career seem most remote from being considered as part of the expanded public articulation of camp that in complicated fashion forms an important element of queer male culture's increased visibility of the past four decades. Warhol, Anger, and Waters made camp films as part of that new public sphere of male homosexuality, but Minnelli's efforts seem more restricted, in their historical moment of Hollywood censorship, in their approach to male same-sex erotics. Yet because camp is so often defined by its own cautious approach to sexual themes and depictions, this may render Minnelli's efforts all the more paradoxically as perfect emblems of what this book considers camp to be—a philosophy not so much of sexuality but of commodity culture.

Whereas Minnelli's work on cinema is defined by its emphasis on visual extravagance, in chapter 2 I argue that Andy Warhol's efforts take camp fascinations with the film spectacle as a product of expenditure in an opposite direction, one based on the possibilities of a film aesthetic derived from efficiency. Warhol's films mirror, in inverted fashion, the Hollywood product, given the latter's capacity for multiple takes and the continual redeployment of technologies and personnel to alter the look and sound of a given shot. Warhol's films insist on the possibilities of a cinema that includes representation of the various conditions of its production—ambient sound, out-of-focus framing, nonprofessional acting, and in-camera editing—and the inclusion of these aleatory elements allows them to make a spectacle of their own economy.

Kenneth Anger's films, on the other hand, are characterized by a style of composition (most importantly through their editing) that must be among the most lavish of any filmmaker, and they bear the marks of extravagance that montage allows its makers. In chapter 3, I demonstrate that the visual rendering of the artist's desires (for men, for glamour, for the very love of color and dynamism in cinema itself) emerges in Anger's work as a complicated handling of film temporality as historical consciousness. If montage retains within it the dialectic sense of the collision of different historical forces, Anger relies on the camera to hold together the very forces of commodity standardization and individuation as beheld in the queer subcultures that his films depict.

Finally, I argue in chapter 4 that within the films of John Waters, the decomposition of the commodity becomes the occasion in which to renew its fascinations, most notably in the "trashing" that he insists on for the institutions of cinema, especially that of stardom. Waters returns camp filmmaking to narrative and to genre, and his films read the scene of the contemporary household and its attempts to contain the perverse desires that it instigates within its members as the setting for his melo-dramas. Waters's films are "degenerate" in a quite explicit sense, for they stage the movement of dissident desires, in terms not only of erotics but of taste as well, back to the spaces that have generated it to begin with, to the strictures of marriage and bourgeois reproduction.

ONE

Working like a Homosexual: Vincente Minnelli

in the Metro-Goldwyn-Mayer Freed Unit

> Vincente [Minnelli] was not a man who was a dictator.
>
> He tried to do it in a soft and nice way. He worked in let's say . . .
>
> I don't know whether you will understand what I say . . . he
>
> worked like a homosexual. I don't mean that nastily. I have
>
> nothing against homosexuals . . .
>
> — *Lela Simone, production assistant at Metro-Goldwyn-Mayer*

Nowhere is the challenge to locate the positive image of same-sex desire in film representation so pronounced as it is in relation to the classical Hollywood cinema.[1] Since Vito Russo's groundbreaking 1977 volume on the subject of gay and lesbian imagery in film in *The Celluloid Closet,* scholars and historians of modernist sexualities have found their task grounded in the opposition between (apparently nonexistent) "positive" Hollywood representations of queer men and women and all too plentiful stereotypical vilifications of male and female same-sex eroticisms. Critical treatments of the relations of queer sexualities to the production of cinema have thus largely taken two approaches. The first stresses the pathologizing effect of Hollywood cinema in its portrayal of queers, with *Rope* and *Caged,* for example, offering to those in pursuit of queer-positive images particularly objectionable depictions of queer life. From this perspective, the presence of queers in Hollywood studios seems a remote possibility. The second approach, then, embraces queer filmmakers outside Hollywood, independent from Hollywood both in terms of the economic conditions under which they make movies and in terms of the array of film styles available for contemplating the role of gender and sexuality in contemporary life. The exceptions to these two approaches are notable, particularly in terms of how Hollywood can be understood as a site of production for queer filmmakers: for example, Dorothy Arzner has rightfully taken her place as a figure of an anti-auteur auteur, and George Cukor and James Whale have only recently begun to be rethought as *queer* directors. In the wake of the assessment that Hollywood has traditionally been hostile to queer laborers (at least at the level that their cinematic visions might reach the big screen) and that therefore it is only outside corporate studio production that queers might make movies, we are left with a historical and theoretical vacuum when we consider that queer men and women have been instrumental in the productions of some kinds of Hollywood film that are not entirely homophobic.[2]

This chapter rethinks the situation by fixing its attention on the films made by Vincente Minnelli in the Freed unit of Metro-Goldwyn-Mayer during the late 1940s and attempting to dislodge these films from universalizing accounts of classical Hollywood cinema. My interest is in accounting for the contributions of queer men, and the specific example of Vincente Minnelli, to the Freed unit, and in rethinking the status of their labor as crucial to the films' hallmark style. Although I will consider Minnelli at the greatest length in terms of camp and queer-inflected production, there are numerous opportunities to discuss queer figures in the Freed unit, the most important being Cole Porter and Roger Edens. Porter composed many of the most popular songs to be performed in Freed musicals; Edens was responsible for the unit's daily operations, and his vocal arrangements are immensely important in the history of the American film musical and the popular song. In this respect, this chapter forms an attempt to render more visible the labor of queers and their sensibilities within the production of a dominant cinema, sensibilities that I discuss in terms of camp. Further, the "queer labor" of camp is a strategic category for understanding the camp markings affected by the production of these films, and therefore queer labor, in the form of camp encodings, functioned for the studio as a way of enhancing the final product by way of "product differentiation." At stake are both a recuperative account of the contributions of men whose difference vis-à-vis sex/gender are largely ignored because of the imperatives of the closet and, equally important, the challenge to our impulses to ignore differences, whether they arise in terms of race, ethnicity, class, or gender, as such differences informed the ideological practices and the material production of Hollywood film in its larger social dimensions.

By treating the question of narrative integration in the musicals of the Freed unit, I demonstrate that the stylistic anomalies of the Freed films that are most pronounced indicate an extra-added labor on those texts. Keeping in mind both how camp has previously been understood as a fascination with artifice, excess, and performance and how a history of queer Hollywood lives continues to circulate anecdotally, I claim here that these features of some Freed productions (which occur most often for this account in regard to the art direction) provide an opportunity to understand camp as a kind of queer labor, but queer in that the erotic dimensions of queer male Freed laborers' lives were masked by camp, and labor in that the conditions for their productive output were predicated on the particular economic practices of the studio in the period that I am describing. Thus I am attempting to bring together questions of stylistic differentiation and the economic conditions for such difference to appear; by extending the idea of camp beyond its being a hallmark of consumption, I offer an analysis of how queer subjectivity emerges within the dynamics of capitalist cultural production for audiences that extend well beyond queer male subcultures.

Freed Productions at Metro-Goldwyn-Mayer

Claims that the Freed film musicals of the post–World War II period can be set apart from contemporaneous musicals of the period cannot derive solely from perceived formal qualities of their mise-en-scène and choreography, and the forms of distinction that we might draw around their anomalous production cannot necessarily be adduced through other kinds of labor history.[3] Striking as these aspects of the films may be, it is imperative to consider the industrial conditions under which these forms of spectacle could arrive at the large screen. When we recall that Metro was enduring numerous challenges in order to remain competitive with other studios, we need to account for the Freed unit's almost singular eventual success as the unit on the MGM lot that earned box office profits.

Important to consider is Metro-Goldwyn-Mayer's unwillingness to reorganize itself in light of its competitors, an unwillingness that positioned the studio after World War II as burdened with high overhead costs, convoluted bureaucratic practices, and fewer exhibition outlets. Tom Schatz describes Metro's organization as "the consummate example of waste and excess," and he amply demonstrates the studio's numerous unhelpful maneuvers to respond to a changing economic climate for the Hollywood studios.[4] Unlike its competitors, Metro did not move in the direction of making fewer and frequently more tightly budgeted films that represented potentially smaller losses if a product failed and greater gains if it garnered healthy receipts. Rather, the abortive attempts to sustain Metro-Goldwyn-Mayer's signet reputation as the producer of Hollywood's most lavish movies resulted in financial disaster for the studio, with one notable exception: Freed productions.

Arthur Freed originally came to Metro-Goldwyn-Mayer as a lyricist, having written with his collaborator, Nacio Herb Brown, the music scores for *The Broadway Melody* (1929), *Hollywood Revue* (1929), and *Going Hollywood* (1932). Early in his career, as Hugh Fordin notes, Freed became known within Metro-Goldwyn-Mayer as possessing a capacity not only for writing song lyrics but also for seeking out performance talent for the film musical.[5] This positioned him ideally to become a line producer on the Metro-Goldwyn-Mayer lot, and by the late 1930s, he had been put in charge of his own unit, which sponsored the Mickey Rooney–Judy Garland vehicles *Babes in Arms* (1939) and *Babes on Broadway* (1941). Based on these successes, Metro-Goldwyn-Mayer allowed Freed to recruit talent for more extensive musical properties, and it was with employees already on the lot, such as Judy Garland and Roger Edens, and in conjunction with figures such as Vincente Minnelli, Gene Kelly, Cole Porter, and Betty Comden and Adolph Green, all of whom were brought from New York, that Freed was given comparatively large budgets to realize such projects as *Yolanda and the Thief* (1945), *Ziegfeld Follies* (produced 1944, released 1946), and *The Pirate* (1947).[6]

It is remarkable that the Freed unit was budgeted in such comparatively lavish terms, as Metro-Goldwyn-Mayer was currently undergoing significant pressures from a changed post–World War II Hollywood economy. At a moment when it would have seemed imperative to rein in budgets and to supervise production more closely, Metro's executives allowed for a relatively autonomous production unit that was simultaneously a place of exclusivity. Lela Simone, an important figure for the unit's day-to-day operations, recounts that within the studio, unit members were mockingly referred to as "the royal family." Stanley Donen recalls that "you had to want movies more than life itself, and all these things were unsaid and unspoken. But that's how you got in . . . that's how Freed selected you."[7] Freed himself referred to the unit as "my own little Camelot."[8] The process of selection to which Donen refers is often remarked on as Freed's most marked contribution to the Hollywood musical; Freed recruited talent for the unit and then often seems to have given the unit's employees a large measure of creative independence.

In this sense, the unit exemplifies the transition in postwar Hollywood from the producer system to the package system. Janet Staiger describes this change as one from a mode of production organized around a larger number of films being put into production with a staff that labored on vehicles in serial fashion to a shorter-term arrangement in which fewer productions were realized, often hiring on a per-production basis.[9] Of course, the transition was not immediate, and the Freed unit operated as a hybrid; I call attention here to Staiger's analysis to remind us that the opportunity for queer men to labor in this venue stemmed less from the impulse by Metro to sponsor a queer subcultural setting and more from the studio's interest in extending profits. This means that the question of the economic does not have to arise in the last instance, but helps to explain how the distinguished Freed style, in large part a queer style, became visible. Further, Freed productions continued to secure their large budgets because more often than not, over the course of Freed's supervision, they showed healthy profits.

Freed pictures *were* eventually profitable. In spite of their large budgets, the general pattern of the films was to be their increasing box office success, not to mention the prestige that the Freed productions earned in the critical and popular commentary on them. The problem for the studio was that they would have been profitable for the comparatively autonomous system of the package-unit system that figured in Hollywood's future, but not for the producer-unit system. For one thing, the heavy demands of musical production on studio resources meant that Freed produced only two to three films per year through mid-1953, and in most years after that only one. If the unit had been able to put more films into production per year, Metro might have sustained the more customary producer-unit practices of the earlier classical mode of production; the problem here was that the scale of budgets for such films made producing more of them unthinkable in terms of the demands for studio capital and human labor investment.

While musicals were for any studio a large commitment to undertake, the films coming out of the Freed unit were particularly expensive and labor-intensive projects. And generally speaking, musicals offered by other units within Metro-Goldwyn-Mayer and by other studios were profitable at the box office, but Freed films, particularly those produced later in the unit's history, such as *An American in Paris* (1950) and *Singin' in the Rain* (1951), proved to be particularly successful with audiences. My focus, though, is on earlier Freed films, some of which, from the viewpoint of the studio, were tremendous disappointments. Among the films of the 1940s, *Ziegfeld Follies* would show a small loss, while *Yolanda and the Thief* lost substantial money, and *The Pirate* proved an outright financial disaster. Nevertheless the earlier films have come to enjoy a status within hierarchies of camp *readings* greater than that accorded later Freed efforts. As Jane Feuer suggests,

> A queer subcultural reading would elevate these two Minnelli masterpieces [*Yolanda and the Thief* and *The Pirate*] of the 1940s above the currently more esteemed Freed Unit musicals of the 1950s— *Singin' in the Rain* and *The Band Wagon,* whose sophistication stems more from their smart Comden and Green scripts than from elements of excess in their *mise-en-scène.*[10]

Later Freed productions of the 1950s would herald a compromise between camp visual style and tighter narrative integration, and it is remarkable that despite money losers like *Yolanda and the Thief* and *The Pirate,* the unit continued to secure its financing. Indeed, Freed budgets did not diminish but expanded from production to production.[11] In this, the studio seems to have gambled by investing in stylistically idiosyncratic productions that held no guarantee of showing a net profit. What Metro potentially stood to gain were films markedly different from their competitors, difference that could (but did not always) reap returns for Metro-Goldwyn-Mayer's initial investments. Here I can only suggest that the later productions would more carefully balance the camp visual elements (no small feature of *An American in Paris,* for example) with the demands for "streamlined" (i.e., assertively heteronormative) narrative. In this respect, though, the earlier productions that I am discussing stand out as emblems of the unit's experiments with cinematic art direction, experiments whose failures at the box office served to aid in the refinement of subsequent films' camp style.

In the context of the remarkable contradiction of Freed productions within Metro-Goldwyn-Mayer, where a unit within a troubled corporation was allowed to produce seemingly with little or no executive supervision beyond that of Freed himself, camp style allows us to distinguish Freed productions from other Hollywood films and in fact from other film musicals of the period. How, though, do we align camp, which has long been understood as a practice performed by audiences on texts (which Feuer outlines) with an analysis of production? The realignment of camp as the labor that queers contributed to the *production* of these films should be underscored with an important caveat: at the very least, we should remember that the corporate interests of Metro-Goldwyn-Mayer in distinguishing its products were hardly identical with the interests of its queer laborers, as the latter brought features of queer metropolitan culture to the forms of mass entertainment. There is, however, the possibility of seeing such interests as coinciding with one another, particularly when the studio can profit from commodities that bear the marks of distinguishing efforts of queer laborers and camp philosophy.

"The Royal Family": Queer Labor within the Studio

When Lela Simone commented that Vincente Minnelli worked "like a homosexual," she was hazarding a description that allows us to see how sex/gender difference and the subjection of labor under capital can be bound up in each other. As a personal assistant to Freed and Roger Edens, and as one of Minnelli's coworkers on the lot at Metro-Goldwyn-Mayer, Simone was in a position to recall much about the production of Freed films in the unit's heyday. Her attempts to articulate a relation between Minnelli's sexuality and the effects of his labor resonate in the way that she expresses the vexations of the closet as they arise in the workplace; her words also encourage us to theorize the possibility of a capitalist enterprise accommodating marginalized sex/gender subjects because their labor could enhance a product's appeal through its differentiated style.

In his splendid monograph on Minnelli, James Naremore argues that Minnelli deserves to be understood as a key figure in translating the idioms of high-art modernism to mass forms. Naremore comments:

> Together with several of his collaborators in the Freed unit, [Minnelli] brought a rarefied sense of camp to musical numbers, making several pictures that were adventurously stylized and ahead of popu-

lar taste. To a degree, such films ran against the grain of dominant attitudes, establishing Minnelli as what French critic Louis Marcorelles
would later describe as "an Oscar Wilde of the camera."[12]

One of Naremore's key insights is that Minnelli's relation to camp is
not a revelation about his sexuality as much as it allows us to understand how the emerging queer metropolitan subcultures would shape
mass tastes and aesthetic sensibilities, and Minnelli's efforts are central
to the shift from the more rarefied fascinations of the New York live
theater to the Hollywood soundstage. Two features of Naremore's argument are especially important: first, that the camp dimensions of the
Freed films were the result of Minnelli's collaborations with other talent, such as Roger Edens and Cole Porter, and second, that one of the
director's repeated auteurist motifs was a devaluation of macho American masculinity, and that later in his career, Minnelli would make his
antagonisms to normative gendering more apparent:

> From the mid-fifties onward, Minnelli's films repeatedly criticized
> American standards of sexual "normality," and although he never
> treated homosexuality directly, he flirted with the issue in *The Cob-
> web, Designing Women, Tea and Sympathy, Some Came Running, Home
> From the Hill,* and *Goodbye Charlie.*[13]

Any commentary about American masculinity (and, by implication,
the status of male heterosexuality), be it valedictory or critical, had to
emerge obliquely, given the constraints of censorship and contemporaneous homophobia.[14] Thus the earlier films, which form the centerpiece
of this chapter, might demonstrate this antagonism less through thematic or narrative concerns about masculinity and more through the
visual cues that serve as a (frequently playful) indictment of American
masculine performance.

Naremore presciently links Minnelli's visual style to that of *Vogue*
and *Harper's Bazaar* (an important relation between cinema and commodity culture that heralds Warhol's training as a commercial artist
and Anger's *mise-en-abime* use of ads, comics, and soft-porn cinematic
imagery). Minnelli's affinity for camp came about during his tenure as a
designer for Radio City Music Hall during the 1930s, a venue in which
to stage live spectacle and one located centrally in one of the queer pre–
World War II metropolises where camp tastes were being invented and
refined. This camp sensibility translated to his later films, for as Nare-

more suggests, Minnelli "worked in a milieu where 'backstage' homosexuality was fairly common, and his best pictures—all of them made during the most restrictive era of the Production Code—are marked by the sort of 'excess' that could not speak its name." Of course, Naremore refers here to the long-standing axiom about male homosexuality, and one of his chief criteria for arguing that Minnelli is an auteur, that his style was unique and idiosyncratic, derives from Naremore's reading of Sontag's definition of camp as the hallmark of the dandy in the age of mass production. Minnelli, comments Naremore, was "the aesthete in the factory."

While recognizing that the comments of Naremore and Simone might appear to be mostly of biographical interest to Minnelli auteurists, I argue that they allow us to see relations between subjects and their ability to labor that marks the results of their efforts as different. I do so not simply to redefine the terms under which, in this case, Minnelli's films can be argued to share auteurist hallmarks but to suggest that the queer employees at Metro's Freed unit during this period formed a collaborative effort to alter the look of the Hollywood musical through their camp sensibilities. Because both the demands of capitalist enterprises (for workers to avoid being articulated as capable of collaborative work) and the demands of the closet (where sexual subjects can give no proper name to themselves as desiring subjects, especially as a social group), it was in the interest of the efforts of Minnelli and his many coworkers to name the visual styles of these Freed films as the efforts of Vincente Minnelli. For example, if we consider the contributions to the Freed product of Minnelli, Roger Edens, and Cole Porter, figures now recognized as having affinities with the queer camp subculture of New York in the 1930s and 1940s, it is not only the case that each was an individuated talent working alone within the studio. These men collaborated at work and socialized in their after hours, forming a vital working team that not only fortified Metro's stature within Hollywood by creating an idiosyncratic product but also allowed them to realize their own artistic projects within the regimented organization of corporate film production.[15]

It is worth wondering about the difficulties of treating camp style as one that might offer clues to affirming an auteurism, be it on the part of the studio or a director, when the hazards of being nominated as a corporation that sponsors queer style or as a queer laborer within apparently "straight" corporate cultures still make demands on us for confirming or denying privatized sexualities as public knowledges. In going about the research for this chapter, for example, I had occasion to interview a current executive at Metro-Goldwyn-Mayer, George Feltenstein, who confirmed for me that not only were many of the men responsible for the Freed product queer, and not only did it seem to him immediately apparent that films such as *Ziegfeld Follies* or *The Pirate* are saturated by camp style, but also that Metro-Goldwyn-Mayer has always hosted a kind of anecdotal corporate knowledge that such were the facts of the films' realizations.[16] In this interview, I was then treated to an account of the various friendships and romantic pairings that formed the in-house history of the Freed unit's queer subculture, whereupon I was reminded that many of these figures and their families are still alive and perhaps quick to summon their lawyers lest I engage in "outing" any of these people.

Fortunately, the interests in this project have been less in offering nominations than in ascertaining the conditions under which these figures labored.[17] Nevertheless this simultaneous confirmation and denial only makes more vivid the historiographic problems of articulating the effects of queer laborers in Hollywood in an age that still promulgates the stigmata of same-sex sexuality. That is, by agreeing to maintain the anonymous status of queers and lesbians, we may ourselves be engaged in the strategies that deny, from an empirical stance, the notion that dissident sexualities have a bearing on the final product.

As a historian engaged in thinking about labor from a position of materialist critique, I wonder if we do not risk relegating the particular queer labor of camp back into what Marx called the "abstraction" of labor, whereby the corporation is entitled to think of the labor involved in industrial production as being offered from an indistinguishable pool of laborers. As we know, Hollywood long demanded a highly regulated and differentiated set of labors that it often attempted to treat as, of course, not necessarily that. Thus the forces of one form of historical consciousness, one that privatizes queer sexuality and its forms of cultural expression, position us perhaps to enact the very subsumption of labor as "undifferentiable," which we know not to be true.

Further, the act of considering a director such as Vincente Minnelli as the emblem of camp auteurist style might allow us to ignore the vital and important working relations between the director and numerous other key queer personnel, such as choreographers, vocal arrangers and songwriters, who were involved in the making of Freed musicals. These strong laboring bonds might offer us a collective of studio laborers who employed their own more privatized languages to create a public spectacle of a subcultural style, and yet these networks were rendered in the studio's internal history and folklore (i.e., its gossip) as sexual and romantic bonds rather than issues of labor and collectivity. In this sense, the impulse to see the production unit as having a unique or idiosyncratic style (over and above the hallmarks that might be underwritten by an auteurist analysis) allows us to situate the collaborative laboring relations among these queer men within their contradictory conditions for production, all the while remembering that Metro hosted these figures because of profit, and not through any vision of a subcultural politics or solidarity (which these figures themselves would find a strangely unrecognizable form of discourse).[18]

In terms of the Freed unit, the fact that a studio was willing to employ queers (even, or perhaps especially, those willing to enjoin with the open secret of the closet) suggests that labor is sometimes inflected by the difference of subjectivity when such difference can expend itself on behalf of profit. By this I mean that the ability to labor—what Marx refers to not as the actual and specific output of the laborer but as the potential labor that capital anticipates and subsequently objectifies according to its interests—differs for various laborers according to the different talents that they bring to the enterprise. Marx writes of capital's interests as the eventual "objectification" of labor, where "the reduction of all kinds of actual labour to their common character" serves the ends of efficiency and profit even as such general labor is informed by a host of features: sex/gender, racial difference, ethnicity, and, not least, class.[19] These labors differ at the level of subjects' potential for making different kinds of commodities, and the possibility for such differentiations is not simply coincidental to the force of capitalism as a system for the making and distribution of objects and, more to the point, value. A larger implication may be that capitalism is predicated on a multitude of differences, besides that of class, that it can exploit.

Camp is an index of such difference, although it is a notoriously ambiguous one. As a sensibility so often linked with dissident sexualities, camp seldom offers itself for immediate identification as that which has been made by a queer man, and the camp commodity can bear ambiguities in such a way that, say in its potential for camp and noncamp readings alike, it heralds queer life and consciousness in its most mundane dimensions. In a sense, what camp offers to us is the commodity that "passes" through the economy much as queers themselves must pass in many of the social settings of their daily lives. Thus what I am calling queer labor is not simply the effort of queers expended on a particular commodity but the particular effort to ensure the commodity's multivalence, in that it can be consumed by queer and nonqueer consumers alike for retaining camp features or not. Camp figures as queer labor in its answer to the demand to pass; the difficulty of identifying queer tastes at work means that the object has served to deflect attention away from those who think in camp ways. Eve Kosofsky Sedgwick outlines the strictures of the demand to pass and the camp response:

> The typifying gesture of camp is really something amazingly simple: the moment at which a consumer of culture makes the wild surmise, "What if whoever made this was queer too?" Unlike kitsch-attribution, then, camp-recognition doesn't ask, "What debased creature could possibly be the right audience for this spectacle?" Instead, it says *what if:* What if the right audience for this were exactly me?[20]

Sedgwick's argument suggestively maintains that the question posed by the camp spectator displaces an interest in absolutely confirming a queer presence on the side of production to the viewer's awareness of his or her particular status as a camp spectator. But what if (to rejoin Sedgwick's question) camp is understood as the specific term for addressing how queer sensibilities labor in venues over which such subjects may have restricted control? (As, indeed, all subjects would seem to be positioned.) The Freed unit operated within the most centrally organized and labor-differentiated form of corporate filmmaking in the United States during a period marked by extensive homophobia. Yet given the camp stylistic flourishes of Freed productions that appeared in such a climate, the "what if . . ." question asks how queer sensibilities could inform a film's look under such circumstances of production.

The emphasis I wish to place on the camp aspects of the Freed unit, then, stems from the articulation that Simone's comments about Minnelli make possible, between the signifying play of camp and the forms of subjectivity marked by labor, a tension that can scarcely be approached through the largely unhelpful forms of identity-speak that have arisen in the past thirty years. It has been a truism of liberation politics in the past three decades that gendered identities derived from sexual activities: that one is a queer man because he maintains an erotic interest in other men. I do not want to deny this claim of identity as articulated with sexual desires and practices. I do, however, want to under-score the political, economic, and cultural dimensions of what being queer has meant to the labor of men and women who have been labeled as homosexual (and whose lives may predate the political act of self-naming themselves as gay, lesbian, or queer). Simone's claim that Min-nelli "worked like a homosexual" means that labors performed by par-ticular subjects, and not identities, can in some cases display the mark of the subject on the product; the net effect of this claim is that some commodities are indeed, as Marx suggested, queer.[21]

In the case of camp arising in Hollywood, we discover two dispa-rate ways of rendering the experiences of modernity by a particular set of men: as gendered subjects who desire others of the same sex, and as laborers within a capitalist enterprise. The strangeness of the juxta-position of the terms "desire" and "laborer" tells us how unaccustomed critiques of sexual politics and capital can be to seeing any features as common to both, and the task of discovering where these social realms overlap is frustrated in light of the strategies of bourgeois gays to deflect attention from their dissident sexualities as they relate to the results of their productive efforts within the larger political economy.[22]

That said, the primary feature of Freed productions that deflected the "what if" question posed by Sedgwick's camp spectator (and the censoring eyes of the offices of Joseph Breen, too) was the ability of queers to labor in the process of creating heterosexual romance narra-tives. Not surprisingly, the effects of queer participation in creating nor-mative straight romance emerge quickly as contradictory. On the one hand, queer labor here enables the dissemination of the purportedly one culturally sanctioned version of erotic and romantic bonding, a hetero-sexual version that customarily enforces the hidden status of queers as historical subjects and encourages their exclusion from representation. This exclusion is intensified by analyses that predict that a given film can only be read in one blinkered way, that is, the romance narrative. On the other hand, the labors of such queer subjects may show up in other ways alongside narrative, here called camp. The difference between what I am offering as camp, vis-à-vis the production of Freed musicals, and the general idea of camp as a reader's emphasis on stylistic excess resides in the fact that, within the analysis here, camp stylistics contributed to the studio's profits while taking advantage of the fact that such signs of visual excess remain ambiguous enough to encourage camp-embracing view-ers as well as those unaware of the visual economy at work. The camp-loving viewer contributes to those profits by simply buying a ticket, but camp style within Freed films circulated to noncamp audiences under the more general idea of their being "stylized" or "witty."

What is then labeled as the integration of straight romance and queer-inflected visual codes is more generally within the camp sensibility what we might call "style," or more particularly a style of excess. Susan Sontag comments on the impulse to call attention to the stylization of a text:

> Stylization in a work of art, as distinct from style, reflects an ambivalence (affection contradicted by contempt, obsession contradicted by irony) toward the subject matter. This ambivalence is handled by maintaining, through the rhetorical overlay that is stylization, a special distance from the subject. No doubt, in a culture pledged to the utility (particularly the moral utility) of art, burdened with a useless need to fence off solemn art from arts which provide amusement, the eccentricities of stylized art supply a valid and valuable satisfaction. I have described these satisfactions in another essay, under the name of camp taste.[23]

Sontag proceeds to comment that such camp stylized art is "palpably an art of excess, lacking harmoniousness, [and] can never be of the very greatest kind," locating her own tastes for high modernism and its limited ironic vista. Sidestepping her dismissal of camp, I would suggest that the sense of integration so often attributed to Freed-Minnelli films achieves the very ambivalence that Sontag is describing. This occurs at the moment in which we realize earlier Freed productions to be breaking with the previous nonintegrating codes of the musical, whereby we could argue that camp stylization informs the films in their entirety, not just within the numbers. Camp style marks a critical commentary on the narrative of heterosexual bonding. Before moving to depict Freed's queer employees as necessarily agents of transgression through their critique of heterosexual romance narratives, though, we should remember that the unit's independence stemmed, within the profit-driven logic of Hollywood film production, from its capacity to fill movie theaters, profits not unrelated to the narrative organization of heterosexual desire and union. The usual prestige accorded the films, then and now, comes perhaps with the demand that we ignore elements of camp production, meaning that popular and critical responses to the films have customarily ignored the very art direction that differentiated the MGM product.

Nevertheless, despite the history-making dynamics of censorship and forgetting, recent accounts have begun to suggest that an interest in knowing the queer features of the lives of Freed employees figures in the popular rewriting of Hollywood. When we consider that commentary continues to be traded within fan culture about the erotic liaisons of key figures within the Freed unit, we are confronted with the fact that these films do circulate with varying historical accounts. Recently there has been confirmation within print media, such as when David Shipman's biography of Judy Garland remarks in passing that Vincente Minnelli was widely known as homosexual within the more restricted domain of Hollywood, and Lela Simone comments to her interviewer that Roger Edens, acknowledged by many as the figure responsible for the success of the unit's collaborative efforts, was known in the period by many to be homosexual.[24] (Indeed, Edens's longtime lover was employed on the lot as a production assistant.) Further speculation, unconfirmed within the popular and academic presses, circulates about many figures, some of whom are still alive and hostile to being named as situated in the queer history of American corporate film production.

These emerging accounts of queer life in Hollywood do not call for an "outing" of every queer laborer within the Freed unit. At the very least, they illustrate the problem of whether addressing particular figures as queer produces a necessarily pro-queer history; at the worst, such nominations on behalf of a history of sexual identity disregard one vitally important feature to recall of the period of the unit's production: that the very anonymity of production, in addition to the anonymity for sexuality, that was ensured for those laboring within the corporate structure of Metro-Goldwyn-Mayer may inadvertently have provided the queer makers of camp Freed musicals with a venue in which to labor. Even in the case of such a prominently identified maker of the popular commodity such as Minnelli, an important reversal around the anonymity of labor emerges, in that the generalized labor that I commented on earlier offers an anonymous erotic sphere for the emergence of nonsanctioned desires.

If anonymity-in-production was a feature of the Freed/MGM setting for more recognizable reasons of profit, then any attempt to historicize the relation of the labor of queers to this anonymity-in-sexuality will have to devise historiographic strategies of its own. Remembering Simone's caveat when commenting on Minnelli that she has nothing against homosexuals, every attempt to specify one figure as queer means that the historian might end up producing *something* for homophobic stances against the queer filmmaker. Therefore it is less important to see current revelations about the sexuality of Hollywood figures as confirmation about what we think we know about a star or director than it is to seize on such comments as the occasion to address the conditions under which such figures labored.

Anonymity as a feature of queer labor in the Freed setting accounts for the problems of the historian as she or he encounters the dissembling abilities of camp, most notably when many of the historian's sources are the most scorned form of historical discourses: gossip. How do we acknowledge the truth value and concurrently question the veracity of a given bit of hearsay? This problem is compounded by the fact that we find ourselves dealing with a subterranean history that is now almost fifty years old, and gossip has a way of accruing half-truths and misnamings to it. There is, however, a way to play to the strengths of gossip by remembering that commentary on the sexual preferences of a particular person circulates as gossip, not as monumental history, because such tale-telling involves the overlapping of sexuality with production, an overlap more usually called the closet. In other instances, historians encounter similarly private and debased historical discourses; these are given the name of folklore. Like gossip, folklore accumulates truth value by its circulation through more personal venues of conversation and storytelling. We should take pains, though, to distinguish the organicist strains of folklore from gossip, as the gossip surrounding queer Hollywood, current and past, is frequently antagonistic to folkloric and nostalgic versions of Hollywood history that circulate within popular venues.

The presence of queer laborers and its accompanying circulation through the circuits of gossip, then, become a forceful way of thinking about the films made by the Freed unit because it allows subsequent viewers and historians to read the films for the traces of queer sensibilities and taste while acknowledging enforced silences around sexual dissidences. Nevertheless what has allowed camp features to be ignored in critical treatments of the Freed films has been the centrality of narrative as a privileged category for critical analysis. In seeking to classify the film musical as sharing features with all films in the enormous ideological edifice called Hollywood Cinema, we risk losing sight of the anomalous features that may in fact distinguish one genre from another. The problem here is not only a taxonomical one but one that concerns our attempts to understand the different positions that varying genres inhabited within the complex ideological practices of cinema and how such genres seized different workers' efforts and different forms of affectively necessary labor.[25]

Camp Style and the Problem of Integration

In an immensely important essay on the complexities of the mass culture text, Richard Dyer, in "Entertainment and Utopia," argues that the fascination of Hollywood film musicals resides in their ability both to coordinate the sense that life under modernity is itself riven with crises and dissatisfactions—what he calls "inadequacies and absences" such as alienation, exhaustion, and monotony—and to represent a world of utopian feelings (and not utopian political solutions) that seem to answer to such frustrations. Dyer argues that the musical in particular is well suited to this form of ideological management in that music itself is an order of signification that seems utopian; that is, it is not burdened with the history of Western modes of representation in which almost every sign comes to have a kind of political status, what (taking his cue from Fredric Jameson's reading of Ernest Bloch) Dyer calls the historicity of its narrative. The musical numbers in the film musical appear to transcend this semiotic weight, and the film musical mobilizes this appearance by making each socially motivated inadequacy into a form of pleasure; thus the exhaustions of alienated labor are answered by the musical's sense of endless energy and enthusiasm, which is marked by dance and song.

> Musicals (and variety) represent an extraordinary mix of these two modes—the historicity of narrative and the lyricism of the numbers. They have not often taken advantage of it, but the point is that they could, and that this possibility is always latent in them. They are a form we still need to look at if films are, in Brecht's words on the theater, to "organise the enjoyment of changing reality."[26]

Dyer has written elsewhere more specifically about camp, but this passage offers an incisive strategy for considering the labor of camp as related to the problem of the films' integration of number and narrative. The Freed films are perhaps utopian not solely because of the more conservatizing features that they display through Dyer's critical taxonomy but because they offer pleasures in the changing realities of the hallucinogenic worlds that they purport to describe, fantastic worlds known not through narrative as much as through their outlandish backdrops, vocalizations, and physical movements.

Betraying any temptation to think that this problem is solely one for the cultural theorist, contemporaneous historical responses confirm that audiences and the industry itself seem to have registered the very dynamics about which Dyer writes. The comments of filmgoers who attended previews of *The Pirate* confirm that studio executives were aware that the film tended to emphasize its own spectacular art direction while sometimes disregarding story lines with narrative economy and clear characterization. There seems little doubt that, in some measure, this seeming imbalance in the films offered by the unit were known to those at Metro-Goldwyn-Mayer who took an interest in seeing the studio's profits enhanced: the studio circulated audience responses to producers and directors within days after an audience in Pasadena had passed judgment on the film. In the preview cards, where anonymous viewers offered praise and disparagement, a repeated emphasis on the art direction arises: "[The] sets detracted from the people and the music was too loud," "not realistic enough," "entirely too surrealistic," "the beautiful background settings were exceptional," "plot rather thin," "truly one of the most exciting pictures from every standpoint, direction, artwork, color dancing, scoring," "beautiful coloring," "slightly fantastic plot not developed in as natural and realistic [a way] as it could have been," and perhaps the most telling, "Minnelli back to the small minority who really appreciate him."[27]

These comments suggest that the viewers had screened a film by Luis Buñuel or Ken Russell, not the product of Metro-Goldwyn-Mayer after twenty years of corporate film production experience. Nor would these responses make sense when we account for the fact that the Freed unit recruited some of the most renowned writing talent of the period for its films and devoted attention to writing and revising its script properties during preproduction and production. Indeed, given these audience responses, it appears that historically contemporaneous viewers perceived these films as residing within the tension between story and spectacle and were commenting on this through their attention to the film's apparent shortcomings in offering a clear and forceful story line. We risk losing sight of this when we emphasize the former as part of the impulse to subsume Hollywood musicals to the larger "ultragenre" of Hollywood narrative cinema. Thus from Rick Altman's account of the Hollywood film musical, I would particularly reiterate his suggestion that genre, as both historical and theoretical category, is repressive. By this, it seems that the aspects of production that pertain to a given genre, in this case the Hollywood musical, not only dictate what will be included within a specific film's making but also by implication delimit what cannot be included in its critical treatment. As Altman argues:

> Genres are not the democratically elected representatives of a group of like-minded texts. They are autocratic monarchs dictating a single standard of allegiance for all subjects. In short, genres are not neutral categories, as structuralist critics have too often implied; rather they are ideological constructs masquerading as neutral categories.[28]

Altman quite rightly, to my reading, argues that the various features of a generic text that different critical projects value, often in wildly fluctuating ways, are not mere coincidences. Critics notice different features of a text for their particular interests: thus the musical can be read as ideological practice, "mere" entertainment, a vestige of folk culture, and so on. The argument for a particular reading relies on the priority of one set of traits over another, and no critical project is exempt from having its hierarchy. Musicals have largely been understood as primarily narrative films at the expense of other features.

There is little doubt that the relation of story to number counts for much in the meanings attributed to film musicals, and the plotline that structures many musicals is that of straight romance and marriage. The world in which a man and a woman meet and find initial attraction, in which their union is frustrated, and where ultimately the prohibitions to heterosexual bonding are overcome through the mediation of the song and dance number is typically the world of the film musical. But there is more to the making of musicals beyond the plotline and its ancillary subplots, all of which are said to be brought to happy closure at the film's completion.

For one thing, song and dance occur in the space of spectacle, and this space seems in excess of the realist codes that lend credibility to the space of the more humdrum story. Perhaps the most dazzling examples of the differences between the codes of narrative and number are those of the Busby Berkeley backstage musicals made at Warner Brothers in the 1930s.[29] For the Freed unit in the late forties, the spectacular number became the benchmark of the prestigious films that Metro-Goldwyn-Mayer was known for making; the large amounts of time, labor, and investment by the studio in the Freed unit stemmed from the requirements of staging such sequences. Here I would draw out the differences in readings that emphasize one aspect, spectacle, over another, narrative.

What seem to have been the memorable features of Freed unit musicals for contemporaneous viewers were their dazzling sets, costumes, use of color (in terms of film stock, set painting, and lighting), and choreography. These specific elements of film production are perhaps most likely what the various viewers' cards cited are locating as the Freed unit's distinguishing style, or to remember the viewer who commented on the "small minority" who might be interested in Minnelli films, that this style was idiosyncratic enough to have both fans and detractors. This style distinguished the unit's films from those of its rivals, even those appearing from other Metro production units making musicals.[30]

Minnelli's work habit of plotting a film's numbers by creating a series of paper dolls and scaled-down soundstages in which to place these figures suggests that his first impulses were to conceive of a film through its mise-en-scène rather than its story line. As Naremore argues, "within the limits of the system, Minnelli was able to say a good deal about sets and costumes (departments that could be intractable), and he usually influenced the overall visual conception of his films."[31] Minnelli himself described his move from Broadway productions: "When I arrived in Hollywood, I didn't look down on musicals as so many people who were doing them did, treating them as a romp, a slapstick, nothing to be taken seriously."[32] The seriousness of the labor that Minnelli expended on Freed films suggests that camp manifests itself in what has more commonly been described as the high degree of visual stylistic integration within Freed productions; that is, camp becomes an important way for thinking about Minnelli's efforts inasmuch as it shaped his work on the films' visual style over and above their narrative.

"Never had a story": *The Ziegfeld Follies*

In a certain manner of speaking, *The Ziegfeld Follies* is not really a Vincente Minnelli film. Although the film is saturated with the lavish visual sensibility that would become Minnelli's signature style and showcases early in his film career the talents that would make him one of MGM's most important directors, Minnelli was not originally slated by Freed to direct this lavishly budgeted ($3 million) spectacle. According to Stephen Harvey, Freed had contracted George Sidney to direct, and Minnelli was brought in only after disappointing portions of the film indicated that Sidney was not the best talent for the project.[33] Further, not all the film's segments in the final cut are credited to Minnelli, with a number of the film's set pieces being attributed to a host of different talents, including Sidney, Lemuel Ayers, Roy Del Ruth, Robert Lewis, and (uncredited) Norman Taurog.

Be that as it may, *Ziegfeld Follies* demonstrates that early in his career Minnelli had already achieved a highly consolidated aesthetic vision in which the emphasis in his filmmaking was on a mise-en-scène that not only competed with the narrative but in fact could become the narrative. The structure of *Ziegfeld Follies* and its occurrence so soon in his endeavors in Hollywood make it key to his oeuvre. Seemingly returning to the backstage musical, *Ziegfeld Follies* consists entirely of comedic skits and musical numbers strung together with only the intermittent page of a playbill to announce the name of the number and its performers; the film offers a series of numbers that are ostensibly the enactment of a live performance of Ziegfeld's Broadway spectacle. No story line serves as a hammock to hold the separate pieces together, other than a wish by the dead and apotheosized Flo Ziegfeld (William Powell),[34] now ensconced in a celestially appointed pink luxury hotel suite in heaven, to see who might appear on his stage in the year 1944.[35] Demonstrating the secondary importance of narrative as a vehicle for the staging of number, *Ziegfeld Follies* could be said to be a film that is all number and no narrative; as Fred Astaire, in a moment of direct-camera address early in the film, proclaims, the appeal of Ziegfeld stage productions was to be found in the fact that they "never had a story." An opportunity for different talents to appear in a Hollywood production that might otherwise never find a place within narrative, *Follies* showcases Lena Horne and Fanny Brice, stage stars too "ethnic" for the more customary middle-brow WASP depictions sought by Metro. Without recourse to (or constriction by) a story, the film provided the opportunity to see African American "exoticism" and Yiddish comic play largely unavailable in a Hollywood vehicle.[36]

Ethnicity, though, is not the only trace of difference that informs *Ziegfeld Follies*. The camp play of Minnelli's direction appears in many of the musical numbers that bear his directorial credit, and in different ways they each form an experiment on his behalf in importing the kinds of visual tricks that had brought him celebrity in his stagecraft. Taken together, the two dance sequences, "This Heart of Mine" and "Limehouse Blues," which pair Lucille Bremer and Fred Astaire, demonstrate Minnelli's fascination with the challenges of moving physical bodies through cinematic space, and each number answers this challenge in importantly different ways. In "This Heart of Mine," which offers the story of a party-crashing roué (Astaire) who inadvertently becomes erotically interested in his intended debutante-victim (Bremer), Minnelli moves the romantic pair out of the public arena of the party into a privatized space of seduction by breaking apart the foreground fourth wall of the soundstage, an effect paying homage to his earlier apprenticeship to Busby Berkeley, in whose films proscenium arches continually disappear and rematerialize. Remarkable in Minnelli's use of this technique is that he preserves the previous space of the ballroom, now a tomblike drum encased in monumental Orientalist-medieval figures designed by Tony Duquette. Harvey reads this bizarre physical presence as one being protected by these looming "courtiers," but the space equally reads as one out of which the characters must escape to play out their fantasies of inappropriate social contact and of erotic bonding (codified through the dance). Preserved behind them, the world of socially sanctioned contact, of normalcy and decorum, is however momentarily encased in a vault, but remarkably the other, external space of their fantasies is equally winterish, marked as it is by leafless trees and a cool blue backdrop. If Astaire and Bremer's dance signals the attempt to find a realm of pleasure and desire beyond that presented in the ballroom, then the mise-en-scène of this sequence hardly provides a utopian backdrop for illicit heterosexual bonding.

Even more to the point, when Minnelli stages the couple's dance on a system of mechanically rotating platforms and treadmills that circle and counterpose them in a series of remarkably awkward poses, the camp engagement with the technologies of modernity, so often concealed in the production of film spectacle, intrude in a seldom-witnessed fashion whereby the dancer's bodies, usually the site of boundless energies and delight, become robotic and clumsy. Minnelli moves the couple to the center of a turntable, where they are subsequently surrounded by a corps of other couples, almost imprisoned by the stark pale thorns of the trees that encircle them.

In contrast to the automated organization of the dance in "This Heart of Mine," the "Limehouse Blues" number uses lighting and editing to mark the spaces of the "real" and the fantastic. Here Minnelli places Astaire and Bremer, now rendered in stereotypified Hollywood-Asian makeup and costume, in turn-of-the-century East End London, where Astaire plays a coolie smitten with Bremer's indifferent prostitute, her

Exile from normativity: Lucille Bremer and Fred Astaire dance
before Tony Duquette's fantastic creations in the "This Heart of
Mine" number in *Ziegfeld Follies*.

attentions being lavished on her patron, Robert Lewis, himself in an
equally ghoulish racialized performance of an Anglo-Chinese Daddy
Warbucks. Caught in the cross fire of a dock gang's robbery of a shop,
Astaire falls into a reverie where he and Bremer are united in world
of chinoiserie-saturated bliss. The marked technique of this sequence
involves the positioning of Astaire and Bremer in a long shot and cast
in the circle of a spotlight; quite suddenly the immense soundstage
is brightly lit into a world most like that of the colonialist fantasy of
Chinese-export porcelain: "jasmine" trees, half-moon bridges, and paper lanterns. Similar to "This Heart of Mine," "Limehouse Blues" offers
the dreamed-of possibility of a heterosexual union as the most fantastic
(i.e., improbable) of things. In both these sequences, the diegetic world
in which these figures perform stages their pursuit as bizarre; here the
camp visual field of the musical number makes male-female bonding
paradoxically into the exotic and, in the case of "Limehouse Blues," the
impossible.

In one of his most elegant and mocking numbers, "The Great Lady
Has 'an Interview,'" we witness Judy Garland sending up the star images

Garland and her fans: "The Great Lady has
'an Interview' " in *Ziegfeld Follies.*

of dramatic actresses of the period, Greer Garson being the most notable target for Garland's breathless pomposity.[37] The Great Lady announces her boredom at appearing in the demanding roles that have garnered her attention, and the press corps that surrounds her provide the musical troupe through which she can springboard into a song, "Madame Crematon." The song provides the opportunity for the fictitious actress to perform the light comedy that she wants to do but from which her star persona prohibits her in engaging.

Two elements of the Great Lady sequence offer clues to the camp sensibility that underpins the number. First, the dance troupe–press corps appear as a queer entourage that has descended on the star's house as a contingent of adoring fans eager for a glimpse of her. Dancing in through the entrance door under the disapproving eye of her butler, they link arms and merrily kick-step their way into the receiving room. The dance ensemble depicts an important relation of queers to the figure of Judy Garland, because the young men in this number seem to adore her as fans, but not necessarily as straight men interested in making a sexual score. Dressed identically in dark suits and neat ties, they dance with themselves as much as they do with Garland; in fact, given her initial hauteur, it is their ease with one another that displaces attention from the star back to themselves, and in which she can relax. Garland becomes, through her release into comic play in a nonseductive situation, a star capable of bonding with her "camp followers," depicted in this scene by the male chorus.[38]

Second, the art direction of the star's home is executed in a style that is paradoxically spare and yet overwrought. On a lush background of walls treated in mocha-colored silk hangs an oversized baroque mirror, under which a white moderne table sits with a craggy floral arrangement of seemingly prehistoric orchids. The effect is one of refined vulgarity; expensive materials and extreme lines offer the camp attention to the ways that high and low distinctions of taste can be blurred for comic effect.

The film's penultimate number, "Babbit and the Bromide," is the only pairing of Gene Kelly and Fred Astaire committed to film, and despite the critical tradition of seeing this sequence as a disappointment, it offers one of the most daring and pronounced of Minnelli's camp labors in *Ziegfeld Follies*. The more customary critical response is typified in Steven Harvey's comments that

> this was a unique opportunity for the two dancers to face off in their opposing choreographic styles—Kelly's sinewy athleticism versus Astaire's weightless grace. Instead, they meet diplomatically in a cautious middle ground. After some brief, competitive hoofing, as the song progresses to its climax, Astaire and Kelly pair off in a stately same-sex waltz, a mock jitterbug, and a synchronized, hip-swiveling tap. The ironic result is that while the song mocks the paralyzing effect of unstinting good manners, the Astaire-Kelly dance is itself an anemic model of proper etiquette in motion.[39]

While the ostensible content of the song's lyrics situates the two figures as stultified by the dull repetition of social niceties, the pairing of Kelly and Astaire as men meeting in the park plays coyly with the long-standing queer male practice of finding anonymous sexual partners in public settings. That they can hardly ever remember each other's names as they meet over a period of years (marked by their graying hair and change in costume) plays with this anonymity, and the camp dimensions of this sequence are underscored when they smirkingly refer to each other as "Rita Hayworth" and "Ginger." Curiously, the backdrops and costumes in this sequence are atypically subdued for a Minnelli number, indicating that even this obliquely flirtatious acknowledgment of the erotic alliances of camp demands a corresponding erasure of the film's luxuriant style.[40]

The musical numbers that Minnelli contributed to *Ziegfeld Follies* form perhaps one of the most varied and complicated experiments in a young filmmaker's oeuvre; yet these numbers are the product of a camp artist with an accomplished visual sense exploring a host of different filmic techniques without the burden of feature film storytelling. In most other cases, the dance cast and set decoration could easily become elements of a secondary order, after the purportedly overarching and determining structure of the plot. But *Ziegfeld Follies* offers no plot, and thus the dancing and sets are what the numbers "mean," in contrast to any feature of a story that might be played out. Liberated from the constraints of cause-effect relations, even from the idea of events themselves, *Ziegfeld Follies* plunges into the camp pleasures of texture, masquerade, and performance.

"Not the Marrying Kind": *Yolanda and the Thief*

Narrative-number integration thus emerges as a hallmark of Freed productions, in that the unit's earlier films offered such a pronounced split between story and musical performance that the studio mandated that the production unit strive to make the two textual features more commensurate. This does not mean that the problem disappeared, and indeed the fact that the unit was made to concentrate on film narrative indicates an abiding crisis through which we can read the unit's developing hallmark style for big production numbers and sophisticated music and lyrics. The impulse to integrate more seamlessly the movement from narrative to number meant that the art direction and costuming in the nonnumber portions of the films became even more unrecognizable for the codes of Hollywood realism; if the Freed products came to be known for their higher level of integration, this happened because the narrative portions of the films became more like the musical numbers, at the very least in terms of their outlandish art direction, lighting, and costuming. The musical numbers, with their potential for appearing discordant with the codes of narrative realism, colonized the film's narratives in such a way as to appear natural and spontaneous; the numbers seem less bracketed from the narrative. When, for example, Fred Astaire dances the "Will You Marry Me?" number in *Yolanda and*

Fred Astaire and Gene Kelly in "Babbit and the Bromide" in *Ziegfeld Follies*

the Thief (1945), the motivation for this dream sequence dance is his uneasy conscience over taking advantage of the wealthy Yolanda, the prey for his congames with whom he is simultaneously falling in love. (Her own aunt confirms this when she counsels Yolanda that he's probably "not the marrying kind.") The dream seems more explicable within the story because it has motivation both in terms of the narrative and in terms of Astaire's character, and yet the entire film becomes dreamlike and narratively disorganized the more it becomes like one continuous musical number; we never move out of number and back to narrative, an effect that renders the film as seemingly more integrated.

The potential for reading this perverse form of film musical integration as part of Minnelli's stylistics reveals the camp emphasis on the performative aspects of everyday life. If more customarily the musical number implicates its performers as mystifying the conditions of mundane life, in which it is impossible to break into song and dance with full orchestral backing, a camp emphasis on performance also points in the opposite direction, implicating everyday life as performative, not least of which when it comes to thinking about gender. When the number becomes elegantly situated within its narrative constraints as less abruptly breaking with the realist narrative codes that mark the number *as* number, then it is possible to read the narrative, too, as also baring its performative aspects. Ed Lowry addresses this dual tendency of integration as creating both heightened realism and emphatic performance.

> In Minnelli's films there is a constant tension between his awareness that the Hollywood musical is artificial and false, and his contradictory delight in being able to create that artificiality so well—a conflict which manifests itself in his unpretentious attitude that his "art" is just a job (beautifully expressed in *The Bandwagon,* a film which forwards a professional ethos on a par with the best of Howard Hawks) and an opposing desire to create in a purely stylized and transcendent form (as in the elongated ballets of his musicals), of which the dream in *Yolanda* is said to be the first in film.[41]

Couched not only in the terms under which the Hollywood musical seems "artificial and false" because of its extranarrative codes but also in the sense in which a camp sensibility can point to the limits of romance narrative for addressing all viewers, the contradiction that Lowry describes is not simply one of stylistics but also of the challenge posed by camp as it encounters the realist tradition in which heterosexual romance is depicted. To privilege heterosexual realism, then, we are called on to see the films as visually and acoustically integrated. Describing the films' style as integrated, though, bolsters a reading that neglects the differences of camp commodity production that Freed films so vividly display.

The opening of Yolanda and the Thief provides a moment in which to note the aggregation of several different surfaces that are gathered together in what can only through analytic gymnastics be seen as part of a tradition of Hollywood realism. The opening titles place colorful hand lettering on a brightly painted primitivist landscape, what we subsequently learn is the utopian country of Patria, in which the film is set. As the film commences, the camera moves us into a foreground of the painting, which becomes a backdrop for a country schoolroom, which is set on a grassy bluff where the benevolent (and oddly German-accented) schoolmaster instructs his pupils, mostly by commanding them to sing the national song, coyly named "This Is a Day for Love." Passing shepherds in the background usher the camera into a sunny exterior back lot and the convent in which Yolanda has been raised, and finally into another soundstage interior of the convent. The entire sequence is held together by the musical sound bridges of the song, which is passed from the pupils to the shepherds and finally to the schoolgirls, who reiterate it as they bathe.

The initial images offered in the film, then, gather together a remarkable number of different kinds of filmmaking: wildly "unrealistic" backdrops, extravagant Metro-Goldwyn-Mayer style exteriors, and elegantly stylized interiors, playing out a fantasy of the then-current vogue for all things seemingly "south of the border."[42] We might describe the composition of these multiple diegetic spaces as contributing to an ultimate realism of the film. The fact that the "This Is a Day for Love" number so elegantly binds together, for the sake of moving the narrative from Patria's bucolic beauty to the convent where we find Yolanda, such disparate kinds of film media can be read as in some sense being driven by the story. But questions of narrative economy aside, we have to accept the fantastic opening images of Yolanda and the Thief as a gesture forcing us to accept the film's aesthetic anomalies as in excess of the movie's narrative. As Lowry suggests, "the landscape which we knew could not be real is still no more real, but has been established as the 'reality' of the world depicted in Yolanda and the Thief."[43] However, the "unreality" that the film demands we respect as the place in which the narrative will unfold also seems then to implicate the narrative itself as potentially quite unreal.

The narrative of *Yolanda,* in brief, offers a romance between a naive and wealthy young woman, Yolanda Aquaviva (Lucille Bremer), who is tricked by a con man, Johnny Riggs (Fred Astaire), into believing that he is her guardian angel. Johnny plays on Yolanda's gullibility to convince her to confer her power of attorney to him, but just as he is ready to depart with the goods, he finds himself romantically and erotically drawn to her. His attraction to her surprises Johnny, because he ostensibly does not expect to find Yolanda a figure of erotic contemplation, and his jaded sensibilities lose out to his romantic impulses. Moments of camp playfulness in the film, though, offer another reading of Johnny's surprise at discovering himself in a seduction beyond his overarching greed and cynicism, for there are strong possibilities for reading him as queer.

In the "Will You Marry Me?" number, for example, he wrestles with the trauma of potentially being trapped in a marriage to Yolanda for her money. This dream sequence ballet opens with Astaire dressed in a remarkably dandy outfit, a pair of off-white satin pajamas with byzantine silk cord closures on the shirt.[44] Becoming restless in his bed, Johnny dresses and walks through the streets of Patria's unnamed capital, where he moves into increasingly surreal landscapes in which various women trap him in symmetrical dance steps: washerwomen unfold furls of wildly colored fabric in stark geometric patterns forming a prison out of which he cannot escape. Yolanda then appears, throwing off a series of veils trimmed in coins, and sirens in short dresses and high heels entice him with a cask into which Yolanda has dispensed her gold. The number effectively links Johnny's fear of marriage with his greed, or more properly, according to the dream logic of the "Will You Marry Me?" sequence, his greed is the film's alibi for not stating more directly his desire not to bond with a woman, no matter what her beauty or wealth. I would argue that the film temporarily addresses the question of whether Johnny will accede to the demands of marriage through the camp art direction's treatment of him as queer.

Steven Cohan's discussion of Fred Astaire's performances illustrates how Astaire's virtuoso dances served to feminize him, inasmuch as they rendered him a spectacle to be enjoyed beyond the narrative. As Cohan writes, "Astaire's numbers oftentimes exceed both linear narrativity and the heterosexual (that is 'straight' in the cultural as well as narrative

Fred Astaire wrestles with the mise-en-scène and heterosexuality
in "Will You Marry Me?" in *Yolanda and the Thief.*

sense) male desire that fuels it."[45] Cohan argues that because the dance
might feminize the male actor, the narrative must "retrieve" him to re-
integrate him into the straight romance. Nevertheless the performance
disrupts the narrative by momentarily disregarding the force of the
story for the power of the spectacular dance routine.[46] The settings and
costumes perform a similar function, but we tend not to notice their
potential to antagonize narrative because, of course, most often the
disjunctive features of the mise-en-scène to which I am pointing are
maintained in the film's movement back to the story line, whereas the
acoustic and gestural signs of the music and dance are not.

Thus against the more usual tendency to argue that the innovation of
Freed productions was the high degree of integration of number into
narrative, the visual excesses of the film's numbers cannot be cleaved
from other moments in *Yolanda and the Thief.* The problem with the
ways that integration has been understood is that it commonly serves
as a rhetorical strategy that precludes reading *against* the narrative force
of such films in favor of considering their spectacular numbers. If the
strength of Freed numbers, and the camp proclivities heralded in their
look, is understood as only lending credence to the film's closure around

marriage, the possibility for interpreting the camp signs of the film are foreclosed.

A moment marked by camp play can easily be ignored because it contributes little to understanding the relation between the film's visual style and the tension around whether Johnny and Yolanda will bond. In an early encounter between the two, Yolanda is summoned from her mansion (where she is bathing in a glass-lined tub fed by Bernini-esque marble waterfalls) to meet with Johnny, whom she assumes to be her angelic overseer. In preparation for this meeting, Johnny and his sidekick Victor Trout (Frank Morgan) rearrange the furnishings of the hotel lobby to backlight him on a gilt throne in front of a baroque mural of clouds and cherubim. Yolanda, sporting a kind of mantilla that is meant to affirm her piety and naïveté, has an initial vision of him as he feyly holds his hand out and jadedly stares to the heavens. If we read this as part of a seduction, it would be difficult to see Johnny as an affected aesthete and Yolanda as a schoolgirl unfamiliar with the effete posturings of a queer man. In another sequence at the film's conclusion, Johnny seems bewildered to discover himself married to Yolanda and is further confused when Yolanda's real guardian angel, Mr. Candle (Leon Ames), appears as a wandering tourist who gives them a photo. As Johnny contemplates the picture, a divinely offered snapshot into their future where he and Yolanda are surrounded by their children, he blanches, perhaps not only because of the paranormal dimensions of the picture but because of the familial setting in which he never expected to find himself and whose dangers were so vividly enacted in the "Will You Marry Me?" number. Johnny's aversion to marriage, then, and the sense of entrapment from which he awakens (and which concludes the number) foreshadow the conclusion of the film, for the number is more than a recapitulation of the plot as it has unfolded up until the number is staged; Johnny's shock is anticipated through the camp mise-en-scène of the "Will You Marry Me?" number.

"You Fill the Eyes": *The Pirate*
The Pirate retains a curious status in abject canons of Hollywood cinema as a film that appeals to the tastes of the few; its centrality in biographies of both its female lead, Garland, and her new husband, the film's director, as the film in which Garland began to demonstrate the strain of studio production (tales of substance abuse, long periods of absence from the soundstage) has displaced attention from the fact that Min-

nelli lavished more attention to the production of this film than perhaps any project he ever completed.[47] The film took almost a year to complete, with principal photography extending to an astonishing six months from February to August 1947; it cost the studio $3,768,014, making it one of the most expensive films that Metro would offer, and lost a breathtaking $2,290,000 for the studio in its initial release. This marks *The Pirate* as an important investment in capital and labor that bears further explanation than the more customary one that Garland's tantrums held production up for extended periods and thus made it expensive because of languishing sets that awaited acting talent to fill them. Minnelli, who wrote about *The Pirate* that it "was great camp, an element that hadn't been intentionally used in films . . . I say intentionally," and the film's remarkably consistent visual aesthetic, in contrast to the varied and juxtaposed styles of *Yolanda and the Thief,* beg the question of what Minnelli meant by so describing the film.[48] Naremore takes pains to remind us of the historically inflected critical receptions that met Minnelli's films, suggesting that camp was perhaps the least apparent of terms brought to bear on the film, arguing that "we cannot tell exactly how much of its effect was deliberate," and, curiously, that it "automatically invites a later audience to engage in a whole new range of ironic readings."[49] What the film demands of us automatically remains unclear, but if camp offers any help in deciphering Minnelli's labors on the film, it might help to call attention to the fact that, more than any of his previous films, *The Pirate* showcases the spectacle of Gene Kelly's talents.

If *The Pirate* centers, as Stephen Harvey comments, on Serafin (Kelly) and his "passionate self-love in satin breeches" and is remarkably indifferent to making Garland's Manuela into a romantic partner for Kelly's athletic form of erotic play, then the film comes more closely than any other Minnelli vehicle to articulating its heady visual decoration with male same-sex eroticism; that is, camp and homoeroticism come into a proximity that was, from the standpoint of studio profit, perhaps dangerous. Read through the codes of the genre, the film resists the expected union of the male and female leads and, as Harvey suggests, "ignores a fundamental principle of the genre that song and movement are metaphors for sex. If the stars do their stuff solo, alienation is bound to upstage romance."[50] *The Pirate,* though, is less concerned with alienation than it is with self-pleasure, and particularly the pleasure of Serafin with the spectacle of his own movement, which, barring the film's closing number "Be a Clown" (which has its own problems as a form of romantic closure), he never performs with Garland in a musical number. She is called to witness his image on a number of occasions: the troupe's evening performance in San Sebastian, his trapeze walk across the wires to her balcony, and most importantly, the "Pirate Ballet." In the idiom of the musical, where music codifies sexuality and desire, Kelly's Serafin is more interested in his own pleasures as ones of narcissistic contemplation than in those of Manuela.

Two numbers confirm this performance as one of the male lead's disregard for female eroticism. The "Nina" number suggests that Serafin, despite his interests in the many women who surround him, is indifferent to them inasmuch as he can do no more than assign them the generic name of "Nina."[51] Elsewhere, one of the more bizarre instances of visual play around the erotic distance from Manuela appears at the beginning of the "Pirate Ballet." Serafin is trying to affirm his status as Macoco the pirate through a dance in which he menaces everyone around him, including a white mule that sits in the center of the frame. When the sequence dissolves into another layering of the fantasy, where Serafin is shown pillaging a town, the mule is transformed into a woman whose face we never see. This substitution, of an "ass" for whom Serafin dances, for an unattributed woman whom he sees as more audience than erotic emblem, serves to mock the status of Garland's Manuela as an interest for Serafin. Frances Goodrich's and Albert Hackett's dialogue plays with the same ambiguities, as becomes evident in throwaway moments in which innuendos about Serafin confirm his muscular presence. For example, Manuela speaks of her desire to have a "chickenhawk" swoop down to rescue her, invoking a long-standing bit of gay urban slang for a predatory male trick, and in another scene, when Serafin is being held captive by the local constabulary, the governor looks over Kelly's tightly garbed torso and gushes, "You fill the eyes!"

Finally, another layering of camp play resides, uncharacteristically, in the film's narrative. Manuela, a landlocked virgin, yearns for the pirate Macoco to liberate her from the provincial Caribbean island on which she lives, and the film derives its comedic play from a series of misrecognitions: that Manuela's sweaty and fumbling fiancé Don Pedro Varga (Walter Slezak) is in fact the real Macoco, that Manuela is happy to settle for matrimony and domesticity when in fact she longs to escape her impending marriage, that Serafin is not the pirate he claims to be but only the head of a group of itinerant players. Indeed, the first important criti-

Making a spectacle: Gene Kelly's athletic presence in *The Pirate*.

cal consideration of camp within a Freed film attempted to consider the film's story as a camp romance narrative. Richard Dyer argues, in the context of reading Judy Garland's ability to make fun of her own star status, that *The Pirate* offers a "spectacular illusion," containing as it does costume, disguise, and the mocking of gender performance; and Dyer's reading ultimately emphasizes the camp narrative possibilities contained within the film's failed closure. Expecting as we might a union of the two main figures Manuela and Serafin (played, respectively, by Garland and Kelly), the film instead delivers not a marriage but another musical number ("Be a Clown"), which itself sends up the conventions of the musical by asking us to laugh with the film's stars.[52]

The Pirate is by any measure a vivid example of camp tastes, and its narrative anomalies are not the sole feature that should tell us about where camp production energies were more usually devoted, to the visual fireworks of the films, not to the story's tampering with romantic expectations. Read against the more narratively integrated of Minnelli's subsequent musicals, *An American in Paris* and *Gigi, The Pirate* marks the enterprise of conceiving of a film through the priority of the visual organization of the mise-en-scène, and the investment of labor and capital in the film make it an emblem of camp's labor. Paradoxically, the fact that the film lost more money in its initial release than any other Minnelli film musical discussed here marks it as a tribute to camp's labors and helps us to perceive the vagaries of camp as an index of value, both critical and industrial; it stands as a kind of beautiful failure that tampers with capital's attempts to capture all forms of physical and intellectual exertion in the name of profit.[53]

Minnelli's talents would, at least for Metro-Goldwyn-Mayer, be better harnessed in his later career, with *An American in Paris* requiring an expenditure of a full $1 million *less* than *The Pirate* and garnering a healthy box office of $1,346,000. The later film, which displayed a much more prominently heterosexual romance between the couple (played by Kelly and Leslie Caron), offers its visual styles in as elegant and complicated a manner as any of the films discussed in this chapter and has enjoyed a canonical status that Minnelli's earlier film musicals have largely not. In this regard, *Ziegfeld Follies, Yolanda and the Thief,* and *The Pirate* can be seen as one of the most remarkable experiments in American filmmaking, corporate or independent, in achieving a particular collective vision in the name of the proper name of a director. It seems fruitful to rediscover the features of these films that evade the more usual search for narratirized representations of queer desire at the expense of the remarkable camp visual feasts to be witnessed in these productions.

Conclusion: Labor without Identities

The call to engage with these films in terms of camp as queer labor should not point us toward too easy a valorization of either the studio or the men who produced them. In the first place, we should remember that the studios at the very least were always driven by motives of profit, and the visions that Metro allowed its employees to realize were in the end for the promulgation of the corporation. Second, most of these men might have balked at the prospect of being addressed through the terms of subsequent sex/gender categories; if they were privately devoted to the pleasure of same-sex relations, at least publicly they knew only too well the penalties for being named as homosexual.

Nevertheless the recuperation of their moment can tell us about the difficulties of the present one: we have by no stretch of the imagination superseded or rendered irrelevant the conditions under which they labored. Indeed, those who bear witness to present controversies—over outing, over the status of liberation politics in the wake of critiques of identity, and over the relation of sex/gender to current modes of production—would do well to remember that these problems did not arise recently or coincidentally. Further, the status of Hollywood can sometimes serve as too limiting a category by which to describe modes of film production, relations of subjects to production and reception, and the heterogeneity of genres as they appeared within various moments.

The Freed unit films of Vincente Minnelli should not be seen reductively in the context of camp; narrative in its complex relation to number remains key to the films' appeal even in their own moment as studio-described "family entertainment." Rather, we should remember that these musicals embody the kinds of negotiations among variable determinations that so many kinds of popular entertainment can sustain. I would, however, claim that unless we can make some leap between the bits of gossip lore that situate the films in differing accounts of Hollywood history and the potential for remarking on the stylistic anomalies of the films, we foreclose the possibility for acknowledging an articulation between queer producers of popular culture and their idiosyncratic products. Such a leap marks a beginning for rethinking the question of the visibility of marginalized makers of popular film; just as Astaire's Johnny in *Yolanda and the Thief* emerges from his dream shaken but unsure of what it means, the historian of camp production can perhaps trace the presence of masked queer tastes only by remembering the strange details that seem to have been so easily forgotten.

TWO

Andy Warhol and the Crises of

Value's Appearances

I suppose I have a really loose interpretation of "work" because
I think that just being alive is so much work at something that you
don't always want to do. Being born is like being kidnapped. And
then sold into slavery. People are working every minute. The
machinery is always going. Even when you sleep.

—Andy Warhol

Think rich, look poor.

—Andy Warhol

Andy Warhol said that his films were better talked about than seen,
and there is some truth to the fact that his movies do not entertain,
in the more usual sense of providing a distraction from the conditions
of everyday life under capital.[1] Warhol made films that attended to a
host of important features of the world in which he lived, not least
among them boredom, sex, drugs, death, fashion, gossip, music, politics, movies, and stardom, and he explored these topics through a startlingly innovative approach to the material aspects of film, continually
reinventing the formal features of the moving image by adapting to
and extending the technological limits of the medium.[2] That these films
should be considered complicated or "difficult" is a testament to their
capacity to challenge and redefine our expectations of what cinema can
do, the kinds of knowing, seeing, and hearing it can produce. In a decade of perhaps the most immense experimental energy in American
noncorporate film production, where Jonas Mekas's Filmmaker's Cine-

matheque showcased productions by Jack Smith, the Kuchar brothers, and Kenneth Anger, Warhol's films achieved something important and remarkable, and they did so because they marked the movement of camp from the delimited and private queer circles of the 1950s to the center of American cultural production. Jonas Mekas commented about Warhol's films that "the whole reality around us becomes *differently* interesting, and we feel like we have to begin filming everything anew," because they "stopped everything dead, like beginning from scratch and forced us to reevaluate, to see to look at everything from the beginning." Not discounting the importance of other underground filmmakers, Mekas's comments offer a distilled sense that Warhol's films attempted to do something risky in the world of underground cinema: to situate the formal and thematic experiments of the moment in relation to the dominant modes of cinema, that is, Hollywood. As David James comments, Warhol's cinematic output was engaged with "taking art film ever and ever closer to Hollywood,"[3] and there is no small paradox in the fact that Warhol's films gain their experimental excitement because they are dialectically situated in response to Hollywood; rather than choose to ignore the presence of studio production in the shaping of consciousness and representation, Warhol's films embrace *and* interrogate Hollywood, leading to an effect that Patrick S. Smith describes as one of "appreciation and doubt," surely one of the most succinct renderings of camp interest for the things of mass culture.

This chapter examines a handful of Andy Warhol's films in order to understand their status as camp philosophical objects, to detect where they make it possible to see Hollywood film through appreciation and doubt. I argue that the strategies of camp in which Warhol had been schooled during his rise to prominence during the 1950s, in New York's gay demimonde and in the advertising industries whose stylings he helped to transform, give shape to the kind of antagonisms that Hans Magnus Enzensberger writes about when he comments that

> every transistor radio is, by nature of its construction, at the same time a potential transmitter; it can interact with other receivers by circuit reversal. The development from a mere distribution medium to a communications medium is technically not a problem. It is consciously prevented for understandable political reasons. . . . Tape recorders, ordinary cameras, and movie cameras are already extensively owned by wage earners. The question is why these means of pro-

duction do not turn up at factories, in schools, in the offices of the bureaucracy, in short, everywhere there is social conflict.[4]

The possibility of adapting the modernist technologies of recording to make visible and audible the social conflict about which Enzensburger writes offers a situation for considering how Warhol's camp aligned avant-garde practices in relation to mass forms. In some regards, this is not necessarily new to the extent that the avant-garde has historically since Vertov, Eisenstein, and Pudovkin sought to use the technologies sponsored by capital to interrogate capital's own social effects; what is new in the case of Warhol's camp lens is the sense that he unleashes the spectatorial energies of Hollywood film's viewers to forge a new non-Hollywood aesthetic that has its own political effects, not least the realization of Hollywood's particular handling of the labors enacted to produce stardom. In this regard, my intent is not to argue with other assessments of Warhol's cinema in this period that recognize its powerful mobilization of "perverse" desires or that insist on Warhol's capacity to stage forms of social difference. As Thomas Waugh writes:

> Since Warhol's 1987 death, we have left behind the formalist disavowals of the primacy of sexual representation in the Warhol oeuvre. Critics of the modernist, postmodernist, or heterosexist persuasion routinely failed to mention that the male stripper in *Sleep* (1966) is nude, and somehow forgot that *Haircut* (1963) and *Horse* (1965) include a slow male striptease and a cowboy strip poker game, respectively.[5]

There seems no small task in discovering how deeply saturated Warhol's entire artistic oeuvre, and not solely his cinema, was by queer desires, and the vital critical project of recognizing these aspects of the work has recently emerged and indeed is part of this book's grounding. While Warhol's work was consistently situated within the fascination of male same-sex sexuality, equally important is the fact of the frequent avoidance of any mention of those varieties of sexualities in many camp-informed representations. While emphasizing the immense importance of male homoerotics for much of his art, I want here to offer a way to see queer camp aesthetics at work in those films (where sometimes we do not witness any explicit depiction of homosexuality) and to see how camp's attendance to the centrality of the commodity and of labor in contemporary life is another form of queerness to emerge in modernity.[6]

Worth remembering is the history of the production and circulation of Warhol's films because such a history helps to explain the kinds of critical attention that have so often cleaved camp apart from Warhol. After five astonishingly productive years from 1963 to 1968, when he produced *hundreds* of films, Warhol no longer engaged himself with the hands-on making of film, and in 1972 he withdrew the bulk of his movies from circulation. Although a handful of them circulated in the succeeding two decades, largely in informal (and sometimes illicit) fashion, only in the past ten years, under the auspices of the Andy Warhol Film Project at the Whitney Museum of American Art, have these films again become accessible. The films disappeared at a key juncture, that of the moment of Stonewall and the emergence of a particular brand of Western gay and lesbian identity politics, and this conjuncture marked the crucial absence from any larger public notice of Warhol's visual and acoustic documentation of the social life that led to the liberation politics of the past three decades. I agree with Waugh that commentary on the homoerotic content of the films has often been curiously absent in critical and historical accounts; worth wondering about further, though, is whether the films' disappearance from circulation did not contribute to such failures of attention by gay and lesbian critics, lending them yet again to other forms of canonization by different regimes of (heterosexualized) aesthetic and political value. In the 1970s gay liberationist debates over camp's political efficacy, these key texts might have made a significant difference for understanding the function of the work of sexuality for the production and circulation of commodity culture; then again, they may only have been too firmly embedded in a camp critical articulation of the fact that desire is an effect of Western industrial production, largely because Warhol's camp is so firmly anchored to his lifelong concern with the exertions required of humans to fashion the world that they make. Warhol's camp philosophy, of which he offered an epigrammatic version in his 1975 volume *The Philosophy of Andy Warhol*, returns to the grounding effect of work to human life: sex, drag, art, domesticity, and finally death are visited again and again through the category of work.

Not surprisingly, the films not only thematize work but in fact make it part of their formal and technological strategies, and Warhol's cinema can be read as a demand to know what happens when the routinized rules of industrial cinematic production—as rules of the organization of labor—are discarded. In the act of ignoring the customary expectations of the Hollywood cinematic product, his films reveal that the corporate text is not all that efficient after all and is perhaps obeying another set of logics beyond those of cost accounting: they also regulate desire and bodies in their somatic and institutional dimensions. Taken as a counter-cinema (but one bound dialectically to the corporate product), the film experiments of Warhol allow us to see how the studios' capturing of labor in the product (what Marx refers to as labor's "congealing" in the commodity) is inefficient. Remarkable about Warhol's cinema, though, is that it makes its own "efficiencies"—to use carefully the things of film (film stock, acting talent)—part of the formal and aesthetic play at work in them.

Labor

Warhol's host of experimental techniques, such as the strobe cut, in-camera editing, out-of-focus framing, image looping, and dual projection, all derive from an insistence on another kind of efficiency that could inform film practice. Against the Hollywood mode of narrative economy and continuity editing, his films play with the challenge of making film as efficiently as possible, largely by giving over more control to the technology itself. If the camera is initially out of focus, as it is in the first reel of *Poor Little Rich Girl* (1965), then let the blurry, painterly image of Edie Sedgwick form its own attraction. *Sleep* (1963) finds exertion in the act of recording (by both performer and filmmaker) and then discovers a technique that allows the artist to conserve his efforts through iteration; in the repetition of film reels, it extends five and a half hours of footage to an eight-hour screening. The strobe cut, placing its explosive white frames between edits, announces the edit (rather than concealing it, as in Hollywood) and makes visible the condensation of real time as it is recorded on film; the extended opening shower scene in *Bike Boy* (1967–1968) uses strobe cuts to omit what failed to interest the artist and, through a minimum of effort, fixes the lens on the parts of the male body that are subsequently emphasized in the visual field. This cinema makes the queer labor of camp integral to its project not only through the films' subject matter (the continuing stream of pungent bitchy commentary by Ondine, Ed Hood, and the network of women friends such as Viva and Brigid Polk) but also through the labor *on* the films themselves. Warhol makes camp into an artistic and philosophical project through which to discover what happens when the laborer takes seriously capital's mandate to streamline one's efforts and, in a perverse form of Taylorism, to do *less* in order to produce *more*.

Paradoxically, Warhol has come to figure in many popular and critical imaginings as the artist most customarily associated with the anticerebral pleasures of popular media and consumerism, and if the legacies of pop art are to be detected in the cultural productions we inhabit thirty years later, certainly Andy Warhol's visual and acoustic sensibilities seem almost everywhere at once: in the grainy footage of MTV videos, in the wildly swerving camera work of *NYPD Blue,* in the minimalist posturings and "heroin chic" of Calvin Klein Inc.'s advertising campaigns of the 1990s. Yet if Warhol's film experiments borrow their lasting power from their ability to convey the excitement of a historical moment in which so much of the social life of the industrial world was being reconfigured (and in this respect, they retain a quizzical status as documentary), they equally share a relation to the experience of contemporary life *through* its dominant cinema and how that cinema might be reworked (literally) for other new meanings.

Warhol's access to cinema came to him in the most mundane of ways: in 1963, he purchased a handheld Bolex motion picture camera and began experimenting with it. Using the profits from his other enterprises in painting and sculpture, he expanded his project of cinematic experimentation through the 1960s, continually rethinking the possibilities of cinema to represent the materiality of social life that his silk screens of Hollywood stars and newspaper headlines had already begun to attend to. The sense of experimentation in the production of his films was no small feature of this work, and Warhol made plain that he was hardly licensed in any professional manner to go about his enterprises in the medium. Further, he proved eager to talk about the labors involved in making his films and what he saw as the potential effects of them, if at times acknowledging that his developing aesthetic was frequently born of his unwillingness (often scandalized as a form of seeming laziness) to abide by accepted notions of visual "quality." Notoriously refusing to edit his films in standardized regimes of film continuity, he allowed for the juxtaposition of shots to appear often through the chance of what happened to be recorded, just one technique among many that I call Warhol's "aleation."[7] Rather than conceal these facts of his artistic work, Warhol made them a feature of the widely disseminated reportage about him, and he was keen that the knowledge of his own lack of training might encourage other amateurs that they, too, could work to produce visual and acoustic media. In a 1966 interview in *Tape Recording* magazine, Warhol presciently speculated that the rise of the then-emerging home video technology would become a vital force for redefining habits of sexual representation:

> Tape Recording: What else can people do with their home video recorders?
> Warhol: Make the best pornography movies. It's going to be so great.
> Tape Recording: You think Mr. and Mrs. America will . . .
> Warhol: Yes. And they'll have their friends in to show them.[8]

Driving home his sense that the camera and the microphone might be deployed to a variety of settings to create new meanings and new social practices, Warhol anticipated the expansion of the pornography industries in the decades following, especially that made by amateurs for consumption by other amateurs. Important to his commentary here is that sex and its representation are already named through professional distinctions (the "mere" amateur) deriving from the differing forms of remuneration (wages, accreditation) found in capital's apprehension of labor. Be that as it may, Warhol embraces his amateur status as a maker of moving images, allowing him to make all variety of antagonistic visual forms about the imbrication of sex and labor in productivity.

We might wonder, though, whether these same technologies might be used to monitor and control and indeed preserve standing social orders (note the insistence on "Mr. and Mrs. America" as the institution vested with home video), and it would be naive to insist that such amateur practices do not instantly counter the most pernicious surveillance effects of such technology. Yet the impulse here, underpinned by the more radical impulses of camp, aligns Warhol with the idea that "mere" consumers can adopt film and video to record and interrogate their own lives. (And Warhol was not speaking in solely speculative terms; in the same interview, he offers practical advice for using specific lenses and filters to achieve particular visual tricks, and experimenting with microphones to create a variety of sound effects.)[9]

The production of film by even an apparent amateur such as Warhol, though, is of course overshadowed by the dominance of Hollywood cinema in twentieth-century America, and no film intended for widespread exhibition can be framed without the sense that it bears some relation, however antagonistic, however avant-garde, to the Hollywood product. Warhol's numerous biographies tell us that he maintained a lifelong devotion to Hollywood film, and Thomas Waugh and Michael Moon have explored the resonances that Hollywood held for the shy, queer, working-class son of *Mitteleuropean* emmigrants. Despite the saturating presence of Hollywood, of which Warhol dreamed in his Pittsburgh youth, the creation of Warhol's cinema of the 1960s was a response to, but not an exclusion of, the presence of Hollywood, and its camp dimensions are sponsored in large part by the sense that fandom and its acts of spectatorial devotion are commensurate labors to those of studio corporate production.[10] In this regard, Warhol's films operate as another part of an economy of the circulation of desire, inverting more customary notions that spectators are consumers and reconstruing film viewing as production in itself and productive of films—films such as those made by Warhol and the people who appear in them. If one form of camp is the joking appreciation of a film star shared by queers in the more private domains of the bar and the bedroom, then another more concretized form appears in the films that one camp-thinking queer, Andy Warhol, produced for five years. Revisiting these films three decades after their making, we are struck not only by their sexual playfulness (as noted by Waugh) but also by their continual reference to Hollywood, if not in Hollywood's own forms of textual organization, then through recognition of the emulation and response carried on by its spectators. Warhol's movies are about the critical, camp act of watching movies.

If Warhol's films are to be understood as an examination of Hollywood and popular culture, it is important to recall that Warhol came of age in the postwar settings of queer urban subcultures.[11] Within these settings, Warhol gained a profound exposure to the camp sensibilities that allowed those subcultures to define themselves within the space of the expanding metropolitan life of the West, sensibilities that were from the outset created in relation to popular media. As I discuss the status of irony more extensively in the chapter on John Waters, here I would only point out Warhol's output as instructive in this matter, in that the productive irony at work in his film images resides in the apparent indifference of the makers of these texts (director and actors included) to the fact that they are not in the center of capitalist film production; the (feigned) ignorance of their performances allows them to stage another relation to Hollywood than one solely of exclusion: consumption becomes productive. Tally Brown, a Factory fixture and a commentator of wit and insight about the period, remarks about Warhol that "I think that [what] most people misinterpret about Andy is that whatever he says is absolutely direct, is exactly what he means, and people interpret it as a put-on and start looking for ironic meanings to it and it meant exactly what he said. Once I came in and he and Lou [Reed] were weaving very ugly plastic crosses . . . white plastic crosses. And he said, 'Isn't it terrific?' And somebody who didn't know him would have thought that it was a put-on, but it wasn't. He meant that he thought it was terrific."[12] Brown's account is interesting not because it allows us to adjudicate Warhol's sincerity but because it announces the possibility that the ironic stance *attributed* to him (the "put-on") fails to account for a form of investment (both financial and affective) that is assumed to be unreasonable or inappropriate but occurs nonetheless. That Brown remembers a potential put-on about taste (plastic crosses) and the seeming prohibition against finding pleasure in the cheap (a fascination that Warhol continually expressed) stresses again camp's attraction to forms of disparity in the value codings of capital as those places that are most intellectually and artistically productive. If what is at stake in these investments of intellectual labor is irony, then perhaps what Warhol's work emphasizes, through his feigned ignorance, is the impact of choosing the *wrong* commodities in the particular given historical designations of good taste.

Glamour

Warhol's cinematic endeavors were immense, and any attempt to summon a critical taxonomy of his movies will of course seem to form its own selective exclusions. Be that as it may, if we consider camp to be a critical attention to modernity through the queer labors found in these films, and Warhol's cinema to form a specific commentary on cinema as a central modernist technology of representation, his cinematic oeuvre falls into three different kinds of film output. All of them stem from the impulse to see what happens to the world outside Hollywood when it becomes susceptible to the glamorizing lens's ambivalent and ironic effects: (1) the stardom of the static object, (2) the stardom of performance, and (3) desire's narratives by and for the star. Within this taxonomy one can read all of his films as a sustained experiment (bolstered by the amateur status that Warhol insisted on for his films) that came upon greater complexity and achievement as the films showcased more sophisticated forms of editing, use of sound, and camera movement. (I do not want to prioritize Hollywood modes of continuity as a form that

Warhol's films are attempting to emulate so much as I want to reassert that his films were a *response* to the regulated images and sounds within the classical Hollywood product to which his camp visions were dialectically bonded.) Further, these categories are not cleanly separated by chronology or biography—what is offered here is not a narrative of progression—and indeed his films earn the name of "experiment" in that later films revisit earlier challenges, while earlier attempts inform subsequent endeavors. I *would* argue that because of larger budgets, more personnel, and the impulse to garner nonunderground and nonqueer audiences, the later films of 1967 and 1968 become organized, in comparatively flexible terms, as narratives, over and above the earlier efforts; and the apparent failure of these later vehicles to find audiences and Hollywood underwriting will, as I hope to demonstrate, help us to understand the limits of camp critical sensibilities for corporate modes of film production.

Warhol's films responded to Hollywood by creating their own versions of glamour. In large measure, camp interest in Hollywood cinema has been driven by spectacle and glamour, over and above narrative and spectatorial identification. This makes sense when we recall that the corporate product, particularly in the classical period to which Warhol was responding, offered narrative cinema of astonishing heteronormativity, and as we have seen in the case of the Freed unit, camp's queer traces become apparent mostly through the mise-en-scène, not the filmic events or dialogue. By spectacle, I mean that the cinematic image, be it the image on the film screen or the 8 x 10 glossy of the movie star, is frequently arrested from its bond with the narrative and fixed in other sets of meanings. In this sense, the camp of Warhol's films accentuates the production of Hollywood and its related industries *as production,* at least to the extent that they show how the media of popular culture might be manipulated to produce meanings unintended by the culture industries, this despite the fact that outside the domain of corporate production, one is largely prohibited from knowing what is involved in such studio efforts. The camp impulse to emphasize the Hollywood production of spectacle, vis-à-vis glamour, stems from the all too frequent perception of how queer life has mostly been excluded from Hollywood films, except for the occasional depiction of pathological homosexuality or a "sympathetic" account of the apparent miseries of queer existence. Rather than ignore the Hollywood product because of its censorship of dissident sexualities, Warhol's films take up its iconography at the moment in which it departs from narrative; most often this takes the form of star glamour.[13]

If not invented by the Hollywood studios, certainly the refinement and dissemination of glamorous images in contemporary life must be one of the studios' most significant achievements. By way of definition, we might say that glamour is the sense that an image achieves what could never be made to happen in our own everyday efforts; we are held in the thrall of the glamorous image because it depicts people and lives that are not our own and, barring our own inclusion in that sphere of production, probably never will be. This is not only because we are prohibited from emulating the glamorous image by virtue of our various physical shortcomings but because we have little sense of the complicated efforts demanded in the enhancement of stars through makeup, costuming, lighting, and film stocks. Glamour, then, is profoundly a mystification. When we behold the image of a star, say in the voluptuous surfaces of a photograph by Hurrell or the renderings of Dietrich as captured by Von Sternberg, the glamorous image entreats us to defer to its power without recourse to understanding under what circumstances the image was made. We are subsequently prevented from an analysis of glamour because glamour is antithetical to the notion of labor; the failure of such analyses is to be marked in the primary metaphor of fans' responses to movie stars, that of a star's godlike status that renders the fan helpless in the sight of the star's image.

One name for the star's special status is that of charisma. In his groundbreaking star study, Richard Dyer offers Max Weber's formulation of charisma, "a certain quality of an individual personality by virtue of which he [sic] is set apart from ordinary men and treated as endowed with supernatural, superhuman or at least superficially exceptional qualities." Dyer reads the power described in Weber's definition as how stars are ideological embodiments of particular historical notions of femininity, beauty, morality, and so on. Vital for this discussion of Warhol's films is Dyer's suggestion that

> star charisma needs to be situated in the specificities of the ideological configurations to which it belongs, so also virtually all sociological theories of stars ignore the *specificities* of another aspect of the phenomenon—the audience.[14]

He adds, "I would point out the absolutely central importance of stars in gay ghetto culture" and suggests that "if these star-audience relationships are only an intensification of the conflicts and exclusions experienced by everyone, it is also significant that, in any discussion of 'subversive' star images, stars embodying adolescent, female and gay images play a crucial role." The ways that queer male fandom has attended to star imagery, though, have been notoriously complex to document, especially given that many queer men have *identified* with female stars such as Judy Garland, Lana Turner, Joan Crawford, and Bette Davis, over and above their male counterparts Gary Cooper, Clark Gable, Cary Grant, James Dean, and Montgomery Clift.

The link between queer men and female stars occurs through a perception on the part of the queer fan that glamour marks the achievement of becoming through the expense of labor something that he is not allowed—that is, the privilege of representation. For the female star, that "something else" is perceived as the star's possession of her exceptional beauty (of course, mystified through its enhancement by clothing and makeup), while for the queer male fan it is the demand to have his efforts merely to exist mirrored in the world of dominant representation, something unlikely in the regimes of masculine performance. The queer male fan's devotion sometimes takes the form of drag—its spectacularized version of the structural affective homology being played out—but more commonly appears through the intense devotion of queers to a specific female star whose image offers an embodiment of strength, vulnerability, and humor. This is not an argument for reading such devotions by queer male fans as the effort to become either the woman being glamorized or the male star whose conventional masculinity is sanctioned by the Hollywood product. Rather, these fan investments tell of a knowledge of the gendered divisions of labor in corporate studio production, whereby female stars are not seen producing themselves, even as they struggle to exist (a struggle most commonly marked in affective terms); such paradoxes of appearances form a homology on which the labor of the camp viewer forms its investments.

Nevertheless, if the effect of glamour is that it purportedly appears through a complete lack of effort, that the star simply *is* glamorous, then the achievement of glamour occurs through an immense investment of time, capital, and effort on the part of the studio.[15] Indeed, we should take pains to remember that apart from glamour's concealed labor, some aspects of spectacle might encourage audiences to sit in awe at the expenditure of money and labor. In the creation of immense soundstages for historical epics or action pics (such as De Mille's Roman circus in the two versions of *Ben Hur* or the current action pic's ability to blow up entire buildings), spectacle often demands our wonder at the magnitude of the project's undertaking. In contrast, glamour seldom seeks equally to remind its recipients of its enormous undertakings, as audiences are seldom called on to marvel at the fact that a star has been rendered even *more* beautiful.

Warhol's *Empire* (1964) tests the limits of glamour's effects and by doing so stands out among the entire Warhol oeuvre. In this eight-hour and five-minute film, the image of the Empire State Building is recorded from sunset to early morning, the silent screening rate of sixteen frames per second stretching the film's duration. Callie Angell suggestively reads this film as concerned with the building's status as an emblem of spectacular metropolitan life as the (then) world's tallest skyscraper and emphasizes that the film is a visual document that serves as an "early example of film installation, in which the projected film achieves an objectlike existence comparable to that of more conventional art works," while also offering that because of its recently installed exterior lighting, *Empire* is an image of the "performance and stardom that the building's dramatic new appearance would have suggested to [Warhol]."[16] The building's spectacular status as the most prominent feature in the instantly recognizable New York skyline—both as an object to be seen and as a place from which to see—makes it an emblem of cinema. In Warhol's vision, though, the prestige accorded the building is curiously derived from its inverted status, to the degree that its immobility fixes it in the frame of the lens, a lens that Warhol uses more often, as we shall see, to discover the dynamism of movement—speech, gesture, event. *Empire* is about the beauty of passivity, devoted as the film is to recording the inert and unlaboring fixed object of the Empire State Building.

Most critics, notably Angell and Peter Gidal, have decided that *Empire* is concerned with the passage of time, and while its monumental screening duration offers a kind of perverse shock at endurance (as opposed to the more customary modernist thrills of instantaneity), there seems a critical consensus to ignore the joke demanded by the film's astonishing running time. Recalling Warhol's comment about his films being better talked about than viewed, *Empire* demonstrates a camp will to extravagance, a will that can make a star out of even the inanimate. In this regard, *Empire* makes the Empire State Building into the most exemplary form of the star, where the star's complete passivity allows him or her to become an object for the camera's appreciative gaze. It is telling that alone among all of Warhol's films, *Empire* should showcase a nonliving object. Although other experimental filmmakers have used the camera for similar purposes (*Ballet Mécanique*, the films of Charles and Ray Eames) in the name of a spectatorial meditation, Warhol's films showcase stars as effects of labor, and while not dispensing with the contemplative aspects of this film, *Empire* also makes overwhelmingly apparent the labor of the spectator simply to maintain a somatic presence for this film. Perhaps this makes *Empire* one of Warhol's funniest and most serious jokes.

Whereas *Empire* stages the stillness of its subject for cinematic gaze, many of Warhol's other films of 1963 to 1965 record the energies of those who surrounded him in this period. In this regard, films such as *Haircut (No. 1), Poor Little Rich Girl,* and *Camp* are what I will call his camp performance films, in the sense that they situate the men and women who appear in them in terms of how much these subjects must work to make themselves ready for the camera. In his *Philosophy,* Warhol writes that

> along with having sex, being sexed is also hard work. I wonder whether it's hard for (1) a man to be a man, (2) a man to be a woman, (3) a woman to be a woman, or (4) a woman to be a man. I don't really know the answer, but from watching all the different types, I know the people who think they're working the hardest are the men who are trying to be women. They do double-time. They do all the double things: they think about shaving and not shaving, of primping and not primping, of buying men's clothes and women's clothes. I guess it's interesting to try to be another sex, but it can be exciting to just be your own sex.

Warhol is not exaggerating when he comments that he has scrutinized the different demands to perform whatever it is that one thinks of as his or her "self," and no one seems exempt from such demands; thus the films of camp performance return repeatedly to record the efforts of gendered performances.

If Warhol's performance films need to be read as a response to Hollywood glamour, are they a critical response? Seemingly not, when we consider that Warhol seemed determined to find a way to make films in Hollywood, a theme played out in biographical accounts by himself and others.[17] The films, though, seem like a failed homage to Hollywood, because they can only fail to import the labor and the image that the glamour icon enjoys. Nevertheless the performance films reveal Hollywood's attraction for its queer fans and camp's acknowledgment of queer exclusion from the bulk of dominant film practice. These films forge a queer knowledge about Hollywood, but one borne by the impulse to invert Hollywood's demands and its effects. Where the customary branding of Hollywood's factories as "studios" forgets its regulated modes of production, Warhol's studio—bearing its traces of the artist as experimenter—boldly (and playfully) claims the name of the Factory. Where Hollywood stars adhere to normative standards of beauty and performance, Warhol's superstars are spectacularly freakish.

The performance films challenged the notion of what makes a star, not because they achieve a labor identical to that of the production of the Hollywood star, but because they exhibit the "failure" of these subjects to be suitable for the glamorizing lens even as they labor exhaustively to become photogenic. In their stubborn insistence that drag queens, effeminate boys, and debutantes were worthy of the camera's attention, the performance films reveal that the Factory stars genuinely labored too, and the camera attests to their exertions. The films were firmly tied, even in their ironic play, to the fantasy of the Hollywood studio system as way of disclosing who works and yet is not rewarded for his or her efforts. At the heart of the Factory was the notion that anybody might potentially be propelled to the center of fame (at least, the Factory's version of it) by having a camera fixed on them. Indeed, Warhol encouraged the sense of a Hollywood-like studio, depicting the Factory, well before he made films, as being filled with stars, literary figures, and jet-setters.[18] The failure of the Factory's "stars" to insert themselves into the settings of studio production alludes to the fact of a critical consciousness made available by the camp valences of the works enacted by Warhol—despite the appearances of such attempts at glamour, Warhol's films fail to renaturalize the mystified underpinnings of studio glamour.

If *Empire* is about the stardom of things, then virtually all of Warhol's other films make a point about the stardom of human subjects and the manufacture of their glamour; simultaneously the films emphasize glamour as it figures in the queer male spectator's relation to Hollywood. Even more to the point, if we situate *Empire* as the lever for understanding camp's critical dimensions, we perceive how the stasis of the Empire State Building, rendering it the perfect object for cinematic contemplation, renders all other subjects of Warhol's camera as yet other objects: the performative efforts of Warhol's actors to become suitable for film are dialectically bonded with the inert object that stands as a challenge to make gesture and speech more interesting than immobility and passivity. Warhol's human actors fight against *and* simultaneously for becoming objects and in doing so stage the contradiction of glamour: they cannot in any singular way be or become ideal for the camera. In this regard, they enact a logical tendency within Warhol's film form, itself produced by shaping remarkably marginalized figures into Factory stars. In his immensely important book, *Andy Warhol's Art and Films,* Patrick S. Smith evokes the film factory's druggy and erotically charged atmosphere, a carnivalesque space in which male hustlers on amphetamines, Park Avenue debutantes, and the occasional Hollywood star encountered one another. Smith argues that "Warhol wanted to discover the possibilities of 'found' personalities who live the esthetic of beauty on film. To be a 'superstar' is to be a given state of being," and many of the "personalities" that Warhol was finding were queer men who in some degree shared the camp pleasures he had discovered in his life in New York. Smith describes the Factory as a space where "Warhol would just watch, utterly *absorbed,* his fascinating entourage who would match witty insults, change records on the phonograph—this included battles between those who wanted to hear rock music and those who listened to Maria Callas—and engage in sexual encounters. Warhol allowed unseemly infighting and encouraged it by fabricating rumors concerning the private lives of his entourage."[19] While not ignoring the presence of all manner of perverse and illicit subjects who populated the Factory during this period, it is difficult to ignore in Smith's description the sense that what we witness here is a crossroads of metropolitan queer male life; straight men seldom fight over Maria Callas. This remarkable confluence—not only of queer men but of all kinds of "perverts" and of technologies of recording and reproduction—was new to the extent that it linked these figures with producers and marketers of middlebrow mass taste (galleries, cinematheques, fashion houses), and in this regard the meeting of avant-garde and industrial spheres marked a unique and inaugural moment in American modernity. If we juxtapose the kinds of performances beheld in the Hollywood product by iconic divas such as Dietrich, Crawford, and Turner with the performances Smith describes, we might consider how the latter endeavor to secure a filmic presence that they know themselves to be unlikely to achieve within Hollywood galvanizes Warhol's attention as he stands back to let such efforts become apparent by allowing the camera to do its work.

Tally Brown, herself showcased in several of Warhol's films, comments about this milieu and the figures who populated it that "their need to be famous without taking the time or the trouble to develop the resources or, possibly, having the ability" made for a new way of thinking about performance and its mediation: what if one recorded the efforts of exertion and failure as much as one embraced conventional success and the standardized product?[20] Brown here offers a language for understanding how Warhol's films are about being unfit to star, and how inadvertently that can make one a star nonetheless. Taking the time, having the resources, having the ability, are versions of productivity in a political economy devoted to efficiency and standardization; while the "positive" version of such productivity appears in the Hollywood studio system, its underside, a kind of mirror of exploitation in the sphere of another form of production, is discovered among these fans who perform for Warhol's camera. The production of stardom, then, emerged as an important feature of Factory work and unveiled the often hidden networks of queer men in which Warhol had been moving since his arrival in New York in 1949.

The interest in discovering stardom in the everyday world, though, expanded to include all variety of cosmopolitan types; this is borne out by the making of the *Screen Tests.* In the approximately five hundred *Screen Tests* made between 1964 and 1966, Factory visitors and regulars were filmed, seated in close-up before a static camera, often in a manner that proved to exceed the subject's patience and to press him or her to perform an extemporaneously invented self, or to reveal the discomfort in not having anticipated that such might be demanded on that day. These films play on the language of testing in that they challenge their subjects to endure the camera's technological limits: they will probably fail in their energies long before the steel and glass of the apparatus do. The *Screen Tests,* in the very name that they appropriate from Hollywood, seemed to promise the production of larger film projects and created for the Factory the effect of being a film studio, complete with the aura of stardom for the figures in the *Screen Tests.* This is not so dissimilar to the promises that Hollywood's own self-promotion has long made, continually trading on fantasies of being "discovered" and rewarded for being beautiful and clever. Warhol's own self-promotion would take up the same tropes of the "democracy" of beauty that Hollywood has long offered. Despite the labors demanded by glamour culture, the logic of studio glamour stated that film performers became stars because, on the one hand, they came from "nowhere" just like everyone else and, conversely, unlike everyone else, stars owned a special hold on the cinematic imagination and indeed the cinematic apparatus itself. Unlike Hollywood, Warhol's *Screen Tests* held no greater appeal than the opportunity that they provided to gaze on the Factory superstars remote from the context of film narrative; that is, they did not yield future productions of narrative film that might showcase the spectacle of the star performance.

By framing the figures in the *Screen Tests* as potential movie stars, Warhol begs the question of whether the labor of glamour is achievable within the everyday while simultaneously suggesting that the use of the camera after the advent of Hollywood could effectively create something akin to "aura" where often it would seem unlikely. Warhol's *Screen Tests* appear to anyone acquainted with Hollywood's own as sharing only the name, inasmuch as Warhol's *Tests* display his refusal to groom or coach his subjects to make themselves into anything remotely resembling a standardized vision for the camera; distinct from Hollywood's screen tests, the Factory's version of the tests makes plain the individual subject's efforts to produce him- or herself for the lens. Despite their comparatively primitive quality, Warhol's *Screen Tests* produce their assorted figures as stars even as the films' subjects display all of their apparent un-Hollywood qualities, and while the *Screen Tests* may embody a seemingly retrograde longing for the aura of Hollywood stardom, they also demand that we notice how the personalities they describe are not stars in the corporate sense. In this regard, Warhol inherits the avantgarde tradition of deploying an industrial technology to antagonize the role of that technology (here, movies) within contemporary life. But, the project of the *Screen Tests* is equally informed by the camp impulse to put high and low together: those unintended for the glamorizing Hollywood camera are allowed to appear before it nonetheless.

A compelling case for understanding how Warhol's films addressed the contradictions of glamour within his own cinema is to be found in *Paul Swan,* a sixty-minute piece dating from 1965.[21] *Paul Swan* seems to offer a documentary of an aging icon from American dance of the 1920s. The film consists of Swan, now in his eighties, performing various set pieces from his repertoire; he announces to the camera the various selections, with such titles as "A French Country Dance" or "The Four Elements." In part, the film offers a rather grim depiction of the older dancer in a dim set, with only a tattered backdrop, a folding chair,

The labor of performance: Paul Swan in *Paul Swan*. Film still
courtesy of The Andy Warhol Museum.

overexposed lighting, and a tinny piano accompaniment with which to
offer his performance. As the film progresses, Swan changes in and out
of his costumes, struggling to pull his tights on, angry about a lost pair
of shoes, fidgeting with his Roman centurion's cape and helmet.

It becomes clear in the last third of *Paul Swan* that Warhol, who char-
acteristically remains silent behind the camera, seeks less to direct Swan
than to see the dancer direct himself. In the failure to edit out the seg-
ments of Swan's clumsy costume changes and in the resistance to offer
any form of advice through which the dancer might enact his performative tricks on camera, Warhol stages Swan as an emblem of another lost
cultural fringe, one populated by the likes of Isadora Duncan and Swan
in the 1920s. In his impulse to show Swan as a worker of his own kind of
stage magic, made all the more demanding on Swan given his age and
the kind of movement required of him, Warhol reveals an ambivalence
toward glamour that defines, to varying degrees, many of his films.

This ambivalence is one of knowing how much work is required of
(here, inadvertent) "stars" and yet simultaneously embracing them for
their willingness to do that work, on camera no less. Of course, the effect
is intensified by having a figure well past his peak, for whom there are

extra-added tasks to secure his image, made more visible by his presence in the real time of *Paul Swan.* One responds by admiring Swan's determination to continue to dance and by concurrently sharing with Warhol the discomfort at how awkward the star's attempts to achieve glamour have become; we can recall Warhol's comments about the amount of time and effort required of drag queens in creating their own performances. In that light, we appreciate all the more how the performance films such as *Paul Swan* make evident not only that we struggle to enact, at great cost of labor and time, our "selves" but that such activities may form a response to cinema itself, in which we do so thinking about how we appear not only to other social subjects but also for an imaginary lens waiting, as Warhol's did, to record and bear witness to such efforts.

Thus Warhol's work takes up the production of glamour in the everyday, in which nonstars produce themselves for being looked at. In *Haircut (No. 1)* (1963), four men are seen,[22] one carefully cutting another's hair while the third packs a pipe and takes long, hypnosis-inducing drags from it.[23] With no edits save the reel changes, they go about the work of snipping and combing, all the while chatting casually and ignoring the presence of the camera. While they cut, they pose themselves within the frame, forming at moments abstracted compositions as their bodies are various distances from the camera; even in domestic moments, they take pains to remember their appearances. *Haircut (No. 1)* drives us back into the realm of the mundane only to reveal the efforts required of us all to appear within that quotidian life: even if we don't function as stars, star culture functions within us as we go about preparing ourselves for the world.

The fact of their grooming themselves in the decidedly homoerotic dynamics at play in this film is hardly a coincidence. As the film closes, the actors fix their gazes directly on the camera, seeming to respond to some unheard request from the director, and in this final tableau they display their handiwork. At the conclusion, they begin to laugh, as if on cue, and we are left with this silent and ambiguous gesture that could be a mockery of us or an entreaty to share their pleasure. Particularly striking about this final segment is the serene distance with which they fix our gaze: these are expressions seemingly taken directly from the Hollywood icon. Cool and remote, like the faces of Harlow or Crawford, the stars of *Haircut (No. 1)* share with us the pleasures of being seen and *knowing* that one is being seen.

We can hardly ignore, though, in *Haircut (No. 1)* the fact that the action

All dressed up: queer coiffeurs in *Haircut (No. 1)*.
Film still courtesy of The Andy Warhol Museum.

takes place in a rather squalid loft and is lit by a bare bulb within the frame. The men's clothing displays the tattered flourishes of bohemian style, at the time also signaled by their comparatively long hair. In this setting, it becomes apparent that we are nowhere near the glamour mills of a Hollywood studio, and the film presents us with the question of what impulse would drive the minute attentions given by these men to their appearance. In part, the film serves to remind us of the immense difference between those whom Hollywood cinema understood itself as appealing to and, in this particular case, the inadvertent fans who model themselves on it.

The figures of *Haircut (No. 1)*, whose last stares Stephen Koch puzzlingly calls "murderous" and for whom Koch struggles to conceal his class-based revulsion, play with stillness, with their bodies, and with their status as things to be looked on — with eros and with laughter — in ways that require us to acknowledge their world as one built on such labor-intensive glamour. Koch writes that *Haircut (No. 1)* is one of Warhol's most significant films in that it fixes on the problem of immobility for the motion picture; the film is "about a cinematic paradox of movement and stillness, borrowed, among other things, from the aesthetic of the painted portrait and transposed to film."[24] Although there is little to dispute in the general claim offered here about the importance of the film in relation to high art production of portraiture, another intellectual genealogy situates this film's project with popular culture, where stillness might more ordinarily be identified with the boredom of life in modernity. Yet boredom is not the absence of activity but the seeming insignificance of activities that seem unworthy of attention (and, here, specifically filmic attention); when the figures of this film play with film time and somatic time, they unfold the difference between those two versions of temporality as dominant cinema has sought to exploit it. They, and Warhol, bring a camp inversion to that which is deemed worthy of cinema by making the uncinematic into something worth watching—repeatedly, no less.

When we array *Haircut (No. 1)* alongside other films from Warhol's earliest film productions, such as *Sleep* (1963), *Kiss* (1963), *Blowjob* (1963), and *Eat* (1964), the effect of the audience having to struggle to attribute any glamour to the image becomes even more pronounced. The frequently vocalized claim that these films are boring suggests the important feature of glamour in which spectators, cut adrift from the power of any narrative that might be given by a film, are forced to derive their own meanings from the image. This is not to say that we are released into some purely meditative realm, but that the associations with glamour are imported through other impulses, most notably that of voyeurism. *Blowjob* is probably the most vivid example of this, for the film appeals to prurient interest in the glamour icon merely through its title, and what it offers is a highly glamorous cinematic portrait of a young man who is purportedly being fellated. Tightly framed in such a way that we see only his face, his expressions pass through various looks of ennui, excitement, and finally, for the viewer given to taking the film's title as that of a documentary, orgasm. Yet seen as kin to the glossy star photo of Hollywood publicity, *Blowjob* reminds us that glamour often functions through spectatorial fantasy: We do the work of attributing special qualities to the image. This is particularly pronounced by the fact that *Blowjob* is so often assumed to be depicting an act of homosexual oral sex; anecdotal accounts of the film's production notwithstanding, within the film's denotative register, there is no reason to assume such. Such fantasies that surround the film's making usher us to the labor of spectators to find in the image a rendering of the world that gives pleasure, but crucially it is a labor borne largely by the viewer. Perhaps among all the performance films, *Blowjob* is most like *Empire* in the delight it discovers in the passivity of the filmic object; the sense that the camera can do to the subject what it likes (in this case, by *not* moving or cutting) is extended to the viewer, whereby viewer fantasy becomes contiguous with the circuits of production and value coding—after all, the title informs us that this is a "job" and one that the spectator undertakes as much as the director and the actor. That the film offers no "money shot" (the pornography industry's nomenclature for the explicit representation of male ejaculation) indicates a job in which one does not receive remuneration and has to compensate the omission of visual confirmation with fantasy and speculation. While *Blowjob* would seem to confirm the passivity and indifference of its actor to the camera and to the audience and his ensuing boredom, it equally sponsors something quite opposite—productivity in the realm of reception.

If the keynote to *Blowjob* is boredom, then the film plays on a joke about the boredom of sex and the boredom of audiences in watching films (even when those films claim to or actually depict sex) that force the viewer to fantasize to create something alluring from what she or he is watching. When Gregory Battcock offers that "early Warhol movies emphasized the cinema as a medium for experiencing time, rather than movement or event," it is the passage of time with no recourse to some event transpiring within it that forces back on us all of our wishes to think that we are witnessing some kind of countermove to Hollywood.[25] *Sleep* plays with this wish, to the extent that the film does not record in real time the actual duration of a night's sleep but repeats reels as if to see whether we will endure the boredom of the film in order to detect any repetition, a hallmark of narrative. Further, part of the premise of *Sleep,* as Warhol describes it, is about stars and acting: it was "really convenient to film, since the first thing you do when you want a film star is 'check his availability.'"[26] Playing with the language of Hollywood publicity about the possibilities of recruiting star talent based on their work schedules, *Sleep* wonders about whether a celebrity might not have his efforts as performer seized at all moments, even those of which he is not conscious. When Warhol comments in this chapter's epigraph that being alive is work, then the work of remaining alive even when one sleeps might be seized on as a performance worth recording. Like *Blowjob,* though, *Sleep* demands that the audience work to find its interest in the cinematic document (or, perhaps, fall asleep too). Warhol's ability to place such demands on his audience in part stems from his knowledge of a particular kind of spectator who might in fact give film such close attention. That spectator is the trained viewer of Hollywood cinema, attuned to the camera's power to create glamour, to attribute an aura to an act (here, slumber) that may be able to make no greater claims to having a singularity to it than any other human activity.

The difference between Hollywood icons and the stars of *Haircut (No. 1)* goes a long way to dispel the democratic fantasies we might have about Warhol's work, whereby we inhabit the temptation to see his films as revealing the populist strains of commodity culture. By this, I mean to warn against reading the performances of *Blowjob* and *Sleep* as simply revealing the possibility that anyone can share in the promises of stardom because the camera can be fixed on them. Where Warhol's cinema does seem to offer insights to the effect that all fans can position themselves (through the labor of fantasy) to become suitable recipients for the Hollywood product (in this particular case, queer male fans whose lives often fail to register as significant for Hollywood representation), it remains apparent that the dynamics of value production are heavily weighted toward those who enjoy profit over and above those who enjoy their spectatorial reveries. In his own formulation that the beauty of America resides in the situation that everyone, common folk and Elizabeth Taylor alike, drinks the same kind of Coke, while anybody can *buy* the same kind of Coke, where Coke figures within the chains of value production is significantly different for those who consume or profit from it.[27] Substituting Hollywood for Coke, the stakes become much higher, as the ideological freight of Hollywood in modern life is often predicated on the exclusion of many of its biggest fans from even being represented as even simply being fans. Commenting on the milieu of camp-loving viewers in which Warhol worked, Richard Dyer argues that

> this simultaneous buying into and debunking of Hollywood was done by those groups of people closest to it in terms of sensibility (producing sensuousness and glamour and/or trading in sex) yet most rigorously excluded from it at the level of representation.[28]

For Dyer, his fascination with Hollywood ultimately precluded Warhol from being critical of its effects, for "the overall tone is a detached embrace of what Hollywood stands in for recognition of its phoneyness."

Dyer seems to be suggesting here that critical responses to Hollywood can only emerge in relation to the "real" and the "phoney" forms of identity that can be elaborated in the visual register of film; the problem with this critical distinction is that it must ultimately dismiss Warhol and his performers as themselves the agents most guilty for the sins of a dominant cinema. According to Dyer, "by the time we get to Warhol notions of the authentic self have been discarded, to be replaced by the desire to be as inauthentic as possible."

Camp is helpful in this regard for understanding how Warhol's film forms a critical recapitulation of Hollywood through the fact of star performance, and Warhol's *Camp* (1965) is an exemplary text for examining how performance, fragmented and devoted to nothing beyond itself, shifts the terrain to one of playful critique. *Camp*'s opening shots offer a group of Film Factory figures, including Tally Brown, Jane Holzer, Gerard Malanga, Jack Smith, and Paul Swan, arrayed in the Factory as a phonograph record plays in the background. Gerard Malanga announces, "Andy Warhol presents 'Camp,'" and the various personae move singly toward a microphone to perform in response to the question "What is camp?" We see Paul Swan dance, alone and then with Baby Jane Holzer; Mario Montez offers his own dance and spray paints a teddy bear, and finally an unidentified woman sings "Let Me Entertain You." In the next reel, after Malanga reads a poem, "Camp," Tally Brown improvises at the microphone with both song and commentary while also suggesting that "I don't happen to believe in the existence of camp." Subsequently Jack Smith invites us to "open the closet, can we?" and as the camera pans to a cabinet, he opens the door to reveal a copy of a *Batman* comic sitting on a shelf inside. At the film's conclusion, another unidentified woman rises to dance.

The structure of *Camp* is improvisational in feel but in fact reveals a significant elaboration of camp as the effort to embrace popular forms with an eye to individuate them in the everyday, and in this regard two moments are key. First, Tally Brown's clowning with song lyrics (crooning, "A cigarette with lipstick traces / a shrunken head in unexpected places . . .") and simultaneous disavowal of the possibility of such play's existence vivifies camp's driving impulses to forge something unique and momentary out of the mass-produced object while having fun in denying that such is taking place. Brown's comments elsewhere on the experience of performing in the Factory are instructive about the conditions under which such performances about camp could emerge:

I always appreciated from Andy that his attitude was totally permissive, which is: you could partake as much or as little as you wanted to or, in the cases of most of the people, needed to. Andy did not, as one whole school of thought has it, exploit people. He never coerced you to do anything you didn't want to. What it was was a conviction of his vision, his permissiveness, where [he] allowed people to do as much as their compulsions made them do. In other words: he created a perfect outlet for people who were exhibitionistic or needed some wild outlet, which they didn't—couldn't—weren't skilled—you know—weren't taught to perform in other ways.[29]

Brown ushers us to an important feature of Warhol's work, namely, that it has continually since the 1960s inspired a critical response that hinges on the idea that Warhol made use of his friends and workers in the Factory for reason of profit: that in Warhol's art and films lies the central fact of exploitation. This, of course, was at the heart of Marx's critique of capital, where Marx found the division of labor in class societies devoted to the creation of wealth as predicated on exploitation.

It is absurd to ask whether Warhol's relation to those around him is one of exploitation: all relations under capital take on that valence, and thus it is more productive to consider how the exploitative features of his work differ in specific fashion from the more general aspects of exploitation as we understand them to define modernity. Marx suggests that in fact, each society can be known for the peculiar nature of its exploitative relations; capitalist social relations are thus characterized through the fundamental proposition of property, where exploitation takes the form of the extraction of surplus value by industrial capital from the proletariat, and access to surplus itself is predicated on the ownership of property and capital.

When Brown comments that Warhol's relation to his performers is not one of exploitation, she is perhaps not being naive but insisting that the exploitative dynamic he staged is not the more recognizable one that Marx defines. She comments in the same interview that "nobody was behind the camera. The camera was just on," and she describes the scene as one where the technology of recording produces an excess (a surplus: of affect, of gesture) that it cannot control; and I would argue that the film is staging a different kind of exploitation, its camp form, deep in the heart of the modern metropolis in order to bear witness to all those labors that cannot and will not be seized by capital's cycles

Jack Smith opens the closet in *Camp*. Film still courtesy of
The Andy Warhol Museum.

of production and value coding. The fact of *failure*— the failure to succeed in conventional terms, to find a way to adjust to the boredom and
alienation of everyday life, to insist on doing something else, even if it
means doing it badly but in one's own peculiar style—is the testament
that Warhol makes here to those many men and women who fought for
another form of consciousness in that historical moment.

The second important moment for this reading of the film appears
in Jack Smith's invitation to "open the closet" and to discover *Batman*.
Smith's gesture captures a small and remarkable truth about the nature
of identity and the commodity: if we want to discover a truth that lies
at the heart of desire, it will turn out to be not the image of the beloved but, in true Genet-like fashion, a piece of trash to be discarded.
We might discover that the heart of queer signification is its capacity,
however ambivalently, to offer our affection to what Warhol often called
"the leftovers" and to build a new world from such fragments. If Warhol is guilty of merely mimicking Hollywood, in his modes of production, in the nomenclatures of stardom, in making cinema, then we are
challenged to read this most astonishing of moments—the only in the

decade—in which we are given the chance to see the contents of the closet and to find out how little there was. After all, all the action was taking place outside.

In the final period of his hands-on filmmaking, Warhol turned his attentions to the narrative form, but even these films seem underscored by an abiding interest in the cinematic icon over and above the structure of the film text through the temporal and spatial arrangements of the narrative form. Given that the production of his earliest films had emerged during the period in which he turned his attentions from the space of the painted image to the cinema, an abiding fascination, over the course of his entire film production, with the nonnarrative moving image fulfills a certain not unexpected logic. Throughout his cinematic endeavors, even into the later period marked by the appearance of such efforts as *My Hustler, Bike Boy,* and *Lonesome Cowboys,* it is the relation between cinema and spectacle that underpins Warhol's movies. Thus even as narrative appears as a structural concern for these later films, they remain largely organized through the concern with the labor of appearances—what it takes as an actor to become suitable for having a narrative constructed around him or her. In this regard, I argue that these films are narratives of desire for the cinematic image—both by the central figures around whom the films are organized (usually younger and conventionally attractive men) and by those who encounter these men, often in the context of prostitution.

It is worth noting that these films are also sometimes seen as evidence of Warhol's capitulation to a more commercial cinema, and certainly his own comments on the expansion of his film technique into the longer narrative format indicate an interest in garnering increased budgets (with the hope of external funding) and larger audiences for the product; the epigrammatic version of this move takes the form of accusing the artist of "selling out." The coincidence of this phrase in the situation of making films about the exchange of sex for money is maybe not as inadvertent as one might think, because they are indeed about the movement of the cinematic icon (here, the actual actor) into a diegetic world concerned with securing his erotic favors. Warhol's artistic concerns (both cinematic and otherwise), even before the movement toward narrative, were consistently involved with the dynamic circulation of mass imagery; in a manner of speaking, the narrative films simply thematize this circulation within their worlds.

The perception, then, that the earlier films bear the hallmark of some-

thing more like the curated art image while the last films made by Warhol were cynically embedded in the realm of commerce fails to explain
the kinds of narratives he produced. David James succinctly describes
the problem when he writes that "such a categorical distinction between
different Warhols is a precondition of the valorization of one over the
other and to a biographical narrative by which either a good artist sold
out to the media or an elitist, pretentious one became popularly accessible."[30] James wisely demands of us to reconsider this unhelpful and
binarized reading of Warhol's turn to narrative in other terms, notably
around the function of Warhol as a proper name for a complicated new
mode of production that is neither entirely avant-garde (i.e., independent of corporate production) nor part of the dominant practices of
Hollywood. "The various stages of his work, considered as formal and
iconographical constructions, run parallel to an evolution in his role in
its production; while it apparently involves substantial ruptures, in fact
it only extends the scope of a limited pattern of operations that can be
summarized as his systematic withdrawal of authorial presence as the
means of asserting authorship of the process of production and propri-
etorship of its fruits." Couched in the terms of my own argument, it
would seem that the historical arc of Warhol's film production is not
about his withdrawal from the production of avant-garde films and the
trajectory toward an auteurist popular cinema to which his name was
spectacularly attached but instead, his career traces the meanings of a
cinema defined, as James points out, more by its interest in the film *image*
and less in filmic *events.* More to the point, the narrative films bear the
hallmark of an enduring focus on the glamourous icon, related to the
cinematic still images of *Haircut (No. 1)* and to the star publicity still, an
image that often both instigates narrative, as in *My Hustler,* where the
figure of Paul America sets into motion a series of failed seductions, and
arrests narrative—as at various points in *Bike Boy* where the image of
Joe Spencer seems to suspend forward narrative movement in a druggy,
strung-out temporality that fails to produce any sense of a story with
a strong closure. Thus Warhol's camp means that even in his most narratively streamlined of films, the individual shots hold a special and inverted priority over and above the stories that they tell—even when
those stories are largely about queer desire and its circulation.

Bike Boy, a 1967 color and sound feature release of ninety-six minutes centers around the exploits of the eponymous bike boy, played by
Joe Spencer, and uses the loosely affiliated sequences of Joe's movement

Joe Spencer performs in *Bike Boy*. Film still courtesy of
The Andy Warhol Museum.

though various metropolitan spaces to offer, through the remarkable
disparity of image and sound track, a dizzying amalgamation of queer
male desire, commodity fetishism, and camp commentary. *Bike Boy* is a
tour de force of bitchy theatrics about the effort required to get Joe into
bed, with a joke at the center of the film appearing at its start, where we
as spectators have already visually scored him in advance. The film begins, rather famously, with a direct shot on the nude Joe as he showers;
in an extended opening sequence, punctuated with Warhol's signature
strobe cuts, the camera tilts and zooms in on Joe's body as he lathers,
rinses, repeats. This is a startling occurrence in cinema and figures in a
number of critical commentaries (Dyer, Koch) as a signal moment in the
representation of queer male desire: the sequence offers the undiverted
gaze of a camera (and one authorized no less by the proper name of a
director) on the male form with no narrative situation whatsoever. It
does so without the excuse of this being a mere glimpse, running to an
astonishingly long eleven minutes, and in so doing, *Bike Boy* begins by

anchoring its project to this record and refuses to offer any explanation of the event: no pathology of the subject, no excuses of the artistic pose, no alibi of athletic appreciation. The failure of a narrative context is compounded by the fact that Joe repeatedly returns the look to the camera, suggesting that this is no secretive or furtive glance being caught between him and the camera; the dynamics of exhibitionism and voyeurism are acknowledged within the oscillation between Spencer and the Warholian lens.[31]

After this remarkable opening gesture, the film records in serial fashion (similar to other Warhol vehicles such as *I, a Man* and *The Loves of Ondine*) the protagonist's movement through six conversations, most of them with such Factory fixtures as Brigid Polk, Ingrid Superstar, Ed Hood, and Viva. In these sequences, we see Joe undressing and posing, staging his body for the visual delight of the other characters and for the film's audience. His muscled performances, however, fail to elicit much of anything that could be called an "explicit" erotic response within *Bike Boy*'s diegetic world, and in fact most of the film is devoted to the negotiations between Joe and his potential clients as they indirectly attempt to get him to agree to the price of his sexual favors.

Bike Boy makes a point of its organization around the relation, but not coincidence, of sexual pleasure with consumption; Joe is seen moving through not only the private spaces of bedrooms and kitchens but also the retail venues of a flower shop and a men's clothing boutique. The latter sequence, falling immediately after the shower scene, in fact constitutes one of the film's most important moments from the standpoint of the present analysis because this portion of the film crosscuts between Joe and an unnamed young blond man, both of whom try on clothing with the assistance of the presiding shop clerks, two aggressively funny and opinionated queens who insist on helping the men as they choose the furnishings for their sexual play. Aside from the obvious scopophilic pleasures of watching the pair in various states of undress, the sequence's camp dimensions are produced by the sound track as we overhear the conversation between the two clerks as they comment on the customers' choices in clothing. "Can you imagine these people buying these clothes?" one of them whispers breathily, distilling the delight and the absurdity of such a scene whereby the commodities, jammed together in remarkable density, are made to bear the brunt of signing the desires of the subjects who wear them. The scene is completed by a consultation between the clerks and Joe about the appropriate cologne;

one clerk finally has to explain to the seemingly dim Joe the reason for the cologne's expense, "You're paying for the bottle."

It would be easy to dismiss this portion of *Bike Boy* as a bit of sub-cultural documentary on Warhol's part. Nevertheless this portion of the film cuts to the heart of what this book argues about camp as a response to the commodification of life under modernity. The magnificent camp gesture toward the product in the sphere of consumption ("Can you imagine these people buying these clothes?") tells of a critical capacity that frames the objects of the industrial world in both the power of their appeal (such as when the camera seizes on the underweared crotches and tightly T-shirted torsos of the customers) and the exclusions that the commodities can tell about ("Can you imagine . . ." is an entreaty to try to imagine something else besides the scene presented).

The film closes with two sequences in which women figure promi-nently, and if camp is allowed to be antimisogynistic, these moments would be its most graphic illustrations. Capturing Joe's encounters with Brigid Berlin and Viva, it becomes evident that Joe wants to be fancied by them, and while their interest in him as an erotic object cannot be discounted, the film takes pleasure in demonstrating how they have little interest in Joe if he solely presents himself as an inert and passive thing to be admired. Brigid Berlin takes pleasure in humiliating Joe with regard to his suggestion that she is a lesbian, countering the clichéd definition of a woman who is uninterested in a specific male as indifferent to all men. The heated argument that ensues is a tour de force of feminine humor and strength in the face of normative masculinity and ushers the spectator to the segment of the film featuring Joe and Viva.

Here we are presented with the image of the pair contorting them-selves over a sofa that forms the spare backdrop to their seductive sex play; Viva clearly is in charge, telling Joe that she picks up men to alle-viate boredom and strongly hinting that Joe is not the answer to her current ennui. At one point, she announces, "I don't think you know how to kiss: How can I have any fun fucking you if I don't have any fun kissing you?" Later, after they have partially stripped and are rolling around the sofa, she laughs at him and produces a distressed look on his face, to which she responds, "I'm just laughing at you because you're so funny." *Bike Boy* here becomes momentarily utopian in its sexual poli-tics, because Viva's self-possession disrupts Joe's attempts to dominate her; he is attempting throughout the film both to insert himself into the sexual economy of hustling and to declare himself independent from it, and *Bike Boy* offers an important vision of the contradictions that arise not simply around the commodification of sexuality (seen perhaps more trenchantly in the shopping scenes) but from the crisis of Joe's attempts to commodify his masculinity.

Viva's closing comment to the film ("you're so funny") offers a counterpart to the shop clerk's earlier laughter at the absurdity of what transpires before him, and the two insights give shape to *Bike Boy*'s project: the shift from his status as erotic emblem at the film's opening to his being scorned by the playful women. If Joe is attempting to organize a life based on his capacity to hustle, both the spectator and the women in the film, then he goes about his efforts with only the most limited of success—we never see him either get paid or score sexually. Paradoxically, the work is done by everyone else around him (the shop-keepers, the women, Warhol himself) in order to produce as an erotic icon that ultimately they largely fail to find of much interest. The importance of his status as a sexual object is confirmed not by the other actors in the film but by the devotion of the camera to him, a devotion episodically undercut by his treatment by the women and queer men whom he encounters. In Warhol's incidental tale of this bikie's life on the make, there is no doubt that sex work is work—the challenge is to know who is performing it.

Bike Boy presents us with two framings around the glamorous image, one that visually defines the hunky male icon whom Warhol's camera does not fail to represent as desirable (lit and situated for long periods for erotic gazing by the spectator) and the narrative world where he is rejected. This is complicated by the fact that the film shows us how glamour is produced through the consumption of clothing and fragrance, and we might want to conclude that the other characters in the film desire Joe as much as the spectator is encouraged to, but they instead mock and reject him. The critical wedge of camp appears in the ways that they express how the revelation of glamour's production undercuts its erotic appeal—that the work of sex work removes its sexual appeal and makes it susceptible to the camp play witnessed in the commentaries of the shop clerks and of Brigid Berlin and Viva.

Forming a more explicitly queer counterpart to *Bike Boy*'s tales of straight prostitution, *My Hustler* (1965) inverts the status of the hustler: here everyone wants to score with him, but the hustle is to hustle *him*— to subvert the sexual economy by withholding the wages he might earn and to secure him for sexual pleasure.[32] Divided into two long sec-

Conditions of labor: John MacDermott and
Paul America in *My Hustler*. Film still courtesy of
The Andy Warhol Museum.

tions, *My Hustler*'s first sequence situates the camera at a distance from
two spaces that it sutures together through zooming and panning, between the deck of a Long Island beach house, where we see Ed Hood,
John MacDermott, and Genevieve Charbon, and the adjoining beach,
on which the hustler, Paul America, lies in the sand. Sitting in front of
the house, Hood announces to MacDermott and Charbon that he has
brought the film's eponymous hustler to the beach for his own entertainment, and he warns them about any attempts to seduce the hustler
away from him for the weekend. MacDermott and Charbon take up the
challenge to see who might usurp this financial arrangement (conve-
niently managed, as Hood proudly proclaims, through the services of
"Dial a Hustler"). Hood then coyly tells Charbon, "You take some perverse psychological pleasure from stealing them from homosexuals" and
suggests to MacDermott that his own investment in this competition
stems from the fact that MacDermott himself (called by Hood a "tired,
aging old hustler") is now unable to participate in the sexual economy
and can only fail to attract other men with his physical attributes. After

Charbon moves to the beach and is seen (but not heard) chatting with Paul and swimming with him, the film inconclusively ends this sequence without having suggested whether anyone has succeeded in hooking up with Paul. Vital to this sequence is that although it would appear that Charbon has managed to insinuate herself with Paul, we continue to hear Hood's commentary on the action; like the shop clerks in *Bike Boy*, it is the bitchy commentary that now frames the utopian scene of Charbon and Paul America as one established through exchange and competition: heterosexuality is now imbricated with the economy of queer male pleasure that sets the terms for straight sexuality.

The image of Paul America, like that of Joe Spencer, enjoys a significantly appreciative treatment at the behest of the camera, evoking in its cinematography the blond California surfer boy as the figure of sexual attraction; like *Bike Boy, My Hustler* insists on the critical difference between the internal gaze of the other characters on the male figure and that of the audience. Unlike *Bike Boy*, this effort employs different formal techniques. Whereas the latter experiments with the strobe shot as a form of in-camera editing, here the long take, panning and zooming the camera (itself always in a fixed position), move the spectator between the spaces inhabited by America and Hood, Charbon and MacDermott. The difference in approach is key to *My Hustler*'s insistence on locating the viewer in relation to a vector of queer desire, as Hood and MacDermott are seen craning to watch Charbon's interaction with America, and we come to realize that we are watching queer men watch an enactment of straight seduction. Warhol uses the visual image and dialogue of the two men watching to comment on the action quite similarly to the voice-over commmentary of the shop queens in *Bike Boy*. Richard Dyer describes this triangulated structure of the film's attentions to Paul America (whereby we see and hear Hood's and MacDermott's responses to the action on the beach) as significant because

> they give us the sight of the object desired, give us the pleasure sought by the man, but they also draw attention to the devices that are permitting the object to be seen and establish distance, so that when Paul is in the frame we may nonetheless be aware that only we the audience, and not the speakers (overheard on the soundtrack commenting on Paul) can gaze so closely.[33]

Similar to Warhol's earlier efforts, the role of the camera for implicating the audience's own impulse to gaze at Paul is strongly at odds with

Hollywood, reminding us continually that, as Dyer offers, "the frisson, especially for the mid-sixties audience, is also that we are able just to sit there, in a public space (a cinema) rather than secretly at home, and look with uninterrupted lust at a man." Yet even as the film offers this vision of the male figure without the more customary excuses offered by dominant cinema for such erotic gazing, *My Hustler* frames our vision of the male icon in terms of his status as a site of exchange, enacting such access to male pulchritude through questions of labor and value coding. Inverting matters, though, Warhol makes the hustler's potential customers and bedmates work to secure him, instead of positioning the male prostitute as a sexual commodity procured easily through the offer of money. This begs the question of whether money is the only form of exchange in the relation of customer to hustler, as what Charbon and MacDermott import as a threat to Hood's glib assumption that he and he alone (however temporarily) owns Paul is the fact that language and bodies might themselves be the token through which one wins the bet at hand; they can perhaps lure Paul away from Hood through promises of pleasures other than that of the money form he is guaranteed to garner from his being a "Dial a Hustler," but in doing so they will have revealed the nature of his status as a commodity and the way that money is bound up in this economy that is very queer, indeed. The work involved, then, becomes apparent in the fact that both the male and female competitors in the wager must obey the form of exchange that Hood has already installed before them. He can trump them simply by insisting on the promise of sex for money that has brought Paul to the beach to begin with. Charbon's and MacDermott's efforts are framed by this contract: they may employ whatever strategies they might to seduce Paul, but such exertions are always done with the knowledge that they must give way to the precedent set by Hood and his money.

The first reel of *My Hustler* achieves its narrative suspense through the question of who might attempt to seduce Paul away from the money/sex-as-commodity nexus, and it is worth noting that the two competitors whom Hood invites to this contest are a man who, according to the film's dialogue, has been discarded by this economy by virtue of his age and a woman who seemingly has less money than Hood and must rely on her good looks and charm to participate. (We never hear either of them challenging Hood's status simply by offering to pay Paul more money than he has been offered by Hood.) In Hood's character, Warhol draws attention to the rich queen who seems to have mastered the economy that elsewhere might marginalize him; as an effeminate middle-aged man, Hood's wealth establishes him as the figure who names the terms of exchange. The effect is not one that vilifies Hood so much as one that locates his dominance within the domain of leisure and consumption, and in this regard the film discovers that value can be determined not only through labor but through consumption. That the object of consumption is another man's body, to whom the other figures are barred by a lack of money, drives home the kinds of circulation that *My Hustler* is attempting to disclose whereby queer men participate in the fluctuations of capital and its value codings. Warhol produces a film about how queers produce value in consumption, and the first half of the film ends with the question of whether this determination must be obeyed or might itself be subverted.

When at the beginning of the film's second reel, the action moves inside to a static shot of a bathroom where MacDermott and America bathe together, we discover a potential answer to this question, which perversely enough returns us to the function of the hustler's labor to sustaining this economy. Here we see the two hustlers, one young and the other apparently experienced, as they share comradely advice about the life of sex for hire. Interspersed with shared insights about the benefits of getting their teeth capped and the virtue of shaving with Noxema, they debate the different things to be gained in hustling, such as whether dinner or cash might be preferable forms of payment. Mac-Dermott counsels America about the kinds of money to be made by prostitution, all the while eyeing his rival and his seductee. It becomes clear that if the film's first reel made a joke about gaining visual access to Paul as one kind of "scoring" with him (thus the initial reel's emphasis on the zoom and the pan), then MacDermott, in this logic, has won the bet, at least for the moment, in his capacity to share visually the small space of the bathroom with Paul. We hear Paul's voice, which we have not in the first half of the film (his vocal presence here marks an access to him that not even the audience had previously been able to enjoy), and the exchange between Paul and MacDermott about the life of hustling, the world of their labor, draws them together in an unexpected tangle within the contest—revealing the situation of their mutually shared profession gives MacDermott priority over his competitors. His failure to interest Paul sexually, having revealed that every human exchange in this setting becomes an economic one (he jadedly counsels Paul that "everybody's hustling, and looking to get hustled"), and indeed his own labors to succeed as a prostitute have largely come to an end. After their lengthy exchange, in short fashion the frame is filled in the foreground of the bathroom doorway, where in rapid succession Charbon, Hood, and the newly appearing Dorothy Dean all stand in silhouette, trying to lure Paul away from MacDermott's commentary.

Compared to the first reel's dynamic and playful camera work, this sequence feels claustrophic and limiting; if the initial game was to beat out the other competitors in access to Paul, the second reel makes that access a dismal rite. Koch writes that *My Hustler* becomes the first Warhol film "in which the work's fundamental qualities as film don't happen to be particularly interesting,"[34] and he suggests that the camera fails to allow us to see much beyond what he calls the "clichéd tics of the national vocabulary of masculine body language" enacted by Paul America and MacDermott in the film's latter half. Yet if elsewhere Warhol's camera had made a point of providing a stage for various marginalized performances to make their appearance, *My Hustler,* like *Bike Boy,* reveals the determination behind masculine macho to resist disclosing itself as another set of acts in the production of sexualities. The camera's immobility in the second reel of *My Hustler* thrusts into view the image of masculinity's production, and if the results sometimes disappoint the film's critical commentators, we might begin to apprehend what Warhol was trying to tell us about (Paul) America.

When confronted with Warhol's reworking of a Hollywood genre, in the form of *Lonesome Cowboys,* it is not a simple substitution of queer male desire into the form of the (apparently) masculine Western that we witness; in this film, the closest approximation in his career to a Hollywood movie, we get a sense of why Andy Warhol might have nurtured fantasies of working within Hollywood. Were *Lonesome Cowboys* solely the substitution of queer male desire into the form of the Western (a genre whose more general sexual dynamics, Corey Creekmur has argued, need to be understood for their homoerotic and homosocial valences), it would already mark an important contribution to the history of experimental film about sex/gender.[35] Undoubtedly, the film does this; while trading on features of the mise-en-scène that mark the Western, such as the setting and costumes, *Lonesome Cowboys* suggests the breakdown of the Western genre in the face of its previously unarticulated homoeroticism. Depicting the tension between townfolk (Viva and Taylor Mead) and cowboys (Tom Hompertz, Louis Waldron, and Joe Dallesandro), the film has been understood by some critics as illustrating the latent homoerotics that underpin the Western, offering, as Peter Gidal claims, a "masculine ritual" that is

> performed with a naturalness that is unprecedented; it exposes the sick confrontations in the usual Western, where perversely *latent* homosexual wishes are played out to the full, disguised by the acceptable notions of gun-fights, round-ups, brawls. . . . It is the disguising of these values that is sick, not the values themselves. Repression of *anything* is sick in that repression leads to (or betrays) an unfulfillment.[36]

On the other hand, Dyer argues that the film is "probably a good deal less coherent and critically conscious" than Gidal would have it. This leaves us with either having to see the film as embracing a "natural" homosexuality implied by the Western or, according to Dyer, understanding it as tampering with the codes of the Western's manliness to such a degree that it fails to achieve a naturalized gay pleasure, exposing the film as a failed critique. This opposition is a curious one because it situates the film either as representing male same-sex pleasure on the screen as something that derives from a knowledge of the Western but that the Western has never been in a position to admit or as importing something so foreign to the Western that it fails to disturb the masculinist codes of the genre, preserving them intact. That something, when described by Dyer, is the film's camp rendering of masculinity:

> When Ramona and Taylor Mead first see the cowboys riding into town, Ramona says, "Maybe they're real men," to which Mead replies, "Oh not real men! Ramona I must protect you." The levels of irony in the delivery of these two improvised lines are so unresolved as to defy analysis. Does Ramona want them to be real men? Does Viva already know they are not? . . . Just where is the irony directed—at the very idea of "real men" or at the idea that these gay boys might be it? And would their being real men make them more or less desirable?[37]

I would direct the problem of whether these figures deserve the name of "real men" to the question of the *value* of masculinity for the Western. It is not a question of whether "real" homosexuality is more commonly repressed in the Western, as Gidal suggests, inasmuch as we need to understand the productive function of same-sex desire for the Western; but it seems neither the case that the film is sabotaging a "positive" homosexuality by invoking the appeal of "real" (i.e., somehow not queer) masculinity, and Dyer's frustration with the ironic delivery of this problem signals the film's deliberate ambivalence at confirming a "real" masculinity to which the film does not see its own cowboys as belonging. Indeed, the film offers possibilities for reading these figures as straight (they trade in the icons of sanctified masculinity: boots, spurs, Stetsons), and yet they also have homoerotic impulses that become articulated as homosocial gestures. In fact, their sexual aggression against Ramona (Viva), in which they rape her, and their subsequent tenderness (Gidal's "naturalness") go a long way to understanding the relation between male homosociality and the repression of women, and from this nexus emerges what is Warhol's most pressing insight in this film, namely, that the Western film may often be organized around a villainized version of male same-sex desire whose treachery can be known through its violence toward women. The Western's importance historically as a lucrative product for the American studio system, then, derives from the genre's capacity to offer a vision of male homoerotics that ultimately it can condemn, a vision built on the ambivalent performances of many of the film colony's most important actors in the Western (one need only think of Montgomery Clift in *Red River*).

When at the film's conclusion, Eric and Tom leave for California, it becomes apparent that only by exiting the Western (two of the cowboys leave for the beach: the setting of *My Hustler*) can some other representation of queer desire and its relation to women be figured. *Lonesome Cowboys*, then, forms a critique of the Western, but it is a camp critique in which questions about the Western's validation of masculinity are brought to bear through the figure of Taylor Mead, Ramona's "nurse," and the function of labor in the film, inasmuch as Mead operates as a supplement to Viva's already pronounced feminine appeal. Mead's effeminacy initially seems to figure on the side of the civilized in *Lonesome Cowboys*, and if Ramona is heard questioning the status of the cowboys as "real" men, Mead's comments confirm the threat of *straight* masculinity from which she should be protected. The evocation of effeminate queer men in the Warhol Factory, where queer men, often in drag, and women formed an alliance that combated the biases of straight male critics to the work of pop art's camp dimensions, would have had particular resonances for contemporary audiences. Indeed, the hostility toward masculinity voiced at moments in the film would suggest that part of the film's effect is to offer no identificatory pleasure for the straight male spectator, a turnabout from the usual expectations of the Hollywood

Western. The customary place of the straight male within the Western, protecting femininity from the advances of outlaw and "savage" aggression, is taken over by the effeminate Mead and ultimately leads to the nurse's humiliation at the hands of the cowboys. Warhol's positioning of Mead in *Lonesome Cowboys'* revision of the Western forms the critical wedge that displaces an understanding (or, to recall Dyer's comment, "defies analysis") of the film as arranged around the classical organization of the Western's purportedly typical oppositions of civilized-savage and female-male. I write "purportedly" because once we have witnessed this displacement via the camp commentary offered by Mead's character, it is difficult to return to the genre of the Western without having to interrogate the stability of those oppositions, via the question of "real masculinity," in the first place.

Warhol after the Sixties: Camp as Retrograde

There is much to the argument that Warhol's ability to interrogate the place of popular culture had transformed into the intent to create the popular itself. Warhol's career after 1968 reads as a failure both to offer alternative visions of cinema and, Warhol's energies notwithstanding, to achieve the power that he so yearned for within the production of mass culture. Despite this narrative of Warhol's "selling out," which populates Dyer's and Koch's analyses and those of numerous others, there remains an important question about how such an account (outlined by James: first Warhol was radical, then he was reactionary; or first he was elite, and then he was popular) fits with the concurrent dynamics of emergent identity politics.[38] Warhol's departure from his filmmaking (but not his sponsorship of Paul Morrissey's films, which carried the imprint of Warhol's financing, if not entirely his artistic vision) handily coincides with the appearance of gay and lesbian identity politics. It seems worth wondering how the forms of post-Stonewall gay and lesbian political discourses so remarkably diverged from the kinds of questions posed by Andy Warhol in his art and films that it might have been inevitable that his films became, as he himself argued, unwatchable—not because they failed as entertainment but because their camp dimensions interrogated the value codings of a consumerist society that much sexual dissidence would ultimately seek to validate and inhabit.[39]

In 1969 Warhol reappeared in New York life, recuperating from his shooting attack and redirecting his energies and disavowing, at least in private, the Factory of the 1960s. Simultaneously the Stonewall riots marked a watershed moment in the visibility and tactics of gay and lesbian subcultural politics. In 1972 Warhol withdrew the films of the 1960s from public circulation, and the effect has been to efface the fact that so many of the films antagonized the notion of stable identities in contemporary gender politics.[40] The disappearance of these works in the post-Stonewall moment serves to remind us of the importance of underground film in the setting of 1960s intellectual debate. More importantly, much of Warhol's sensibility was assimilated into the production of popular nonunderground cinema, most notably in terms of the breaking of censorship codes around the production and screening of pornography; if in the 1960s Warhol's ability to interrogate pop culture seemed radical, by the 1970s those interrogations were adopted in the styles and themes of mass-market films.[41]

From the viewpoint of "gay-positive" politics, Stonewall marks the moment that Warhol's project became depleted, for the energies and sensibilities of the Factory scene became for many in the new gay liberation politics the hallmark of repression and self-loathing. If previously the project of pop art had been to fix a critical and often humorous eye on the specter of popular culture, and that eye had been trained within the camp subcultures of 1950s and 1960s queer New York, gay liberation could draw no quarter for the potential perception of gays as somehow aberrant in their viewing (let alone sexual) pleasures. More to the point, the act in which gay viewers, whether they thought of themselves as camp or not, enjoyed Hollywood cinema became a taboo. As Andrew Britton claimed:

> Anyone who has ever had the misfortune to endure a conversation with one of the tribe of Bette Davis' camp-followers will know that [this] kind of appropriation of the star's image . . . leads to . . . self-recreation as an oppressive stereotype.[42]

Britton argues that the pregay queer man's fixation with a glamour icon prevented him from the political act of naming himself in positive terms, the implication being that since he could never really become Bette Davis, attention to her could only serve to render him as a "stereotypical" fan. A significant omission from Britton's account are drag queens, who in fact do "become" (as much as one is humanly able) Bette Davis or Joan Crawford, but for the sake of forging positive gay identities, such an omission was key.[43] Yet the problem for Britton was also one that involved the processes of spectatorial identification and sexual identity. Without the inverted identificatory processes of camp in working with Hollywood film, the two could not be the same. Much as the dynamics of identification would come to be questioned by feminist work in psychoanalysis, any pleasure, however strangely it might be called "identification," felt by queer male spectators with the star image meant that precious resources for forming positive identity would be squandered. Couched in my arguments about camp's critical strategies, the queer man who camped could not become a gay man because he squandered his productive energies in his devotions to the mass text while he should, apparently, have been rebuilding himself as a social subject worthy of valediction. Andy Warhol would not be the man in whose image such rebuilding should take place.

The two critical strains arising concurrently after 1968 around Warhol's film productions offer a way to see how much this artist, whose film works attest to an important intersection between sexuality, value, and capital's social organization, failed to satisfy either demand on his work. First, in terms of the argument that the tendency in the Factory was increasingly to imitate Hollywood narrative film (cf. Koch), one can only point to the narratives involved and suggest that they are, as I hope to have demonstrated, not so much derived from Hollywood film form as critically grounded in it. Second, given the "gay-positive" attitude toward Warhol that saw him as embodying a retrograde camp emblem, he could do little to help secure the newly invented political category of the "gay man" for his art and films. This may have made him, for some gay audiences of the 1970s and 1980s, something of an anachronism, but it also meant the loss of a camp critical project whose longer history within modernity has largely been lost.

We thus discover that the implications of gay liberation politics for Warhol's work were enormous and not always felicitous, not because Warhol's art needs defending but because the insights that its camp strategies reveal seem difficult to apprehend within the dull normativities of identity politics. Complicating matters is the fact that the nomination of "gay man" seemed hardly to sit well with Andy Warhol himself, and not for the most inspiring of reasons. That Warhol might be understood as a gay-identified artist could horrify his patrons, a tie the artist was loath to endanger. Gay liberation political voices did not see him as a model, and he most likely did not see himself as an avatar of a utopian new sexual subculture, to the degree that it seemed little concerned with questions of labor and production. The problem was that his work was so deeply informed by camp, and camp still had to be reckoned with by emerging gay politics that saw it as the hallmark of prior oppression of homosexuals. Britton argued in 1978 that

> camp has a certain minimal value, in restricted contexts, as a form of *épater les bourgeois;* but the pleasure (in itself genuine and valid enough) of shocking solid citizens should not be confused with radicalism. The positive connotations—an insistence on one's otherness, a refusal to pass as straight—are so irredeemably compromised by complicity in the traditional, oppressive formulations of that otherness. Camp is simply one way in which gay men have recuperated their oppression, and it needs to be criticized as such.[44]

Britton maintained that camp could offer nothing to gays but a form of conciliation to the conditions under which they had largely failed to be represented, but more to the point, camp had become such a vital feature of popular culture that it could not always be articulated as a form of expression of gay identity politics in the 1970s. At the heart of that movement of camp to popular representation was Andy Warhol.

In the context of this argument, I would argue that the tendency toward narrative within Warhol's filmmaking was not necessarily retrograde, difficult as it is to construe a film like *Lonesome Cowboys* as solely imitative of Hollywood narrative film; and while Warhol's departure from the earlier experiments of his filmmaking signals for some critics a disavowal of the earlier Factory practices, it is important to renew the later films with the sense that narrative itself can, of course, be experimental too. The assumption of his political and aesthetic debasement in the movement from the Factory of the 1960s to its later incarnations might apply to a filmmaker who gained access to Hollywood financing, but by and large the assumption of Warhol's corruption into the popular (without recourse to an antagonistic stance to that popular) tends to be read through Warhol's biography, where his increasing association with Manhattan's high society meant that his interests in camp critique distanced him from his former avant-garde stature.

Indeed, were we to resort solely to biographical interpretations to explain Warhol's eventual leave-taking from film, the unfortunate story to be told lies not only in Warhol's own life but in the cultural politics to which he had given shape. The 1968 shooting, the prime event in Warhol's surrender of the old Factory for the later one, bears great weight in a story to be told of his transformation into a high-society figure, telling as it might of his conversion into a benign documenter of the rich and famous. Nevertheless the financial explanation deserves attention, too: Warhol had spent a goodly amount of his income from his fine art on his movies, and at the moment in which it appeared that he might recoup his investments by gaining access to wider distribution, Hollywood had usurped him by taking on the cachet of an alternative cinema without having to deal with the strong women, bitchy men, and amphetamine queens who populate the underground films.[45]

More important, the camp critical impulses under Warhol's name had been rechristened pop and had by the period of his later films taken on a larger dimension than could be tied simply to the figure of Andy Warhol. If the fantasies of fame that had driven the Factory for so many years were finally realized, the notoriety of pop would spread beyond his control. Warhol's own assessment of Hollywood's power might have told him something about the increasing irrelevance of him personally to the popular culture that he had reshaped, for the domain of corporate production holds little respect for its own innovators:

> Out in Hollywood, I kept thinking about the silly, unreal way the movies there treated sex. After all, the early ones used to have sex and nudity—like Hedy Lamarr in *Ecstasy*—but then they suddenly realized that they were throwing away a good tease, that they should save it for a rainy day. Like, every ten years they would show another part of the body or say another dirty word on screen, and that would stretch out the box office for years, instead of just giving it away all at once. But then when foreign films and underground film started getting big, it threw Hollywood's timetable off.[46]

If Warhol understood that the camp underground's potential to extend the boundaries of what constituted acceptable cinema had posed a challenge to Hollywood, by the end of the sixties, Hollywood had returned the bluff. These techniques, widely praised by contemporaneous critics of the emerging underground cinema, proved difficult to adapt to the popular cinema of the moment, and Warhol's explicit depictions, particularly of dissident sexualities, earned him no rewards within the Hollywood industries whose funding he longed for throughout his professional career.

As much as Andy Warhol seems to have discussed his fantasy of breaking into Hollywood—expressing at various moments the desire to make monumental films, the most notable endeavor having been his **** (*Four Stars*)—there is little indication that he pursued this desire in any official or serious way. No correspondence with any studio suggesting such has come to light, and Warhol's career as a graphic artist in the previous decade would at least make it plausible that among all the underground and avant-garde figures of that moment, he was the best suited to move into the corporate sphere of production: he knew how to achieve results that pleased those who were fiscally in charge. This failure—even to try to engage with Hollywood money—is a curious turn of affairs and would bear some speculation. Perhaps the studio that he had put together was an achievement that satisfied him enough, or maybe he realized how much work was involved in making cinema and found that such duties distracted him from his other work—painting, sculpture, and the art form he was to achieve in his social life in Manhattan in the following two decades. Callie Angell has suggested that his films were probably becoming increasingly expensive to make, and that the drain on his resources was too great to sustain—even as his films, particularly *Chelsea Girls* and *Blue Movie* seemed to have the potential to gather larger and more diverse audiences. Be that as it may, if we displace this discussion away from the entirely biographical, we might ask: How did the camp movies he had made redefine the ways that film could be a medium for philosophical enquiry into the experiences and effects of modernity? The kinds of knowledge *and* pleasure that film can produce, and the kinds of questions that his films asked—about the social life of industrialized humans, about the activity of looking and knowing, about the unexpected things to be seen through camp—were already of such immensity that he had, in five brief years, pushed the medium of cinema to a startling new place where it could help to examine those things.

THREE

"A Physical Relation between Physical Things":

The World of the Commodity According to

Kenneth Anger

In the same way the light from an object is perceived by us not as the subjective excitation of our optic nerve, but as the objective form of something outside the eye itself. But, in the act of seeing, there is at all events, an actual passage of light from one thing to another, from the external object to the eye. There is a physical relation between physical things. But it is different with commodities. There, the existence of the things qua commodities, and the value-relation between the products of labour which stamps them as commodities, have absolutely no connexion with their physical properties and with the material relations arising therefrom. There it is a definite social relation between men, that assumes, in their eyes, the fantastic form of a relation between things. In order, therefore, to find an analogy, we must have recourse to the mist-enveloped regions of the religious world. In that world the productions of the human brain appear as independent beings endowed with life, and entering into relation both with one another and the human race. So it is in the world of commodities with the products of men's hands. This I call the Fetishism which attaches itself to the products of labour, so soon as they are produced as commodities, and which is therefore inseparable from the production of commodities.

—Karl Marx

The cover of the spring 1964 issue of *Film Culture* displays a photograph of Kenneth Anger and the Angel of Death. Anger, done up in tight black motorcycle leathers, rests his right hand on the handles of a garishly chromed motorcycle; around the "hog" are arrayed a host of talismanic props (a cartoonish skull, a head of Pan). Presiding over this whole affair is an effigy of Death, tricked out in customary sickle and black hood, and the whole tableau is anchored to a mock gravestone on which reads "The Reaper: Meditations." If the journal's editors were interested in its marketing through the appeals of male pulchritude, Anger's movie star good looks of course did not hurt matters, but the significance of Anger's image appearing on so important an issue of "America's Independent Motion Picture Magazine" could hardly fail to identify him as one of the most significant figures of American noncorporate film culture. This image powerfully reinforces Kenneth Anger's status as a commentator on the grisly imbrication of commodity fetishism and the aesthetics of the necrotic that his films and writings seize on at the heart of American modernity.

This particular issue of *Film Culture,* in fact, appeared on the heels of the New York City Police having seized several underground films on the grounds that they were obscene; acting under the orders of the district attorney's office, in March 1964, police detectives had already impounded Jack Smith's *Flaming Creatures,* Jean Genet's *Un Chant d'Amour,* and Anger's own paean to leather-and-bike culture, *Scorpio Rising.* The editorial board of the journal, writing in appeal to the readers of *Film Culture* as the "Film-Maker's Cooperative Anti-Censorship Fund," argued that "the City and the State have turned against the avantgarde in the arts," and that "an important shift in the ways of life, in moral attitudes, is about to take place in America." Led by Jonas Mekas, this collective voice presciently identified an important political stake in the work of the American arts movement, hardly a surprise to any student of the historical avant-garde and its relation to forces of domination and exploitation. What does come as something of a surprise, though, is the fact that the political images at the center of this struggle were concerned with dissident sexualities, and not the more customary kinds of leftist positions that we might expect under the name of the political movements of the 1960s. Further, the depictions of homoerotic play beheld in the particular example of Anger's *Scorpio Rising* are entwined with evocations of the fetishistic play of an American subculture and the concomitant exploration of the relations between the fascination of the commodity and the fascist imagination.[1] Worth examining in all of Kenneth Anger's film and writing is how his productions are so centrally focused on homoerotic desire in relation to the emergent political imaginations of modernity.

In this chapter, I argue that the camp dimensions of his work form a critical project that continually attends to the metaphysical languages of both life under capital and the fascist aesthetics that form one expression of those languages.[2] Perhaps no living artist is more responsible for revealing, through the camp critical lens, the fetishistic fascination of the mass produced commodity of which Marx writes in the foregoing argument, and if Anger's recent output as of late seems to have lessened in volume, his impact on film culture bears daily witness. This is true not only of his films but also of his writings in the *Hollywood Babylon* volumes, where Anger surfaced a subterranean history of the film studios' suppressed self-history and in so doing examined not simply alluring bits of film industry hearsay but, more trenchantly, how the industrial production and distribution of film star gossip functions within the larger matrix of social regulation contained in the nomination of "Hollywood." I conjoin readings of Anger's films and his *Hollywood Babylon* volumes through the idea that Anger's efforts derive their dynamism through a dialectic continually restaged in his works between the seemingly liberatory libidinal pleasures set into motion by consumption (what I am in this chapter naming as the fetish) and the potentially annihilatory energies bound up in such pleasures (here called fascism).

All Dressed Up: The Curious Theoretical Life of the Fetish

In her introduction to *Fetishism as Cultural Discourse,* Emily Apter situates the anthology's project as one that addresses, in her splendid phrase, "the sexuality of things." Commenting on what holds together the critical strategies of the various disciplinary fascinations with the fetish (in some cases, perhaps itself fetishistic), she writes:

> Desublimating the aura of falsity and bad faith in consumer consciousness; unmasking the banal sexisms of everyday life; undercutting aesthetic idealism and the seductive spectacle of kitsch, camp, or punk; exposing the postmodern infatuation with transgression, "gender trouble," and erotic fixation; smoking out the Eurocentric

voyeurism of "other-collecting"—fetishism as a discourse weds its own negative history as a synonym for sorcery and witchcraft (*feitiçaria*) to an outlaw strategy of dereification.[3]

At the heart of this description of recent critical fetish talk appears an appeal to camp as a strategy that might dislodge the reified status of the commodity. Apter senses camp as insisting on the fetish as an appearance of something else besides the dense node of incommensurability it has been made to bear in the colonial bourgeois imagination, an incommensurability born between European ideations of value and the modes of thought of the colonized that themselves could not, literally, be made sense of within the economic and political epistemologies of the Western imperial mind.

The place of "sense" and "sensation" for the fetish within this scheme is vital to its sexiness, as the seemingly apparent material and erotic appeal of the commodity, which make it liable to become a fetish, are held in abeyance from other measures of its value, such as its production via exploited labor and its circulation. Binding together all manner of approaches to the fetish (such as anthropology, art history, literary criticism), but most notably psychoanalytic and materialist critiques, is the fetish's status as an icon of value's unpredictable career as it moves among the fragments of modernity: body parts, commodities, words, images. In some measure, one can think of the work of ideology as the management of the unreasonableness of the fetish, as the fetish continually reappears *differently* for each subject but appears to maintain some form of social recognition; even as the fetish feels like a private relation to desire and to value, it also maintains a curious status as not entirely cryptic, either. If on the one hand, one does not share another subject's particular fetishistic fascination, one cannot claim that the act of fascination is not a discernible social fact. The fetish, then, is the name given to the seeming reasonableness of one's own erotic and monetary investments and the acceptable unreasonableness of that of others.

Anger's camp vision seizes on the fetish and its failure of reason because camp, too, is concerned with the pleasures to be maintained in the inappropriate distribution of value through the erotic valence. Marx's choice to identify the fetish as a kind of metaphysical holdover from older forms of belief, of course, betrays in some measure his status as a European, equally naming the beliefs of the "primitive" and subjected mind of the colonized as invested *unreasonably* in the power of the fragment; but it is also worth extracting from Marx's comments that he is indicting the metaphysical longings of Western modes of thought, too. It is here that we stand at a threshold that helps to discern the conjunction of commodity culture and the quasi-religious figurations present in Anger's films, and my readings of his cinema will insist on its being situated within a dialectic of modernity most easily named in terms of the aesthetics of homoerotic longing and the appeal of the commodity (Apter's notion of its "sexiness").

Boy Toys: The Masculine Icon in the World of Commodity Fetishism

If Andy Warhol deployed the camp love of glamour in his films' appreciation of those most marginalized by dominant representation (despite their love of Hollywood), for Kenneth Anger, glamour meant a return to understanding how the everyday is, to recall Walter Benjamin, re-enchanted through the commodity. Anger's films sought to depict subcultures equally on the fringe of representation, but his cinematic vision introduced a different set of figures: the sailor, the "macho" biker and hot-rod junkie, and the hallucinatory figures of the occult. In contrast to the fey characters of Warhol's New York, Anger's interest was in the icons of male homoerotic desire and their appearance in relation to the very emblems of sanctified masculinity.

To draw out the relation between mass imagery and the male queer erotic imagination, a significant question posed by Anger's films is the seemingly perfect complement between "masculinized" forms of consumerism (shiny cars, thundering bikes) and male (allegedly always entirely heterosexual) identities. Although the status of masculinity is treated most expansively in *Scorpio Rising* (1964) and *Kustom Kar Kommandos* (1965–1966), his earliest available film, *Fireworks* (1947), offers clues as to how Anger sought to disrupt the codes of masculinity by jokingly asserting male same-sex desire for such masculinity as a seemingly logical end for such erotic codings as they are discovered in macho aesthetics. From his earliest projects, Anger situates masculinity as performed within and against same-sex desire and, in short, gives vision to the old queer joke that all sexualities are a form of drag and merely play to different audiences.

Fireworks retrieves the sailor, a long-standing queer subcultural emblem for the man who disavows his homoerotic impulses, and working through an associative dream logic, the film beholds a young man (played by the seventeen-year-old Anger) waking in his bed surrounded by still photographs that depict him in the arms of a sailor, pietà-style. He departs his room through a door labeled "gents" and goes cruising. After approaching one sailor, he is attacked by a group of them but is returned home (how, we do not see) and is depicted, through a set of symbolic substitutions, as having sex with his evening's pickup.

Fireworks operates through montage in order to organize male same-sex desire and masculine performance as bonded and coconstituting and as an early effort signals Anger's commitment to montage as a political form—startlingly, we here witness its use to examine the politics of erotics. The anarchic pleasure of this film derives from its ability to encompass any number of surprising visuals into its fantasy world. At the beginning, for example, the young dreamer appears to sport an erection, which is jokingly revealed as an African statuette under the sheets; later in the film, images of a burning Christmas tree and a firecracker hanging from a sailor's trouser fly suggest orgasmic pleasure. In the former image, Anger's playful sense of the fetish literally recalls the stereotypical obsession of the Western sexual imagination with the fantasized erotic prowess of the exotic other, and later the wholesome icon of the Christmas tree is substituted, one fetish (the commodity) taking the place of the other (the token of racial and economic difference).

Worth emphasizing in these juxtaposed shots is the relation of male same-sex desire to the commodity fetish, a combination of embrace and disavowal. The film's protagonist discards the African statuette in a gesture implying that the stereotypical queer male preoccupation with penis size is akin to the exoticization that nonwhites experience at the hands of colonialist discourses; implied too is the fixation on penis size as parallel to the fascination with novelty and giganticism in American consumerism, most pronounced in automobile stylizing and a theme to which Anger will return in subsequent works. Later in *Fireworks,* the hero cruises a sailor in front of a dimly lit scrim that evokes either a bar or department store window, with glinting rows of glassware or jars stacked in repetitive rows. Finally, the garish lights of the Christmas tree and the explosion of the sailor's "firecracker" play out the film's featuring of material goods as central to the camp imagination's interest in the urbanized and modernized world.

Anger juxtaposes these objects with what appear to be more "elemental" media: the film opens with the shimmer of light on water, in which

Tokens of love: Montage in *Fireworks*.

a flaming torch is extinguished; as the hero is attacked, blood gushes forth and is subsequently washed away by milk poured over his body. Perhaps the film's most provocative image is that of the parting of viscera under which a ticking clock is discovered (an image in which Anger seems to pay homage to Leger). It might seem that *Fireworks* is offering a "naturalized" pre- or nonfetishizing homosexuality to which Anger counterposes the images of a despoiling consumerism, but it might be more productive to read the film's camp aesthetic as fascinated with commodity goods to the degree that they can be made to suggest the force of same-sex desire. The world into which the protagonist escapes, the streets on which he cruises for sailors, emphasized through a shot of the lights of the city down a boulevard, suggest that the material world in which he forges his erotic pleasure is marked by the smallest bits of consumerist debris. When, in an early close-up shot, the hero finds a pack of matches marked "United States Navy" in his room, the metonymic power of this minute trace of industrial production suggests a world of male seduction in the setting of 1940s Los Angeles.

P. Adams Sitney comments that "there is a comic or satiric element in the hyperbolic symbolism" in almost all Anger's works, and this comic sense is important to keep in mind when viewing the subsequent effort of *Puce Moment* (1949), surely one of the most striking emblems of the love of texture and color ever realized on film.[4] Originally intended as part of the larger, never-completed opus called *Puce Women* and subsequently included in the larger and changing opus that Anger titled the "Magick Lantern Cycle," *Puce Moment* opens with a shot of the folds of evening gowns being parted and then lifted out of the frame, each successively replaced by another equally sumptuous velvet or lamé behind it. Moved through this series of prosceniums, the spectator emerges into a boudoir to discover that these are all dresses that the unnamed female protagonist contemplates wearing. She lounges in one ensemble, tries on jewelry, and at the film's conclusion emerges into daylight strolling with two greyhounds. Despite its largely being understood by Richard Dyer and other critics as a simple joke, an "homage at once real and ironic to the Great Ladies of Hollywood," we should pay attention to the degree to which *Puce Moment* fixes its attention on the power of film to render the tactile pleasures of costuming and playacting as spectacular.[5] Given that *Puce Moment* follows the monochrome stock of *Fireworks,* Anger's first handling of color film, as even the film's title suggests, is striking in that he devotes it to the saturated colors of dresses and jewelry. After the relatively explicit narrative of *Fireworks,* the drama of costuming witnessed in *Puce Moment* reveals a tendency chronically underplayed in treatments of Anger's work: the visual pleasures of looking at objects and the camera's potential for showing us those pleasures.[6] More to the point of the present argument, *Fireworks* and *Puce Moment* should be seen as part of an ongoing concern within Anger's films to bind together the material world of objects and erotic desire, played out more fully, as we shall see, in *Scorpio Rising* and *Kustom Kar Kommandos.*

Anger reveals the photogenic nature of objects similar to the way that Warhol would discover it in his superstars. *Eaux d'Artifice* (1953) consists of shots of a figure moving through the elaborate fountains of the Villa D'Este. Dressed in the ornate costume of an eighteenth-century courtesan, complete with ostrich plume rising from her ornate hairstyle, the figure moves through the baroque fountains as their plumes and jets form abstract compositions within the frame. The faces of gargoyles and the shapes of urns, balustrades, and railings are photographed to suggest nighttime, and the film was subsequently printed with a dark blue tint to enhance this sense of the nocturnal and obscured realm of seduction.

Anger is quoted as saying that *Eaux d'Artifice* is meant as the "evocation of a [Ronald] Firbank heroine" in "the pursuit of the night moth," but I would hesitate to say that the reference to the author of *The Flower beneath the Foot* and *The Artificial Princess* (himself a fixture in many camp canons) provides any strong reading of the film as containing a lucid story line. Rather, the film seeks to create a sense of mystery about why this figure runs through the gardens as she does, visually dwarfed by the spectacle of the ornate fountains at work; similarly, her costume of an eighteenth-century balloon skirt, bodice, and wig ask us to wonder if there is some historicizing component to her pursuit (or evasion) of some unknown presence.[7] In all these Anger films, any sense of drama that we might attribute to the images comes to us via the art direction and not through dialogue, characterization, or plot. Anger invents in the early film projects of *Puce Moment* and *Eaux d'Artifice* a textural cinema driven mostly through the camp affection for the look and shimmer of fabric, jewelry, and ornamentation.

Kustom Kar Kommandos (1965–1966) is a considerably different treatment of the spectacle of commodities and the erotic performance of human subjects in relation to them. Although originally conceived as part of a much larger project about the subculture of car customization in Southern California, *Kustom Kar Kommandos* displays some of Anger's most elegant camera work and presages virtually every attempt in the filmmaking of the past three decades to deploy popular music in relation to the moving image. As the pop single Bobby Darin's "Dream Lover" is heard on the sound track, a teenage customizer lovingly polishes the bright red "candy apple" finish of his hot-rod Ford. A feather duster swoops over the car's trunk and fenders slowly in what seems almost a striptease, rendering the automobile as lover and star for the affectionately laboring car customizer. Despite its brief running time of barely three minutes, *Kustom Kar Kommandos* moves the camera around its subjects in an elegance uncharacteristic of what we usually expect of underground cinema, and the film stands as an anomaly in Anger's own oeuvre in its rejection of montage for camera movement. Here Anger supplants the camera's mobility for editing, and the painstaking deployment of the camera in relation to the mirrorlike finishes of the car's paint and chrome betrays an immense effort to render the automobile at its most photogenic; the advertisement mills of Madison Avenue never approached a commodity with such affection.

Kustom Kar Kommandos.

If the lush camera work of *Kustom Kar Kommandos* evokes the advertiser's lens, what sets the film apart from becoming a well-wrought commercial, however, is its depiction of a commodity that has been reworked by the car customizer. Anger seeks to show not only the hot rod but also the young aficionados whose efforts remold the car to fantastic extremes; in short, *Kustom Kar Kommandos* depicts this car as unavailable to most consumers but the few within the world of customizing. This is at odds with more customary critiques of the commodity fetish, where we expect to find the object vilified, embodying as it does the exploitation of labor within production. Like Marcel Duchamp's "found objects," which hold a powerful sway within the avant-garde imagination by insisting that the viewer admire the ordinary object's tactile qualities (along with the insight that the found object was clearly never intended to circulate in the exalted domain of art), *Kustom Kar Kommandos*' rendering of the car and its lover forces the hand of commonsensical hierarchies of value. Anger disrupts that order by reminding us of the devotion to commodities that arises within many subcultures, a devotion that is demonstrated through the added work of customizing the hot rod. Thus *Kustom Kar Kommandos* commemorates the eroticized longing for the commodity that most of us *cannot* own, a longing most concentrated in the customizer's gaze on the brilliant surfaces that he polishes and admires.

Through the camera's tracking between automobile and customizer, *Kustom Kar Kommandos* points to the erotic charge of the mass object, leading the viewer's gaze over the automobile's elegant surfaces to the bodies of the hunky car aficionados. Anger jokingly concludes several shots by focusing on the crotches, rear ends, and muscled chests of the male subjects of his film, ultimately forcing the question, through the sound track, of who is the lover crooned to in the song: the car beheld lovingly by the hot-rodder, or the hot-rodder himself caught adoringly by the camera. In this manner, *Kustom Kar Kommandos* serves as a tribute to the car as cult object and anticipates Anger's fascination with other forms of commodity devotion, not least that of film spectators. The explicit connection emerges here in Anger's own commentary:

> The treatment of the teenager in relation to his hot rod or custom car (whether patiently or ingeniously fashioned by himself, as is usually the case, or commissioned according to his fantasy, for the economically favored) will bring out what I see as a definite *eroticization* of the automobile, in its dual aspect of narcissistic identification as virile power symbol and its more elusive role: seductive, attention-grabbing, gaudy or glittering mechanical mistress paraded for the benefit of his peers. (I am irresistibly drawn to the comparison of these machines with an American cult-object of an earlier era, Mae West in her "Diamond Lil" impersonations of the Thirties.)[8]

Grounding an analogy between the commodity form of the car/film star and the customizer/fan, Anger collapses identificatory processes into both desiring the "other" and desiring to be the other. That this nexus appears in terms of the virility of the car owner and the femininity of Mae West suggests that entering into a slavish devotion to a given cult object puts all notions of gendering askew: within the dynamics of fandom and commodity culture, there is no "natural" underpinning of male/female between customizer/car or fan/star. Within this brief realization on film of Anger's more extended and never completed project about car customizers, this narcissistic projection is most striking in shots where we become aware of the car's lustrous finish as mirror surface, reflecting the teen customizer's loving gaze back to him. Indeed, the invocation of Mae West in this passage, as an impersonator of her own image (and a long-standing camp icon), suggests that the "mechanical mistress" of the car only serves as a "vehicle," as it were, for the fan's projection: the task of fantasy is to become one's own object of adulation.

While *Kustom Kar Kommandos* thus revisits the splendid photogenic status of the material world played out previously in *Puce Moment* and *Eaux d'Artifice,* in a more complicated manner it embraces the larger challenges of the fetish and the social formation around it; while the cheeriness of *Kustom Kar Kommandos* offers a vision of those with the love of the surface, I would hazard that, as hinted at through the playful substitution of the letter *k* into to the film's title, it also ominously gestures to the resulting abbreviation "KKK." The parallels between one kind of seemingly benign subculture (customizers) and another insistently violent and rageful one, the Ku Klux Klan, are not to be taken lightly, and new critical vistas emerge in Anger's film to seeing how forms of social fragmentation are potentially dangerous. However, let me be clear: the point here is not that Anger offers a simplistic rendering whereby car customizers and hate groups become one and the same, and as the political analyses of Dick Hebdige and Angela McRobbie demonstrate, subcultures are important sites for the forging of dissident political voices.[9] Rather, I take Anger's vision as more cautionary about the impulse to nurture social difference around the commodity fetish and the potential for almost all seemingly benign forms of identity to become invested in the production of forms of sameness that the fascist imagination takes hold of. While Anger's camera insists on showing us the profound delight to be beheld in looking, without recourse to narrative, there is a sense that in the ten years between the earlier efforts of *Puce Moment* and *Eaux d'Artifice* and the latter efforts of *Scorpio Rising* and *Kustom Kar Kommandos,* his investigations moved to consider at greater length how the subjects and objects he so lovingly filmed were imbedded in the particular social formations of modernity, themselves not necessarily entirely positive or reactionary phenomena.[10]

Though uncompleted as originally envisioned, *Kustom Kar Kommandos'* project of bringing together the dynamics of fandom, commodity fetishism, and narcissistic fantasy emerge in more fully completed fashion in *Scorpio Rising.* An object of cult devotion in its own right, *Scorpio Rising* enjoys a status given to few underground films; as J. Hoberman has suggested, "*Scorpio Rising* points the way toward *Easy Rider* and *L.A. Plays Itself, American Graffiti, Mean Streets,* and every MTV video ever made."[11] Organized into a depiction of ritual, the film offers a dense montage of the codes of motorcycle gangs. Moving from the individuated spaces where various bike boys tend to their motorcyles, lounge about with the television tuned to images of Marlon Brando in *The Wild One* and James Dean in *Rebel without a Cause,* and dress up in their leather paraphernalia, the film depicts a Walpurgis Night celebration in a church, crosscut with appropriated footage of a film depicting Christ and the apostles. It concludes with a dizzying set of edits that compile a motocross race, the Jesus footage, and fascist rallies; the effect is fully intensified through the film's sound track, scored sequentially with contemporary pop tunes such as Elvis Presley's "(You're the) Devil in Disguise" and the Angels' "My Boyfriend's Back."

The power of *Scorpio Rising* figures in its ability to render the subcultural codes of motorcycle gangs as simultaneously liberatory and threatening, because Anger discovers the processes of appropriation of commodities into subcultures and the potential of such appropriation for differing pleasures, not least among them militaristic poses of hard bodies and leather. Yet the political valences of such poses are ambiguous and varied, and not necessarily in the service of a particular male same-sex (i.e., "gay") identity. The film's attention to the ways that the gang members choose to dress themselves, putting on trappings of masculinity (big boots, skull rings) while they gaze rapturously at the faces of Dean and Brando, allows us to read the gang members as enjoying homoeroticism without having necessarily any language (and commitment to an identity politics) beyond that of their dress and their longing for the popular forms of comics and cinema. Anger's earlier films might be read as preparatory to the achievement of *Scorpio Rising,* for in the later film, he more fully stages the discomforting dialectic of modernity that camp's attentions to labor and to the value codings of capital reveal in the eroticized commodity. Caught in this tension between homoerotic longing and the strange sexiness of the mass-produced object, *Scorpio Rising,* more than perhaps any piece of American cinema, identifies the expression of the commodity both through its seemingly expansive, "liberatory" dimensions and through its tendency toward social regulation and power. Complicating matters, we could say that large parts of Anger's film oeuvre, in *Fireworks, Scorpio Rising,* and *Kustom Kar Kommandos,* read homoerotic desire itself through camp's attention to the work of subjects under capital and its social regimens.

Scorpio Rising enacts the homoerotic pleasure of its bike boy protago-

Objects of labor: The fetish in *Scorpio Rising*.

nists while withholding a sense of their having any intent to express their activities *as* homoerotic. The tension between these two tendencies emerges in the use of popular music on the sound track, and perhaps more than any filmmaker within the underground, Anger deployed the sound track for ironic commentary.[12] His use of acoustic materials in *Scorpio Rising* constitutes a form of media montage equal to the visual register of Eisenstein; for example, as image and sound unfold against each other and we hear Bobby Vinton croon "Blue Velvet," we are unsettled to decide who is wearing blue velvet: the voice of Vinton tells us that *she* did while the image track reveals a biker's fly being buttoned. Martha and the Vandellas sing that love is "like a heatwave" while a biker snorts cocaine, chooses his jewelry, and kisses a glass paperweight that enshrines a scorpion. Pharmacological bliss and narcissistic play in these moments take on their homoerotic dimensions in the possibility of the masturbatory self-love that the song names: whatever heats up begins in the bikers' private habits of vanity and self-regard. As Philip Core reads these depictions:

> His "bikies" and roses, skulls and musclemen, all studied obsessively to the sound of rock'n'roll golden oldies, revealed that the taste of

straight teenagers in the fifties, though not generally camp, could become so when used to define homosexual images. Recently many of these images have become common objects of desire, and even the suburbs can look on a leather-clad Hell's Angel holding a bouquet of flowers without incomprehension.[13]

Core's comments help to identify how the songs on the sound track become associatively linked, through the film's visuals, with perverse pleasures, but it seems more the case that Anger is indicting the popular forms he crops into the film, both visual and acoustic, as themselves laced with less-than-wholesome forms of pleasure. Though the culture of 1950s teenagers is not specifically about male same-sex pleasure, as Anger's film organizes these songs, they are also not entirely devoid of the kinds of masochistic longing and violent impulses associated in paranoid fantasies about bike culture, themselves captured through the images of Brando and others. Putting a finer point on this objection to Core's argument: it is not so much that the songs become tainted with the whiff of queer desire by being linked with these images as that the images help to uncover the untoward fantasies at the heart of popular culture in that moment. Although Core helpfully outlines how Anger's work in *Scorpio Rising* was fundamental for the dissemination of camp taste, it remains a question of how Anger asserts the primacy of "teenage taste" for the not so suburban rituals witnessed within the film.

To understand the structural homology between popular forms and subcultural styles and practices witnessed in the film, we might note that we cannot distinguish between the "latent" homoerotic content of biker culture to which Anger clues us and the "overt" camera work that purportedly draws out the biker homoeroticism for our viewing. *Scorpio Rising* is hardly a documentary film, interested in describing the "secret rituals" of the biker cult. Similar to the tension between sound and image at work in *Kustom Kar Kommandos, Scorpio Rising* enthusiastically pronounces that the most hallowed customs of postwar masculinity were indeed to be read as homoerotic. If, as Gregory Markopoulos asserted on the film's release, "*Scorpio Rising* has been made in the image of contemporary America," the image of contemporary America lent itself quite nicely to being seen as queer.[14] In fact, the ease with which bikers could be depicted through Anger's camp lens suggested that their extreme macho held clues to the operations of masculinity more generally.[15]

Scorpio Rising asks that we do more than see biker culture as engaging, however playfully naive, in homoerotic self-contemplation. The film's latter half moves beyond the intimate spaces of the bikers and their private imaginative worlds into a larger setting that depicts Christianity, the occult, and Nazism as bearing some relation to the forms of homoerotics and consumption in American popular culture. The film's expansion of its treatment of biker style to contemplate organized religion and fascism has made its critics frequently uneasy; if so, we can only respect the film's continued power to upset our evaluative notions of "good gay" versus "bad straight." As Dyer ventures, "The forces invoked by *Scorpio Rising*—sadism, male sexuality, immaturity (Puck, the bikers as boys), Nazism—are not ones widely approved of, but it is not at all clear that the film disapproves of them."[16] *Scorpio Rising*'s montage moves, as Anger suggests in his notes about the film, "from toy to terror," suggesting that the biker subculture's affinities to the styles of fascism are neither entirely commensurate nor antagonistic.

This is not to argue that *Scorpio Rising* operates through the paranoid equation of fascism and homosexuality; rather, the fascination with the emblems of power witnessed in biker culture lends itself to an overworking celebration of same-sex desire without acknowledging that desire (indeed, all desire) is caught in the workings of power and domination. Further, the film enjoins our pleasure by offering Little Peggy March's "I Will Follow Him" and the Surfaris' "Wipe Out" on the sound track, making us all the more uneasy with our spectatorial pleasure, particularly because the film does not aim to render fascism as a thing of the past but zeros in on the masochistic pleasures imbedded squarely in pop music. Dyer describes the film's project as somewhat harmless: "the 'silly,' giggly, *naughty* quality of Anger's films is a spirit which at times feels irritating, unhelpful to the cause of gay rights, but at others is a tonic refusal to grow up into the drab oppressiveness of normal straightness." I would hazard that *Scorpio Rising,* appearing well before the gay liberation movement, opens an avenue of questioning between homoerotics and subjection in a different vein from that of political "rights" discourse. As Dyer acknowledges, "Such wilfulness [on Anger's part] is at the heart of the difficulty of coming to terms with Anger's work," suggesting that Anger's films still continue to frustrate analyses that might lead to either wholehearted endorsements or denunciations.

The present argument would steer us to Anger's paradoxical impulse to see (homoerotic) desire as vital to popular signs (muscle cars, the

Crystals' singing "He's a Rebel") while remaining aware of the failure of those signs to articulate such desires explicitly. And if Anger discovers within popular productions the seeds of fascistic longing, it is not clear that we can denounce those connections at the level of accusing Anger himself of simply playing out his own distasteful fantasies. Rather, the film comes as a strong warning to be aware of, at the very least, some ideological complicity between subcultural appropriation of "mainstream" signs and those signs' ability to be appropriated in the first place. If the film campily displays its subjects as playfully dressing up in black leather, it also reminds us, through camp attention to the history of black leather, of Nazism's absurd posturings. My point is not to render too didactic a reading of the film; its measure as a significant work is its defiance of simple political and aesthetic formulations. Instead I would call attention to what seeing the film's camp dimensions gains us in understanding its complicated way of working on homoerotic commodity stylistics.

In one of the most incisive commentaries on the relation between fascist aesthetics and the abiding modernist political fantasy about male homoerotic desire, Andrew Hewitt asks, "What work does the identification of homosexuality with fascism . . . perform in the order of our political imagination?" He continues that "if fascism somehow defies representation, it has nevertheless been represented with obsessive frequency at any number of discursive levels—not least of all as a marker (if not a representation) of the historical dilemma of unrepresentability."[17] Hewitt situates the status of homosexuality as "the love that dare not speak its name" as analogous with fascism's failure to achieve representability and suggests that

> the allegorical press-ganging of homosexuality as a vehicle for articulating a historically resistant fascism relies on the fact that neither homosexuality nor fascism speaks in its own name. The liberal fear of becoming fascist and the heterosexual, homosocial fear of becoming homosexual will prove themselves to be something more than parallel: homosexuality will be consistently figured as the desire that the fascist emerge from the liberal.

Hewitt argues that homosexuality has historically been deployed within (heterosexual) liberal political discourse to stand in for fascism, what he calls homosexuality's "allegorical status"; suspicions about the perversity of fascism and its unconscious propulsions to sameness are tautologically held to be proved, within this straight modernist imaginary, by the association of fascism and male same-sex desire.

Central to this collapsing of fascism and homosexuality together within the modernist political imaginary is the failure to distinguish between kitsch and camp; this failure is key to understanding the features of Anger's work that focus on fascist aesthetics. Hewitt comments that "if kitsch and camp both body themselves forth in an exaggerated representationalism . . . then it is always possible to (mis-) read kitsch in a camp manner. The logic of attribution whereby I identify fascist kitsch with the Other might be read as camp—and an identification with an aestheticized fascist mentality thereby established." The specific question of who is (mis)reading kitsch and camp remains unclear in this passage; nevertheless we can still agree that the fascist iconography and symbols in a work such as *Scorpio Rising* themselves might be the topic of camp play (in this case, by Anger). Failing to understand the camp dimensions of the signs of fascism in this context makes possible the glib and dangerous situation whereby, as Hewitt describes it, "if kitsch and camp can become identical at the level of the object, there is always the danger they will become identical in the subject."[18] That is, there is the danger for the liberal (and often heterosexual) viewer that the camp dimensions of Anger's film may not offer assurances that there are not fascist impulses at work not only in queer male culture but in the popular forms that Anger's subjects consume.

While within Anger's work there seems to have been an impulse to create a nonstraight (in every sense of the word) lexicon of images, the relation of the camp images of consumption and the disruption of value coding witnessed in the play of the film's subjects cannot absolutely vouchsafe passage to the political imaginary (which includes most typical strands of leftism) through these images. To invoke Hewitt again:

> The homosexual, in other words, acknowledges the "fascist within" in a way that the heterosexual liberal subject cannot (recognizes, in fact, that the "within" is a mere function of the definitive "without"). It is not so much a question of the homosexual "being" fascist, as it is of the homosexual acknowledging the supplemental inherence of the Other in the self—the contingency of any being.

The implications of this argument for my own analysis are immense: camp here becomes the possibility of recognizing that the fetishistic play with the commodity form is an abiding one and is revealed in *Scorpio*

Rising by the visual and acoustic montage of biker boys and popular song, caught as they are in what Ed Lowry calls a "diabolical dialectic."

Lowry's invocation of the diabolical might recall Barthes's demand at the opening of this book for a materialist critique to think through the "diffractions of meanings" offered by, for a Marxist philosophical practice, unfamiliar practices that emerge in tension with the various signs and commodities of modernity; such a "demonic" world emerges in *Scorpio Rising* in the form of the ritualized Walpurgis Night, which bears out Anger's long-standing interest in the occult and the "magickal arts" of Aleister Crowley. In this section of the film, where the bikers revel in a church by drinking and stripping one another for sex play, we can detect hints of the power to which Anger attributed occult signification. Yet it was in other films, *Inauguration of the Pleasure Dome, Lucifer Rising,* and *Invocation of My Demon Brother,* that Anger's system of ritualized antagonism (antagonism of virtually *everything*) becomes most pronounced, and to which I turn now.

Glamour and Magick: Anger's Occult

Anger's interest in creating his own alternative world of signification arose early in his filmmaking. For example, notes that Anger provided for his early (and now, apparently, lost) efforts such as *Tinsel Tree* (1941–1942) and *Escape Episode* (1944) provide a clue to the impulses of his first works as deriving from the desire to tamper with the icons of American life. Anger describes *Tinsel Tree:* "Cast: A Christmas Tree. Synopsis: The ritual dressing and destruction of the Christmas Tree. Close-ups as the branches are laden with baubles, draped with garlands, tossed with tinsel. Cut to the stripped discarded tree as it bursts into brief furious flame (hand-tinted gold-scarlet) to leave a charred skeleton."[19] The tongue-in-cheek naming of the Christmas tree as the film's sole cast member suggests that from the start of his filmmaking enterprise, Anger perceived objects to have as great a status as talismanic (i.e., fetishistic and starlike) emblems themselves, and in the case of *Tinsel Tree,* such subjects hold as tremendous a fascination in their death as do the real stars that Anger so devotedly chronicled later in his *Hollywood Babylon* books. Yet if we trust this account, we also are drawn to Anger's working with the medium of film, tinting and scratching the film frame for visual effect, as if the documentary strain of cinema falls short in conveying spectacle. That it is a Christmas tree, the centerpiece of Christian America's central religious and economic holiday, that should be seen "draped in garlands, tossed with tinsel," should tell us that from the outset, Anger intended to antagonize the pieties of contemporary American ideology.

Anger describes *Escape Episode,* made two years later in 1946, as a

> free rendering of the Andromeda myth. A crumbling stucco-gothic sea-side monstrosity, serving as a Spiritualist Church. Imprisoned within, a girl at the mercy of a religious fanatic "dragon" awaits her deliverance by a beach boy Perseus. Ultimately it is her own defiance which snaps the chain.

Anger's reworking of the myth anticipates his subsequent and long-standing interest in the occult, for the occult represented a symbolic system that was adequate to antagonize the complex workings of Christianity and heterosexual signs and narratives within American culture. This impulse to antagonize became most pronounced in Anger's increasing devotion to the "magickal arts" of Aleister Crowley and Anton LaVey, invoking as he does Judeo-Christian satanic figures, the pantheon of Hellenistic gods and goddesses, and figures from the Ramanistic tradition.

Much ink has been spilled in deciphering the images that appear in Anger's occult films, particularly in determining how these films might be read as narrative. Alongside readings of the films that locate them in relation to Anger's attentions to the occult, these works also appear as depictions of queer glamour of the everyday.[20] That is, for viewers not imbedded in the "magickal arts," *Inauguration of the Pleasure Dome* is a film about dressing up and having a party. This is not to underestimate these efforts but to suggest that the pleasures witnessed in them are not solely discoverable by having access to the occult figures that Anger cites.[21] Indeed, the desire to dress up and attend a private party, particularly in the pre-Stonewall era of more private homosexualities, is an important feature of queer subcultures. As George Chauncey suggests, the "apartment" (i.e., private) party was vital to gay metropolitan life and the creation of its languages because it allowed for privacy and social access to other queer men.[22]

Anger's occult films, *Inauguration of the Pleasure Dome, Invocation of My Demon Brother, Lucifer Rising,* and the latter parts of *Scorpio Rising* are structured through moments in which separate figures costume themselves and subsequently enter the spaces of spectacle, where their dress becomes the occasion for them to have special powers. Clearly these figure are allegories for the pleasures of enforced privacy among queers, not only in their depiction of celebrations but in their coded enactments of drug cultures. Key to these films' rituals is the ingestion of various narcotics and hallucinogens; in the case of *Scorpio Rising*, a biker snorts cocaine before leaving his room, and in *Inauguration* the celebrants become intoxicated by drinking from the cup of Hecate. The party-ritual films provide Anger with the chance to offer a multilayered visual display beyond those witnessed in his other attempts, and in all of them, the visual montage, comprising sometimes four or five different shots edited one on top of the other, is meant to evoke an ecstatic, bacchanalian release experienced by the party goers.[23]

We are again confronted within Anger's cinema with the tendency to explode the film's visual and acoustic array well beyond their determinations within any specific and easily discerned narratives. While the complex occult codings through which Anger structured these films undoubtedly inform for some their "magickal" status, these films also release their audiences into the world of shape, color, and texture. To press the point further, if we insist on them having narratives, they are brought about through the pleasures of spectacle beheld by the films' characters. In one key sequence in *Inauguration,* the central figure of Shiva is shown selecting various rings and jewels to wear; only when he eats one shimmering necklace do his incantatory powers come to him.

One does not have to be a devotee of Crowley's cultish arts to realize the way that Anger's occult movies underline the delights of looking (particularly at the artificial and gaudy) and the potential for antagonizing other ways of looking, most usually those structured through more conventional forms of filmmaking. Dyer helpfully comments on Anger's steeping in the lore of the occult by suggesting that the "wild, transcendent forces that convention represses" are given shape in Anger's films:

> The point is that most people disapprove of them (just as conventional morality disapproves of homosexuality, and probably sexuality in general); their disapprovableness is a sign of their fitness for Magick invocation. If they were not conventionally wrong they could not be Magickally right.[24]

But it is not only in their seizing of the images that antagonize conventional notions of religion and sexuality that Anger's films derive their power. Over and above Anger's move to embrace antinarratives is his stylistic display that teaches us how to glory in the things of the everyday, showing them as he does in a "reenchanted" light.

The movement in Anger's artistic trajectory to invent a demoniacal world of icons gathered together under the name of "magick" marks for this argument a lessening of his power to stage the fetish and its accompanying social relations; couched in terms of Marx's assertions about the tendency to attribute metaphysical powers to the commodity, to obey "the fantastic form of a relation between things," Anger's work loses its power by forgetting the energies he found in his bike boys and car customizers. In a sense, what is lost is the dialectic of modernity that camp seizes on in his earlier films, whereby the immense efforts for queer desire to signify as a form of work, made manifest through the appropriations of normative signs such as those of masculinity and popular culture, are lost to the hermetic world of the occult. The tension between the work of queer desire and its repressed status to be represented enlivened the images and sounds that Anger brings together in the film work up to the mid-1960s; his subsequent efforts in the arena of cinema have not inhabited this opposition. In this regard, they seem a return to the more fragmented endeavors of his youth, but with the loss of the vitalizing energies of the commodity world to which he saw queer erotics at work.

History's "Holy Babies": Hollywood Babylon and the Prohibitions of Hollywood

If Anger's films of the occult demonstrate a waning interest in the commodity form, then his energies in that regard have more productively been devoted to his written publications, and with the appearance of the *Hollywood Babylon* volumes in the twenty-five years from 1959 to 1984, it would seem that the camp dimensions of his artistic vision have moved from cinema to the publicity still and the industries of gossip. Anger's rendering of Hollywood history found in the *Hollywood Babylon* volumes has remained largely unexplored by critics and historians of the studio era, and in some measure, neglect of these books may stem from the perception that the *Hollywood Babylon* volumes, or the "Holy Babies," as Anger has referred to them, are ancillary to his film productions, or even more dismissively, that his published writings may appear as accessories to Hollywood publicity itself. While it is indeed true that part of the appeal of *Hollywood Babylon* resides in its shocking and provocative use of tabloid imagery and gossip, Anger's project in the books is not simply one of compiling the detritus of Hollywood's long history of love affairs gone sour, "perverse" sexualities, and gruesome suicides. Worth remembering is that Anger situates his materials in the context of an important argument about the role of Hollywood cinema in contemporary American life. Further, the antagonistic stance toward Hollywood found in the *Babylon* books appears not from a left or Marxist interrogation of capitalist corporate production, the more customary venues for critique, but from Anger's camp sensibilities and from his position as what Ed Lowry calls "one of Tinseltown's harshest fans," allowing him to investigate the industry's compulsively heteronormative representations.[25]

Beginning with the 1959 J. J. Pauvert edition of *Hollywood Babylone* and continuing through the various editions appearing in the United States from the mid-1960s onward, Anger offers a critique of Hollywood, and his is a critical project that derives from his position as a fan. Anger writes from within the discursive strategies of queer male camp, strategies of dissemblance, subterfuge, and ironic play, and because of these countervailing tendencies within his work (Anger's critical sense of Hollywood's near-total exclusion of images of homoerotic desire, his loving embrace of Hollywood iconography), we witness in the *Babylon* volumes a simultaneous delight in the gossip in which Anger traffics and use of gossip-driven fan accounts to rethink the status of Hollywood as a purveyor of purportedly "wholesome" entertainment. Anger interrogates Hollywood in the context of his vast fan knowledges and fan devotions. Similar to the interpretive work of many fans, his is a version of Hollywood forged in tension and in concert with official and unofficial publicity apparatuses. Anger is first a fan of the Hollywood cinema, *if* fandom is conceived as those practices that allow popular cinema's followers to engage with the publicity of the industry while also inventing their own readings of its limits to address their frequently marginal status. By marginal, I mean to suggest that most fans are hardly in a position to shape the meanings of the Hollywood cinema from the vantage point of industrial production. *Hollywood Babylon* stands as counterhistory to an idealized Hollywood offered both by journalistic enterprises that are aligned with the industry (think of *Entertainment Tonight*'s endless nostalgic parade of "old Hollywood" stories) and by figures seemingly remote from Hollywood (for example, House Speaker

Newt Gingrich's invocations of *Boy's Town* in 1995 as a model for civic reorganization).

To make sense of the camp dimensions of Anger's work of interrogating the monolithic construction of "Hollywood History," it is crucial to understand his position as a fan of the subject matter.[26] Queer fandom has historically differed from other fan practices as they are described by critics such as John Fiske and Janice A. Radway in that queers have often had to be comparatively discreet in how they appear as fans and have thus deployed camp rhetorical strategies to circulate their writings.[27] One question, though, that repeatedly arises in regard to fan culture is whether fandom is not solely a compensatory practice, in that fans illuminate the moment of capital's almost complete saturation of the cultural sphere, where studios, record companies, and publishers profit directly from the ways that subjects choose to cope with their own alienation in the making of the cultural commodities that they consume. This argument has particular repercussions for queer fans, in that they appear complicit with the invisibility that Hollywood and contemporary conservative and homophobic social discourses on dissident sexualities seek to encourage.

At the same time, fandom has sometimes lent itself to celebratory descriptions of subjects who fashion their own readings of popular culture. For example, Judith Mayne comments that Radway's work in *Reading the Romance* evidences a high degree of projection on the part of the author, wishing as she (Radway) may that the female romance readers whom she interviews are agents of a different variety of feminism than that of the academy. Mayne suggests that "I doubt seriously, for instance, that the Smithton women [Radway's ethnographic subjects] would agree with the necessity of understanding the reading of romance fiction in the categorical terms of critique or celebration."[28] Mayne's question is not one of whether Radway's interview subjects are "genuine" feminists in need of the critical terms with which to understand how they are addressed by the publishing industry but rather a query of the extent to which we might often wish fans to display a particular form of resistance to the industrial modes of production and distribution. This is no small matter, as Mayne suggests:

> I do not say this in order to imply cynically that no alternative positions of spectatorship are possible, but rather to suggest that one of the most persistent myths of spectatorship (and of theory) that has

perturbed and in many ways hindered the analysis of spectatorship is the belief that it is not only possible, but necessary, to separate the truly radical spectator from the merely complicitous one.[29]

While Mayne describes the predicament of attempting to conceive of historical subjects as complex and contradictory (that is, as inhabiting everyday life), the degree to which she resorts to characterizing readers of romance fiction, and indeed all recipients of popular forms, as "spectators" tells something about the legacy of a particular theoretical insistence on viewers' engagements with those forms as always appearing to create "proper" and suitable subjects for capital within patriarchal constructions of femininity. By thinking of the consumers of popular culture as "spectators," we fall into the habit of prioritizing cinema viewing, and especially the attendance of narrative studio film, over and above other activities that are implied by fandom (reading fan magazines, collecting star images, fantasizing, and daydreaming). Further, the theoretical models for addressing film culture that are gathered under the name of spectatorship can have the effect of forming too rigid a binarism of male/active and female/passive, where there seems little room for the mobility of sex/gender difference to afford a larger variety of responses to popular culture.

Miriam Hansen suggests that one of the most powerful figurations of Laura Mulvey's still-provocative theory of the film viewer, that of the transvestite, has been seriously neglected.

> The figure of the transvestite suggests that female spectatorship involves dimensions of self-reflexivity and role-playing, rather than simply an opposition of active and passive. The perceptual performance of sexual mobility anticipates, on a playful, fictional level, the possibility of social arrangements not founded upon a hierarchically fixed sexual identity.[30]

Situating the fascination of Rudolph Valentino in the 1920s in relation to racist, nationalist discourses of the period, Hansen suggests that women fans became interested in Valentino precisely to the degree that he offered a vision of ethnic, "non-American" male sexuality beyond the current Hollywood fare. In addition, a male star such as Valentino offered a figure in whom women fans may have fancied some likeness (his "foreign" polished effeminacy) while simultaneously fantasizing themselves as objects of his seduction; hence viewer responses among Valentino's women fans may have been characterized by the sexual mobility (i.e., transvestism) to which she alludes. Importantly, Hansen does not seek to rescue Valentino as an emblem of a utopian spectatorial position but rather seeks to "delineate the contours of a female subjectivity, with all its contradictions and complicity, in the institution of cinema and the text of film history."[31] The intertwined nature of such "contradictions and complicity" that arise within fan devotions does not dispel, in the case of Valentino, the importance of racism, homophobia, and nationalism that helped to define his image and through which the star came to have a following, but it does suggest the complexity of female fan responses as they reveal shifting definitions of femininity, sex, and consumerism.

We should heed Mayne's advice and not try to wish the complexity of viewers' experience on behalf of a chimerical "free zone" of reception; likewise, we should also wonder why "compensatory" fan practices might so quickly be disallowed. When we recall "compensation" as not only that which serves as an equivalent (its more usual monetary and legal sense) but also that which offsets an error or defect, in the case of fandom's compensatory power, whereas fans do not garner substantial financial profits from their fan labors, they do draw attention to how official forms neglect their social presence. That fans do not transform the culture industries at the level of altering them as capitalist enterprises does not, at least to me, disallow the potential of fans to shape their own readings and the subcultural networks that value those readings. Equally, fan labors redirect and refashion the value potential of star publicity beyond corporate profit itself: we detect the importance of fan labors in the industry's attempts to exploit fan formations by reincorporating (some, but not all) those efforts into the product.

One remarkable aspect of the phenomenon of queer reception should then be noted, namely, that queer male fan discourses on popular cinema are not simply coincidental to the forging of their own languages and social circles; cinema and popular culture more generally have been vital to forming those things in the first place. As Mayne observes, "The question is not what characterizes gay/lesbian spectatorship as common responses to film texts, but rather what place film spectatorship has had in the cultivation of gay/lesbian identity."[32] That is to say, when we address queer spectatorship, we cannot assume a fully developed identity in advance of a commentary on the cinema; the relation between film, and in this particular discussion Hollywood film, and queers is a dialectic in which neither of those two categories, Hollywood cinema or queer subjectivity, can be seen as stable, unchanging, or unrelated.

One of the most striking challenges posed by the fan writing of *Hollywood Babylon* is that of a contemporaneous readership that would have been actively interpreting the innuendo and dissemblance in these texts. As the historical moment of their writing recedes from us, the possibility of discovering such readings becomes more remote, but I take this as an indication of their power in the moment of their appearance. No scandal, to my knowledge, accompanies the queer authorship of these texts, although the history of *Babylon*'s publishing, with its initial appearance remote from Hollywood, suggests that camp responses to Hollywood star iconography could for a long period only inhabit the margins of film culture.[33]

The *Babylon* volumes dwell on failed marriages, masked sexual "perversions," and the panoply of suicides found among the lives of the Hollywood film colony, but the salacious features of Anger's work can eclipse his overall vision of Hollywood, one that he pronounces at the outset of the project in 1959. Even as he invokes the prurient fascination of stars' lives, Anger reminds us that the traditions of Hollywood cinema revolve around titillation and gossip, and even more provocatively, each new scandal carries with it the power to offer some "new" revelation about Hollywood heretofore unseen—not simply the novelty of an emerging scandal but the sense that a larger dimension of film culture might be glimpsed through the star scandal. Citing the scandalous images of Theda Bara and Louis Glaume, and hinting at D. W. Griffith's propensity for "très jeunes personnes," Anger writes of the more recent scandal involving the murder of Lana Turner's boyfriend Johnny Stompanato by her daughter Cheryl:

> There's nothing astonishing about these [recent events], for the winds of scandal flare again from the pinnacle of the American film industry: the prominent trial "Hollywood versus *Confidential,*" the sensational drama of the Lana Turner with her own gigolo-gangster, write themselves perfectly into the traditions of the American cinema.[34]

Referring to the libel suits brought by Dorothy Dandridge and Maureen O'Hara against *Confidential* magazine in 1957, Anger locates the recent reportage surrounding Stompanato's murder within a longer history of Hollywood scandal. It is Anger's overarching project to show how scandals have long been a staple feature of the commercial cinema's production of its own sense of the lurid. For Anger, the sense that the litigation surrounding *Confidential* might seem to have heralded a transformation in the accountability of the tabloid press only, in fact, served to show how deeply imbedded fan gossip and the discourses of secrecy and revelation that underpin gossip were circulated within the larger setting of popular cinema and its reportage. That is, the *Confidential* trials revealed in more spectacular fashion what had long been crucial to Hollywood's appeal: namely, the perverse, the other, the "unnameable" dimensions of gossip. In a subsequent American edition, Anger notes that the public discourses of scandal changed significantly after the *Confidential* trial only by degree, in their saturation of other domains of star production, for stars could financially benefit from the admission of their sins and had much to lose from their *exclusion* from the uses of gossip and tabloid excitement. Anger suggests that after Maureen O'Hara's suit against *Confidential* was settled, stars "started coming out with their own 'tell-all' autobiographies. Why let others cash in on their private lives when they could rake in the bread for themselves?"[35]

Despite numerous revisions of the first volume of *Hollywood Babylon* through its various editions, it has retained a historical sense of the complicated long-term bond between the scandal-driven press reportage and the studios that appeared to be repressing scandal.[36] Read as a fan's history of film colony gossip and scandal, then, it is significant that the various editions of *Hollywood Babylon* open with accounts of the scandals that inaugurated the earliest moments of Hollywood star-driven tabloid culture.[37] Among these are the 1920 suicide of Olive Thomas, the 1921 death of Virginia Rappe, allegedly at the hands of Fatty Arbuckle, and the 1922 murder of director William Desmond Taylor. Referring to the treatment of these events in the popular press of the 1920s, Anger claims that

> the "star system" was born: at once the dogma and rites of this new cult were established, the entire world fell into step with it. In France, Scandinavia, Germany, Italy, Japan and in India, the cinema relied upon the "cult of personality" and this formula assured its fortunes.[38]

The fortunes of Hollywood, we learn, are pinned not simply to the creation of a star system, a version of Hollywood history that the industry itself has long circulated, but more specifically, as Anger would have it, to the creation of the star scandal system. This insight allows Anger to read Hollywood publicity, from its earliest moments, as a history in which stardom and scandal are closely linked and, indeed, constitute each other within the ideological field of popular culture, with scandalous sexualities forming a large part of Hollywood's dynamics of production. *Babylon* depicts the event of the star scandal as emerging in sync with the screening of the cinematic image and the formation of a star system within the studios. Star gossip, movie magazines, film attendance, and fantasy about stars all form, according to Anger, part of a larger network through which Hollywood has been responsible for creating contemporary notions of sexuality, wealth, consumerism, and class mobility within the global setting for the Hollywood product.

Indeed, one of the most important features of *Hollywood Babylon* is its insistence that Hollywood produces a larger constellation of social meanings than can be apprehended in terms of a particular film and its exhibition. Anger disrupts an opposition between accepting Hollywood *films* as ratifying a wholesome, normalized set of traits (heterosexuality, proper bourgeois values, familialism) and Hollywood *gossip* as a secondary phenomenon that occasionally undermines such depictions through its devotion to stars. Rather, *Hollywood Babylon* refuses to isolate gossip as a lesser feature of star lore and perversely reads Hollywood backward through its gossip to interrogate the too often prioritized (and idealized) notion that Hollywood sought only to suppress its own power to titillate. In the 1959 *Hollywood Babylone,* for example, Anger reprints as an appendix the Censorship Code with an accompanying epigraph from Saint Matthew, warning that "if your hand is an object of scandal, cut it off." Anger seems to have anticipated Michel Foucault's notion of the production of contemporary sexualities through their apparent prohibitions, the net effect of the Code's presence in *Babylon* demanding that we perceive censorship as signaling the presence, not the omission, of contentious sexual representations (but not only that: criminality, blasphemy, alcoholism). Of course, as the paradoxical scriptural injunction reminds us, the problem of locating scandal in relation to the whole "body" of Hollywood (to cutting it off) is that gossip's energies and enthusiasms derive from the fascination with scandal that is allegedly redressed, but in fact may only be heightened, by censorship.

Anger thus offers a reading of Hollywood through its own allegedly prohibited history. One strategy for recuperating such a suppressed history appears in his lavish illustrations, taken from Hollywood publicity, scandal sheets, and his own private archive. Although the text details myriad Hollywood love affairs, bouts with drugs, and careers in demise, the graphics do not accompany Anger's writings as chunks of evidence so much as they invite the reader to speculate about the connotative possibilities for reading them in the ways that Anger suggests are possible.[39] For example, in a chapter in *Hollywood Babylon II* entitled "Odd Couples," Anger offers staged studio publicity shots of housemates Cary Grant and Randolph Scott that might have appeared as "innocent" depictions of two stars enjoying domestic pleasures as two of Hollywood's most eligible bachelors, the captions intoning, "Cary and Randy: at home, at the pool, harmonizing and out at the fights." Nowhere does Anger suggest that Grant and Scott might have been lovers (a long-standing Hollywood rumor that survives today), but such a conclusion is left to the reader through her or his interpretation of the photographs as more than just cheerful publicity about the pleasures of single life, but also a record of queer coupledom within the strictures of Hollywood censorship.[40] I would hazard that part of the appeal of *Hollywood Babylon* resides in its unwillingness to trace specifically the valences of unarticulated desires and repulsions that many of the images attempt to evince in the books' readers. While Anger captions many of the photos with tongue-in-cheek (and let's say it: often bitchy) commentary, the effect of this commentary is to invite the reader to try to imagine the alternative "straight" reading of the material, an exercise in which the ideological fissures of star imagery begin to emerge with dizzying effect.

One might object to the *Babylon* books in that they seek to claim knowledge of the private domains of the lives of Hollywood stars and can only substantiate such knowledge through innuendo. Such literal readings of the books fail to account for the fact that the *Babylon* books assume a familiarity on the reader's part with the practices of reading and sharing gossip, practices that form part of Hollywood's own impulse to profit from gossip-driven knowledge. In the 1965 American edition, Anger offers a definition of stardom that situates scandal centrally within the industry and locates the star icon as an effect of fans' desires to know more than the censored versions of publicity can supposedly reveal:

The Hollywood religion—"Star Worship"—of the Heavenly Bodies began when the flicker-figures doffed their anonymity, taking each a made-up name (obligatorily euphonious—Bunny, Dove, Pretty, Sweet), matched with a made-up personality, and a colorful, spicy "private affair"—necessarily an enormous snow-job—the whole teetering structure supported by press-agents' handouts, planted news items, slush-and-gush fan-magazines, and studio-inspired fan-clubs. The desires and frustrated appetites of the fans were focused into an awesome kind of bug-eyed, Beatlesque, frenzied worship; ready to erupt at any public glimpse of the idol in the flesh, and, more pertinently, conditioned to *pay* and *pay* and *pay* for his shadow at the box office.[41]

By citing earlier moments of star production in conjunction with more recent events (in this case, the contemporaneous appearance of Beatles fandom, but other examples might be substituted: Madonna, Michael Jackson, Britney Spears), Anger seeks to articulate fan practices and the economics of studio profit ("*pay* and *pay* and *pay*") that accommodate them. Throughout the *Babylon* project, we repeatedly discover Anger's treatment of the spectacle of Hollywood scandal as contiguous with filmgoing, leading us to an important question: that of whether gossip, be it produced seemingly in concert with or against Hollywood reportage, should be seen as transgressive of other versions of Hollywood history. If the industry is structurally predicated on the inclusion (which *appears* as an exclusion) of scandal within its own publicity-driven discourses, then are fan knowledges, as we see them played out in *Hollywood Babylon,* necessarily at odds with what the industry might wish for the reception of its product?

To my mind, this problem is illustrative of the strictures that confront "marginal" recipients of cinema of all sorts, queer men not the least among them, and needs to be theorized in such a way that allows for a subtle interplay between fan knowledges and the industry's recognition that such knowledges circulate beyond the control of the industry.[42] It is not simply the case, within Anger's reading of Hollywood public relations materials, that the studios generated a singular and monolithic set of representations, and subsequently all spectators accommodate themselves as they might within particular discursive limits; instead, scandal and tabloid culture indicate those most contentious of matters that the industry might not necessarily address in its more central texts (i.e., the films) but do address in other productions, say of stardom within tabloids and gossip magazines. Anger illustrates the traits of Hollywood life that could not appear on the big screen, at least to the extent that the use of drugs and alcohol, extramarital and promiscuous sex, and blackmail and a host of other crimes could not appear in conjunction with the articulation of star images within Hollywood films. Anger recognizes, though, the fascination with sexual perversity and criminality in relation to stars' "real" lives as they were imagined in gossip and the scandal-driven tabloid press on which Anger dwells.

Having suggested that *Babylon* functions primarily as a camp and queer fan textual production of Hollywood history, it is important here to clarify that many of the books' strategies for recalling Hollywood lore take part in the queer male camp habit of focusing on female star iconography, and it is telling that scandalous sexuality is thematized in *Babylon* around one primary topic: female (largely heterosexual, but sometimes lesbian) erotic pleasure.[43] Despite the books' many references to the homoerotic dimensions of male stars' private lives, read as an exercise in fan textual production, *Hollywood Babylon* centers its concerns on the status of female sexuality and sexual pleasure. The appearance of this theme as an organization of the books is not all that surprising, given the situation of Hollywood within the terrain of contemporary sexualities; what is surprising is the degree to which Anger does not link female sexuality with narratives of dissolution and demise. Despite contravening treatments of the matter to be found within conventional Hollywood film history, which focus on the containment of female sexuality, Anger offers the possibility of finding representations of "prohibited" sexualities within the very materials of Hollywood star discourses that do not wholly condemn such sexual pleasures. For Anger, many of Hollywood's most important female stars circulated as powerful images of how sexual and social regulation and questions of power are sent askew in the wake of images of female star icons.

The portrayal of female sexuality in *Babylon,* in fact, attributes the dissolution of heterosexual marriage to the institution's failure to accommodate pleasure on the woman's part. Anger reverses the usual depiction of marital breakup, seeking to understand how marriage denies sexual pleasure, particularly that of women, rather than seeing divorce as the fault of an excessive female sexuality. In his relatively lengthy treatment of Mary Astor's relationship with George S. Kaufman, Anger fixes his discussion on the discovery of Astor's diary. There Astor wrote of her relation to Kaufman in detail, and her subsequent "downfall" arose from her husband's discovery of the diary and use of it in their divorce proceedings.

Although she was, through the litigious circulation of her diary, held hostage to the demands of proving herself a "respectable woman," Astor was eventually awarded custody of her daughter and given property rights. Anger's account, driven through his impulse to endorse Astor's extramarital sexual pleasure, concludes with the fact that her career did not suffer in the aftermath of the scandal but in fact flourished; as Anger crowingly comments, "it is significant to note that Mary Astor's screen career *did not* go glimmering after all this torrid exposure. Hollywood took note, as it was confirmed that Mary's box office had actually *climbed* after all the to-do over her carefully noted love life."

This latter fact, not lost on Anger, draws our attention to the relation between the press's rendering of a female star's nonmarital erotic life and her continued popularity at the box office, for such publicity served to ratify the star, within her off-screen (but widely reported) private life, as an emblem of erotic pleasure for whom marriage became an institution of control and prohibition. Astor's career did in fact flourish after the revelation of her affair with Kaufman, much in the same way (as Anger reminds us) that other stars' careers were bolstered through scandal: Robert Mitchum's marijuana possession arrest of 1948 and Errol Flynn's 1942 rape trial, in which he was acquitted, serve to remind that scandals can launch a new career and revitalize an old one.

Within the gossip-driven accounts of the lives of female stars, there were of course limit cases, and for Anger's work, the regulation of what could be depicted within Hollywood, both on and off the screen, appears in his handling of two figures, Mae West and Frances Farmer. West became a contentious figure within Hollywood because, according to Anger, she used her motion picture vehicles as a venue in which to play out her unapologetic delight in her own body and those of her favored muscle boys. Paradoxically, if West staged herself publicly as an icon of feminine sexual self-delight, she carefully orchestrated her private life to avoid scandalous reportage, all the while creating an even greater speculation about her erotic prowess; Anger remarks that "while Mae has never been known to lack male company, and has always shown a marked preference for boxers and body-builders to actors and playboys, she has always been most careful to draw the shades."[44] Drawing the shades on her off-screen relations would not be enough to counter the innuendo that her on-screen presence came to galvanize. West became a central figure for the industry's censorship codes, and from Anger's account emerges the paradox of gossip: lowering the shades is always potentially (within the realm of fantasy) a way of raising them. Nevertheless Anger's rendering of West deliberately avoids situating her as a figure of abjection; writing in 1965, he delights in the fact that "today, as always, the one-and-only Mae West could say: 'It's not the men in my life that counts—it's the life in my men.' "

Counterposing the figure of West for Anger is that of Frances Farmer, the Hollywood actress whose career ended abruptly in 1942 with a drunk-driving violation. Anger recounts in detail the events leading to the star's exile from Hollywood through prisons and mental hospitals; the chapter on Farmer, "Daughter of Fury: Frances, Saint," offers a hagiographic account of an artist involuntarily unable to control her antagonism to the police, courts, psychiatrists, and other agents of the contemporary institutions that legislate and patrol ideals of appropriate femininity. Although Hollywood itself later attempted to resurrect Farmer as a figure of independence and powerful femininity, Anger records the demise of her career in order to understand how the industry has consistently handled its talent: by insisting on the allure of its stars but disavowing them when they prove too much of a liability.

On the whole, *Hollywood Babylon*'s distinction from other forms of star discourse arises in its insistence on retrieving the biographies of such "failed" stars as Mae West and Frances Farmer as significant for having been *both* those things: as stars and as failures whom the studios were unwilling to support at the moment in which they appeared to be risks. To hear them described by Anger, the lives of Astor, West, and Farmer are triumphs over the hypocrisy of Hollywood politics, where the studios actively recruited nonconforming talent in order to garner box office profits, all the while remaining unwilling to support, legally or otherwise, these figures when they erupted outside the boundaries of propriety. Yet these women have hardly remained staples of Hollywood star canons from the classical period and in fact enjoy a status mostly within a "trash" aesthetic of Hollywood cinema, to which Anger has been pivotal.

In this regard, it seems that *Hollywood Babylon* may confuse its own version of stardom (a celebration of degeneracy and the perverse) as supplanting another (wholesomeness, glamour), and one response to Anger's writings might be to insist that he "merely" glorifies the nasty and brutish goings-on of the film colony. Although Anger's emphasis on stardom as a site of contestation over what stars mean to viewers replicates the very spectacle he seeks to undercut, focusing on this inclination loses sight of the fact that fan-produced texts, which I understand *Hollywood Babylon* to be, function within and against the powerful and far-reaching star discourses of the industry's own invention.

Within the *Babylon* project's tendency to celebrate its own version of morbid stardom, it evokes camp fandom as a powerful strategy for demystifying star production through the latter's own terms. By quoting so heavily from trade press articles, Hollywood gossip, and publicity photographs, *Hollywood Babylon* appropriates the materials of star discourse and often emulates them; yet *Babylon* interrogates stardom, as a site of scandal, in order to convey how little Hollywood production of the star commodity has changed since the first scandals in the 1920s.

Inhabiting the contradictions of star culture, Kenneth Anger embraces the individualizing and personalized notions of stardom while simultaneously reminding his readers of the industry of which stars are a significant feature, and I am not convinced that this has been an unimportant project. To the degree that the *Hollywood Babylon* books have succeeded, within a popular venue, in making visible the camp fan who doubts the motives of the film industry and the primacy of its self-depiction, the *Holy Baby* project retrieves the debris of Hollywood in order to make sense of fans' alienation from the false promises and bogus claims of star culture. In closing the first volume of *Babylon,* Anger quotes from a bit of Hollywood's own maudlin self-description:

I walk along the streets of sorrow
The Boulevard of Broken Dreams
Where Gigolo—and Gigolette
Can take a kiss—without regret
So they forget their broken dreams
You laugh tonight and cry tomorrow
When you behold your shattered schemes
And Gigolo—and Gigolette
Wake up and find their eyes are wet
With tears that tell of broken dreams . . .

These lines, excised as Anger notes from the 1934 Warner Bros. production of *Moulin Rouge,* offer a now-clichéd rendering of the film colony's ambivalence toward stardom and its allure. And yet by citing them so prominently, Anger points to the ways that Hollywood can occasionally acknowledge that, indeed, it has known all along the complicated pathos of its product.

FOUR

"Beyond the Critics' Reach": John Waters

and the Trash Aesthetic

In the closing moments of director John Waters's 1998 feature film *Pecker,* a character jubilantly shouts out a toast to a gathered party: "To the end of irony!" This assertion is heard in a social gathering comprised of New York art gallery cognoscenti *and* working-class Baltimorans and announces a curious status for the enjoyment of ironic pleasures. What is meant by irony here is not the more general sense of the message marked by a contrast between an apparent and intended meaning, so prized by cultural critics in canonical texts, but the forms of engagement that seem to saturate contemporary mass-cultural forms and corresponding avant-garde responses witnessed in much current painting, music, writing, and film and video forms. Such irony would seem to indicate that the recipients of popular culture know of the popular's debased status before they take pleasure in its consumption: that capital's promises of abundance arrive with the reminder that the fare offered stands in distinct abjection in its relation to a high culture lost to the past. This moment in Waters's film coincides with a host of recent scholarly and popular commentaries that locate forms of contemporary anomie under the name of irony, kitsch, and camp; one might recall Fredric Jameson's comments in *Postmodernism* that the traits of what he calls contemporary parody are hollow and fleeting, hallmarks of a consumerist culture caught in the need for the next expendable thrill. Indeed, it seems that the practices of responding to cultural objects with an eye to embracing their excessive, performative, and humorous dimensions—that is, the impulse to ironize them—might be considered a dereliction of the duties of citizens and readers to take seriously a culture whose debasement signals a weariness with the current political and economic order. Further, that the foregoing moment occurs in a film made by John Waters might strike any viewer acquainted with his output as bewildering inasmuch as Waters has produced an oeuvre over the past twenty-five years based on the pleasures of mocking many of the most cherished institutions of contemporary life (marriage, domesticity, work, glamour) and celebrating the perverse, the marginal, and the bizarre. In short, one cannot embrace Waters's works without knowing of the ironic stance required to make sense of them.

We discover, though, that irony is a depleted term for comprehending the variety of contemporary cultural practices encompassed in its name, and perhaps worth recalling is that the term carries with it its classical meaning, whereby irony was defined as a form of feigned ignorance. To be ironic in this sense is to maintain a pretense of not knowing in order to produce an alternative knowledge of a statement, object, text, or performance: insisting that one is not perceiving the conditions under which the ironic message is dispensed, not possessing its different registers of signification, not acknowledging that one is perhaps the perfect recipient of the statement that one claims only to be overhearing, irony captures a form of complicity between producer and recipient, one allowing for a form of textual camouflage that provides for a hidden, ambivalent interpretation to arise around the message.

Within this sense of the ironic, however, further elaborations are demanded, especially in the context of popular forms, whereby the manufactured ironic text can seem to express an incomprehension about the industries that give rise to it, while on the side of cultural consumption, the ironic response forms an agreement to ignore the culture industry's undemocratic tendencies and homogeneity. In short, irony is taken as the measure of capital's exploitative logics to the degree that the ironic sensibility records the bad faith of both producers and consumers as they turn their back on more exalted cultural expressions in the era of mass forms.

This chapter offers another way of thinking about the status of contemporary irony; here, I argue that the ironic features of Waters's films mark a counterknowledge, one shared by producer and consumer alike, to the value codings within popular cinema itself, and further, that these features indicate the movement of camp intellectual labor into the arena of postclassical Hollywood. The apparent disavowal of the ironic in *Pecker* does not herald the end of the complicated, modernist text as much as it suggests that audiences wider than those educated in the appreciation of canonical high cinema culture can consider the ambivalences of cultural production under capital. The ironic registers of Waters's films, which here are discussed as expressions of camp intellectual labor, are most usually staged in his films in terms of good and bad taste, and the purposeful confusion of those domains by Waters coincides with the fact of his ascendancy as one of the only filmmakers in Hollywood able to secure funding for highly aberrant products about the nature of debased consumption itself and to reach new audiences with the insights of camp (relatively) intact. The measure of the expansion of this audience, I argue, is to be found in the migration of Waters's films to what we too often refer to as the "mainstream" cinema, and although my intent is not to insist that by and large, the industries of cinema do not tend toward homogenization, too simplistic is the argument that the *seeming* standardization of mass-disseminated films implies a concomitant single-mindedness of spectatorship. Indeed, I argue that Waters's films find their place in an intellectual and artistic geneology made available in the aftermath of the era of the cult audience, a cinematic venue where Waters assessed what kinds of interventions might be made into the generic forms of Hollywood moviemaking. Despite the demise of the cult cinema, whose spectatorial investments were marked by a fascination with the contemptible, the scorned, and the perverse, its critical strategies subsequently appear in Waters's work in what he calls the "trash aesthetic," whereby his work embraces all manner of marginal subjects in his beloved Baltimore—eccentrics, the downright mad, transvestites—and seeks to embrace these figures by sharing in their delight in disregarding customary notions of good taste, normative sexuality, and racial identities.

Linked to the camp dimensions of films such as *Polyester* (1981) and *Cry Baby* (1990) is the fact that Waters's films have demonstrated a fascination with the Hollywood genre film, most notably the melodrama or "woman's picture," and his movies offer a commentary and accompanying revision of the ideological functions of the melodrama (similar in many instances to the productions of directors Rainer Fassbinder and Pedro Almodovar). Waters's education as a filmmaker in the underground milieu of New York in the 1960s would seem to locate his artistic concerns in relation to the avant-garde practices of Andy Warhol and Kenneth Anger, whose bodies of work were characterized by their frequent avoidance of narrative and their emphasis on associatively arranged sequences of images that disobey narrative as an organizing logic. Despite a debt to these filmmakers' groundbreaking innovations in formal film practices (a debt that Waters has consistently recognized in his own writings), Waters's cinema is unwaveringly a narrative one and demonstrates a commitment to reaching audiences more customarily alienated from avant-garde practices and more oriented toward feature films; although his films offer strong story lines and distinct characters (hallmarks of the dominant practices of Hollywood studio productions), Waters has over the longer duration of his cinema imported nondominant artistic visual forms and forms of intellectual investments into his movies, all the while producing cinematic narrative.

The important lesson of the underground for Waters's work has been the problem of offering a cinema that can challenge the expectations of the "regular people" (his term) while shocking such audiences at their own pleasure. Waters's films maintain this recognition by revivifying the melodrama and its sometimes concomitant form, the teen pic, genres where one is encouraged to identify with the long-suffering female lead in her struggles. Centering on women characters and redeploying the generic features of the melodrama in innovative ways, *Female Trouble* (1974), *Polyester* (1978), *Hairspray* (1988), and *Serial Mom* (1994) attempt to gather audience's affective investments toward the melodramatic heroine. In this regard, Waters offers a split affectivity, whereby the films recognize the history of film melodrama heroines as they have been situated in camp readings for their performative excess of costume, speech, and gesture while simultaneously taking seriously the demonization of femininity in a patriarchal and homophobic society. Performances by the female characters in Waters's films pay tribute to the teary-eyed efforts of Hollywood icons such as Bette Davis and Joan Crawford while demanding that we recognize the pleasures of suffering as they are sustained by both audience and performer. We witness in Waters's heroines the possibility that femininity contains dual valences: both concerned with sacrifice and domestic duty *and* the delight of feminine performative excess. Such pleasures themselves emerge from affective investments in abjection and self-denial while simultaneously challenging those very structures of feelings.

Commenting, for example, on *Serial Mom,* Waters suggests that he "was trying to make you root for a serial killer. I was trying to find people's limits, how far you can go, and make the audience a little bit nervous, that they're enjoying something they've been taught not to enjoy. Nobody likes serial killers, but this one, not only did she do it, but she got off and you're *glad.*" Sympathizing with the mother whose love becomes aggression, we become conscious of the history of melodrama in a new way, for in *Serial Mom*'s lead character's urge to clean the world and make it over in the image of domestic orderliness, we recall Joan Crawford's Mildred Pierce as she seeks to extend her talents from the home to the world of profit via her chain of restaurants. Domestic labor and its customary bourgeois associations with feminine affect sit uneasily in Waters's films, leading as they do to murderous rage instead of being recuperated, as in the example of *Mildred Pierce,* for household drudgery. One learns from Waters's assessment of melodrama that women's affect can neither be contained within the home nor be extended to the larger world in any acceptable way for phallocentric social arrangements.

Waters extracts melodrama's affective structures and deploys them to confront viewers with the contradictory status of femininity as women's work, and where *Polyester* and *Serial Mom* diverge with their classical Hollywood progenitors is in their impulse to spectacularize domestic femininity and not to conceal or to mystify it.

The potential of Waters's films to upset viewers with their own perverse investments derives from the anticipation that audiences will not necessarily have shown up ready for a shock, and Waters has redirected his energies toward spectators who may have little acquaintance with his cult status of the 1970s. Not knowing of Waters's past career as the director of *Pink Flamingos,* such viewers will perhaps not sit down attuned to what they will see as camp or cult cinema. In this sense, Waters's later career has been less concerned with accommodating "hip," knowing urban spectators than with smuggling a camp reading of the melodrama into the venue of the melodrama itself; Waters distances himself from camp to install it before his unsuspecting viewers in the new formations of the Hollywood cinema.[1]

The melodramatic dimensions of Waters's later films return the present argument to a question of how camp impulses to produce an awareness of the dialectic of the capital and its unstable value codings have shifted from earlier narrative and generic forms (the musical) through nonnarrative (and, indeed, *anti*narrative) practices of Andy Warhol and Kenneth Anger back to the concerns of story-driven filmmaking. Waters's departure from the arena of underground cinema to studio production says as much about the disappearance of the former's audience as it does about the latter's potential to seize new viewers for the evaluative crisis staged by what he calls the "trash aesthetic."[2] In short, even the proclamation of "the end of irony" in Waters's most recent work forms an extension to his ongoing attempts to stage the pleasures of camp to wider audiences than previously.

Genres without Films, Audiences without Spectators: The Problem of the Cult Film

All *cult* really means is that something is popular and no one foresaw its success.
—*John Waters*

A cult film is a film that's never made any money.
—*Russ Meyer*

Allison Graham argues that the cult film marks the despair of the postmodern spectator in locating him or herself in history.[3] For Graham, an audience reared on the banality of television turns to the cult film as a way of insisting on their spectatorial power to discover a different form of mass culture. The cult impulse, Graham offers, organizes a response to the "kitschification" of popular culture through the popular's own materials, and for Graham some of the most savvy of contemporary filmmakers (David Lynch and John Waters prominent among them) have exploited the cult phenomenon by producing films that *seek* cult audiences from the outset. Graham detects the expropriation of post-1960s pessimism in the name of marketing, for what underpins the production of cult films is the recognition that cult audiences have, in advance, voiced their exasperation over Hollywood's "blockbuster" offerings and decided to watch *Glen or Glenda?* for the seventh time at their repertory house, or later on their VCR.[4] The appeal of the cult film, Graham suggests, is its "mystique of failure," in which the realist wishes of an Ed Wood or George Romero are stunted by their cardboard sets and non-actors' nonacting abilities. But cult films appeal through the hallmarks of such apparent failures not only in the sense that they offer cheap visual effects in lieu of the high production values of the Hollywood vehicle but also because they indicate a deliberate will on the part of audiences to disregard the self-proclaimed importance of the more expansively budgeted mainstream release. In this manner, the cult film signifies the will of the cult audience to trump both the low (i.e., attempts to brand a film as a cult product) and high (the blockbuster) domains of film production by forging readings and film canons of their own that stand in tension with the popular Hollywood cinema.

A repeated argument within the critical literature on cult films suggests that cult movie fans seize a role for asserting cultural value in response to the advocacy of Hollywood publicity and various popular and academic critical estimations of what kinds of cinema are worth the price of admission or of critical attention. Nowhere does this become more apparent than in the fact that despite efforts to the contrary, a cult film has yet to be produced in anticipation of a cult audience. *The Rocky Horror Picture Show* was initially offered as noncult fare and subsequently mobilized a cult audience, but its sequel, *Shock Treatment,* designed with follow-up appeal to the first film's midnight audiences, did not secure a cult following. Commenting on the resentment of cult audiences at finding themselves addressed *as* cult audiences, Bruce Kawin describes the pleasure of seeming to discover any film that might inadvertently become a cult pleasure:

> I know when the horror films are not made for me or those who share my tastes: when they are timid or stupid, like *Friday the 13th, part VI;* or empty and unbelieving, like *The Guardian;* or unable to rise to the challenge of the material (in this case, Lovecraft), like *From Beyond.* I know, and I wait for the ones that *are* for me, aware that it can be a long wait. But it is a joy to discover a work or an image that is (all right, *relatively*) free from compromise, as perhaps only the programmatic cult film and the avant-garde film can be.[5]

The shift in Kawin's revelation, from the joy of discovery to the naming of the "programmatic" cult film and its avant-garde cousin as anticipating his joy, unconsciously reveals a tension between the notion of the free, autonomous cult spectator within the cultural marketplace and the fact of his knowledge that the business of film can indeed seek to address him, even if it fails to win him over; thus a cult text resists definition through its formal features and can better be understood through spectatorial disavowal of other kinds of apparently dissatisfying cultural production.

Cult films force the disclosure of the lack of both an identifiable set of traits with which to describe films of the cult pantheon and the frustration of suggesting who in particular forms audiences for these texts. This "failure" (to echo Graham) to my mind is not due to a weakness in the cult film's critical literature, but the strong legacy of the cult formation's insistence on humbling the demands of popular publicity *and* critical estimations of what constitutes cultural value. This is not an argument for cult viewers as necessarily exceeding the ideological limitations of their own positions but a reminder that, like every other invocation of the audience, we are dealing with an imaginary set of viewers who in all probability encompass a range of social positions. Given the limits of what we can know about any audience (and the immense claims forged on behalf of that nomination), it is worth recalling that cult audiences have defined themselves against the expectations—primarily those of the industrial sphere of production—of how aggregated receptions can satisfactorily be lumped together to identify the agent of profit. Cult viewing emerges as a form of labor, or more specifically work-as-play, by spectators both to rethink the history of cinema that gives rise to a particular moment of cult reception and to reorder the value codings of the industries of cinema.

The irony of these two expressions, of Graham's pessimism and Kawin's optimism about the cult film phenomena, is that they emerge after the disappearance of the communal cult audiences and exhibition practices, whose public demonstrations of the will to tamper with registers of good and bad taste no longer seem to sustain particularly younger audiences in the ways that they have. In Graham's estimation, the gradual departure of the cult audience heralds a postmodern spectatorship, one no longer ensconced in the belief of "an autonomous subjectivity":

> While the politics of modernism asserts the primacy and mystery of inner life, the politics of postmodernism that shows most nakedly in these cult films finds little or no difference between social superstructure and psychological substructure, and simply obliterates depth altogether.[6]

Graham proceeds to argue that the cult film figures as "one of the most reliable indicators of our addiction to what Baudrillard terms 'the obscene delirium of communication.'" A perfect mimicry of social practice and individual consciousness is said to be the most crystalline instance of the culture industry's determination of spectatorial pleasure, because the cult film whets our appetite for endless reconsumption of Hollywood's leavings, which in turn is accommodated by the appearance of *The Flintstones* and *The Brady Bunch* on Nickelodeon's cable outlets or *The Flintstones in Viva Rock Vegas* and *The Brady Bunch Movie* at the multiplex.

There seems a perfect validation of Graham's argument in the major studios' current willingness to recycle cult sensibilities into the mainstream product, but I am cautious about the complaint that every instance of cultural production is said to be characterized as anesthetized, flat, and preoccupied with its stylistic trappings to the degree that this necessarily evacuates an accompanying way of discussing spectatorial intellectual work. Indeed, by seeking to blame cult audiences for the current state of nostalgia, Graham misapprehends the fact of Hollywood's power to recirculate older cultural materials as determinative of cult viewership and instead seeks to explain the popularity of the Hollywood nostalgia film by way of emphasizing the malaise of cult viewers over and above their energies to read the depravities of their objects of devotion. For example, the elegant black-and-white cinematography of Tim Burton's *Ed Wood* (1994) serves to remind devotees of *Glen or Glenda?* or *Plan 9 from Outer Space* of just how significant a gap resides between Burton's budgets and Wood's. We might speculate that Burton's attempts to capture the appeal of the cult film in a retelling of Wood's biography diminished *Ed Wood*'s appeal to audiences not because the expectations of the cult viewer (as described by Kawin) at being cynically addressed by a reorganized Hollywood needed to be refused but because Burton's film so explicitly failed to invite the viewer in any way to tamper with the cycles of production and reception that marked the cult viewer's interests in film culture. The cult viewer's fascination with his or her capacity to attend to the wrong bad object of modernity—previously Wood's *Plan 9 from Outer Space,* but perhaps now Paul Verhoeven's *Showgirls*—arrives too late on the scene of degradation: Burton's film serves as an epitaph for Wood's depraved appeal.

The question that abides in these attempts to theorize the meanings of the cult film remains one of whether the disappearance of public cult viewing formations must be so completely subsumed, within critical accounts, to an evaluative hierarchy that privileges in the final instance the Hollywood product, even as Hollywood attempts to incorporate cult film's appeal into its own product. The abduction of the cheap by the expensive does not necessarily lead to assessments that the cultural politics that underpinned cult and trash sensibilities have simply vanished, for pessimism in the name of postmodernity preserves an opposition between high and low cultural production that gave rise to cult in the first place. The tendencies of the industry to produce the homogenized film product with the *slightest* variations that can be publicized as innovation tempts us to disregard the obstinance of cult viewers not to abide by the product's accompanying value codings. Why must we insist that the "quality" look of Hollywood's packaging of the cult sensibility bars the continued fascination with trash as a significant, perhaps even more widespread, attention to the crisis of taste and value that cult viewing patterns played out?

In this context, it is worth exploring Waters's movement from the underground to the domain of the more customarily standardized product around the specter of value's fluctuations, coded throughout his career in terms of taste. The appeal that Waters makes in his films is continually staged through an attention to not only the flux of taste in its wild gyrations through the fashionable and the outdated but through the affective expression of those changes in designations of good and bad taste as they appear in the context of the melodrama. Melodrama's history, as a generic form centrally concerned with the embodiment of capital's organization of femininity and domesticity, furnishes Waters's films with the opportunity to stage not only the bad taste of the outdated commodity but the bad taste of affective expressions as well.

"The Horror Stories of Other People's Lives": Melodrama and Camp Affective Labor

An early scene in the aptly titled *Female Trouble* draws together the ingredients of the melodramatic universe: familial animus, the Christmas holidays, female adolescence, fashion. In the holiday sequence that sets into motion the film's narrative trajectory, we begin with the love of the feminized commodity: Dawn Davenport (Divine) is discovered on Christmas morning searching through her gifts for the one object of her desire, a pair of cha-cha heels. Furious at her parent's indifference to her requests for such outlandishly glamorous shoes, she rampages through the household, overturning the Christmas tree on her mother and fleeing over the suburban lawns to a world where, ironically, she will herself bear a daughter. In the ensuing life that she makes for herself, she struggles to secure a living as a model, and eventually Dawn subscribes to an aesthetic that advocates criminality as beauty. She subsequently goes on a crime spree and, in the closing shots of the film, is put to death by electrocution.

Dawn's movement from one family that she rejects as a daughter to another that she disavows as a mother situates her as being caught in

Divine as Dawn Davenport in *Female Trouble*.

the contradictory logic that criminalizes equally the female desire to be outside the family and within it, but it does so in the context of her investment in the pursuit of physical distinction, a kind of beautifying labor on her body that, failing to approximate normative notions of conventional appeal, unfolds as the camp labor to make herself into a commodity for public spectacle. Working in a theater where patrons can marvel at her criminal femininity as a public spectacle, she bounces on a trampoline and fires a gun into the audience. Divine's performance as Dawn signals the migration of camp to the domain of fashion culture, whereby she enacts the labors of self-improvement so continuously demanded of capital's female subjects, but she performs these labors in such an aberrant way as to display them as the mimicking efforts of work-as-play. Offered by way of a fetish for shoes and clothing, her devotion to beauty is both typified as part of the larger regulations of the female body exerted by the industries of cinema and fashion *and* staged as excessive, and it derives from the need to escape the suburban monotony that catapults her out of the familial scene and lands her squarely back into another form of domesticity.[7]

The sole voice of concern for the film's familial disarray appears in the form of Aunt Ida (Edith Massey), who continually counsels Dawn and her husband Gator that "the world of heterosexuals is a sick and boring life." Ida's admonitions go unheeded, and despite her attempts to break up the marriage of Dawn and Gator, it does in fact emerge that it is heterosexual marriage that leads to Dawn's eventual undoing. What we discover through Dawn's humiliation in the families where she is imprisoned is that femininity as perversion is both created by the family and criminalized by it, and repeatedly throughout Waters's films he has offered a vision of femininity that is captured within this contradiction.

Waters admits to the fact that he writes his screenplays always attuned to the form of a three-reel, ninety-minute narrative feature, and continually his films maintain their narrative momentum playing out the affective dimensions of feminine commodity culture. Although his earliest efforts, such as *Mondo Trasho,* demonstrate the impact of underground cinema on his aesthetic vision through the use of nonsynchronized dialogue and pop tunes on the sound track, they also offer a recognizable plot and set of characters.[8] Though Waters deploys Kenneth Anger's method of dubbing top 40 singles as commentary on the film image, he also integrates the pop tune into the film by sampling lines of songs as dialogue, repeating each fragment for dramatic effect within a narrative structure, and thus while they display a commitment to underground techniques, their melodramatic narrative structure dominates through the most singular concern witnessed within his films, namely, the story of the terror of femininity let loose on a world of suburban banality.

The formal strategies of the classical Hollywood film have been argued, most notably by feminist film critics, to be contradictory when it addresses female viewers, and this contradiction arises from the dual proclivities within cinema to situate woman as the bearer of the sign of sexual difference and to punish her for performing such a function. Rendered into such an impossible position, her image must offer spectatorial pleasure to the heterosexual male viewer as having been somehow contained, for the most important mark of difference is the threat of castration. For the female viewer, this leads to an ambivalence regarding where to devote her energies, for the sight of woman (halting the movement of narrative through glamorous feminine spectacle) only serves to remind the female viewer of her own exile from phallic privilege. Jacqueline Rose describes this as the dynamic of "how the image of the woman can be a disturbance and rupture of narrative cohesion, but also how its transposition into spectacle (woman purely *as* image) serves to neutralise this disturbance, to hold it off."[9] Yet Rose also provocatively wonders "that the image of the woman is the best way of stopping narrative flow without trouble, unpleasure." Otherwise, she notes, a radical cinema of sexual difference might theoretically commit itself to the omission of images of women at all. Rose is suggesting here that there are perhaps ways of portraying woman as not halting the flow of narrative but indeed motivating it through the pleasure of their spectacular incarnations. Were this to happen, we would be speaking of a femininity that exceeds the customary conditions of its appearance.

Although Divine's image is most often summoned as solely an incarnation of queer male drag, her self-conscious attempts to tamper with drag offer an instance of the femininity to which Rose's account calls us. Waters notes that the power of Divine's persona abided in her ability to offend virtually everyone, including other drag queens. He recalls that "other drag queens hated Divine at the beginning because they knew Divine was making fun of drag queens. I mean, you expected her to pull out a knife." Waters is pointing to a commitment by some forms of drag to a more conciliatory femininity than Divine was displaying, a drag that shares homologies with the conciliatory femininity that Rose describes. Yet we can expand on Waters's assessment of Divine's mesmerizing performances of femininity to wonder: who would consider themselves to be in a position to claim that Divine offers an easily identificatory position?

With this dilemma in mind, we might recall that camp's fascination with the wild fluctuations of feminine affect in the melodrama attach themselves to depictions of women that emerge from the crisis of domestic life to offer pleasure to the subjects whose labor is demanded by it. The melodramatic family is perpetually in crisis because it must abrogate the work of the woman to produce the conditions of labor outside the household (men's work) while reproducing subjects for capital (children), and such efforts by the wife and mother remain unremunerated because they are said to offer their own rewards of affective pleasure. If they fail to do so, as in the case of Divine's incarnations in Dawn Davenport, we discover the apparent valuelessness of affect as a form of compensation.

Despite the resistance of Divine to being typed as a heroine of the melodrama (she seldom receives even the affective rewards implied by her work), we should at least note that Waters claims this to be specifically his intention. Yet the image of Divine's "rude drag" catches us in different spectatorial positions as we are positioned through narrative to pitch our sympathies to a figure who might otherwise be named as outlaw. Unlike the beautiful suffering of the Hollywood melodramatic heroine, Divine's image is one of the female becoming more abject through her traumas and yet struggling to maintain, via her glamorous looks, her claims on our attention. That her spectacle of debasement arrives through the vehicle of drag impersonation may compel some viewers to see her as solely mocking femininity to thwart the fears of a heteronormative male gaze. Given the powerful and complex narrative maneuvers that Waters deploys both to consolidate and to confuse spectatorial identificatory pleasure, though, I think that Divine's image must be attended to in terms of its articulation of a failure to achieve a successful (and contradictory) spectacle, a failure brought about by her limited means as "trailer trash."

This is quite vividly a question of class distinction, adding yet another layer to the complexity of Divine's star image. Because I am situating my reading of Divine within a discussion of the fluctuations of value, of which taste is taken to be one symptom, her image of nonprivileged femininity suggests a strong affinity between discriminations of high and low evaluations and the problem of consolidating femininity as necessarily one set of gendered performances. Divine's drag offended as it took on the signs of femininity but did not consolidate them in their more usual bourgeois inflection via the Hollywood female star image. This becomes more apparent when we consider later depictions of Divine within more conventional domestic settings, such as those witnessed in *Polyester* and *Hairspray*. In prior ventures such as *Pink Flamingos*, Divine's characterization played with the conventions of the 1950s "bad girl," outfitting her in tight miniskirts and high heels and depicting her descent into perversion through her exile from the bourgeois domestic familial space. Her subsequent performances, beginning with the character of Francine Fishpaw in *Polyester*, appeared to join her at the moment in which she had been recuperated as a wife and mother, and Waters directs *Polyester* as a series of references to the melodrama and the soap opera as vehicles for the treatment of female pleasure within the family, the medical clinic, Catholicism, and shopping.[10] The film opens with an aerial shot of suburbia, evoking Douglas Sirk's initial shots of a halcyon New England town in *All That Heaven Allows,* and Waters has commented that the film was his homage to Sirk's Hollywood films of the 1950s. Likewise, key moments in *Polyester* reference television soap operas, offering extreme close-up shots of Divine scored with dramatic organ music, and the film takes as a motif the housewifely duty of being preoccupied with dirt and odors, cueing Francine's obsession with smells as the signal that the house is about to be overrun with the filth of exotic pleasures.[11]

The melodramatic energy of *Polyester* derives from Francine's attempts to reconsolidate her family, through her preoccupation with order and hygiene, even as the Fishpaw's family members spin out of control into their own perverse constellations: husband Elmer's s/m affair with his secretary, daughter Lu-Lu's overweening adolescent female sexuality, son Dexter's shoe fetish and criminality as Baltimore's "foot stomping bandit," and the kleptomaniacal pilfering of Francine's purse and household by her mother. Ultimately Francine's exertions to keep her home intact come to naught as she is lured from the sanctified home into an affair with an aging playboy, Todd Tomorrow, played by the démodé fifties teen idol Tab Hunter. The breakdown of the Fishpaw household, with Francine at its center, jarringly occurs within the abandonment of fantasies of suburban wholesomeness, and in *Polyester,* Divine's prior outlaw image unfolds through the fact of her being an emblem of working-class femininity for whom the attempt to become glamorous is always thwarted by her modest means. Her primary foil in this respect appears in *Polyester* in the role taken up (yet again) by Edith Massey. Massey plays Cuddles Kovinsky, a former maid who has inherited her employer's fortune and whose fantasies of social mobility are realized toward the film's closure through the realization of Cuddle's long-standing dream to hold a debutante ball. Whereas Francine represents the failure of suburban motherhood because of insufficient funds, Cuddles offers the possibility that, apart from the family and given enough material means, a woman (and a working-class woman) might achieve her fantasies of success. Of course, we should underline the fantastic dimensions of Cuddles's social ascendancy, and Waters makes plain the outlandish nature of Cuddles's re-creation of herself, showing Cuddles in jodhpurs, tennis whites, and prep-school-girl uniforms, emblems of a faux suburban aristocracy.

Francine, unlike Cuddles, has no resources in her attempts to cope with the suburban devolution that unfolds before her. She suffers through the humiliations of her life in *Polyester* and meets continual frustration when trying to reconsolidate her family. Even her attempts eventually to escape her circumstances are foiled; this becomes most tangible in her love affair with Todd, who represents high culture and social mobility within the film's social ordering (as opposed to Cuddles, who represents a fantasy of high culture). Todd owns an art cinema drive-in (the marquee reads, "DUSK TO DAWN: Three Marguerite Duras Hits," and Francine is shown reading *Cahiers du Cinema* while waiting in the lobby) where access to high culture, signaled by the drive-in patrons' consumption of champagne and raw oysters in the red-velvet luxury of the refreshment stand, promises the realization of a nonsuburban life. Of course, this too collapses around Francine as Todd's motives emerge as wanting to take advantage monetarily of Francine's profound impulse to leave the suburbs behind.

Polyester, unlike its Sirkian forebears, does not offer closure to its narrative of dissolution so much as it abandons the survivors, sobbing and whimpering, on their front lawn in the suburban Baltimore night. Waters's film, appearing in 1981, seems to presage the staging of the crisis of "family values," and it does so by interrogating the effects of the familial instigation of perversity, on the one hand, and the juridical and therapeutic responses to be mustered in response to those perversions, on the other. In one scene, the police trash the Fishpaw house look-

Tab Hunter and Divine in *Polyester.*

ing for evidence of Dexter's criminal activities, shouting, "This whole family is sick!" Later the children, Lu-Lu and Dexter, are both "rehabilitated" through twelve-step programs and arts-and-crafts hobbies that render them macramé-ing and painting zombies. The film's prescient critique of the dynamics through which the family is a source of trauma and an alleged answer to such trauma understands the kinds of ideological undertow involved in taking on the family, particularly in terms of its melodramatic valences. Waters's film is keenly attuned to the fact that melodrama never really "ends" in a historical sense, as the conditions for its existence, and its contradictions, prevail. Although John G. Ives has asserted that the film functions as a "fractured fairy tale," with Massey's Cuddles forming a "retarded fairy godmother" and Francine ultimately becoming reunited with her "repentant" children, where "they really do live happily ever after," it is quite a stretch to imagine that the Fishpaw household can be restored to equilibrium, for it is defined through its continual reassertion of crisis.[12]

The film does, however, situate Francine as its heroic figure, for it understands her as the one character capable of desiring beyond the circumstances in which she finds herself. While the others easily find their drives satisfied through the various fetishistic objects that define them (sex, shoes, money), it is Francine who exceeds the commandments of the family, even as she is maintained as the agent who wishes most avowedly for the family's maintenance. At one point, she attempts to hang herself from the refrigerator, and Cuddles appears as Francine begs, pietà style, "Why hast thou forsaken me?" She repeats the phrase as Cuddles tugs her through a maddened crowd of TV journalists, angry neighbors, and the police, and her plea's unanswerability gives Francine a remarkable pathos, even as Waters renders the situation absurd.

Polyester's display of its characters' perverse appetites showcases how such desires menace the space of the household and its concomitant feminine labors, and in this regard, the film asks us to consider how much the domestic effort of the wife and mother is defined by the capacity to know and demonstrate appropriate affective responses to such familial dissolution. In short, the film asks if there is such a thing as a camp emotion. Given that camp is so widely understood as an embrace of excess and artifice, standing distinctly in tension with affect's valences of genuineness and sincerity, this is perhaps one of the most immense challenges for understanding how Waters's films redirect camp's fascinations with capital's value codings to the melodrama's structures of feelings. If part of the demystificatory capacity of camp is to reveal the unreasonableness of customary adjudications of appropriate forms of value, then we find ourselves pressed to know the value of affect. Or put in terms of the camp tendency to value the wrong thing, what happens when a figure such as Divine's Francine Fishpaw has the wrong affective response to her domesticity? Within the melodrama's organizing logics, the usual solution for familial disturbance is that the woman's affective performance miraculously helps to resolve the crises of domesticity (displays of joy, grief, hysteria, and so on are demanded for the reconstitution of the household). Francine, however, weeps and gushes to excess, but usually at the wrong time, and thus in the instances of Waters's films, we witness the outcome of the inappropriate emotion performed to the wrong degree. These performances emphasize the sense that melodramatic affect is characterized not so much through its being grounded in sincerity but in the economy of the household, a relation that becomes more apparent when played out, as it is in Waters's films, through inappropriate performances of emotional display by the female heroine. That the depictions of these performances centered for an extended period within Waters's films on the figure of Divine, though, is complicated by the fact that Divine was not a Hollywood female star but a suburban Baltimore drag queen, and thus we should attend to the complexities of her star image as it accompanies her film performances.

Trash Stardom (Part 1): Divine

Divine embodied physical and sexual excess in a way that challenges the critical commentary on her. Gaylyn Studlar suggests that

> although she finds sadistic satisfaction in killing, Divine's sexuality is expressed mainly as a narcissistic exhibitionism. Because her exhibitionism breaks free of female passivity and the aim of producing male pleasure, it becomes an autoerotic, perverse act that recalls the late nineteenth century notion of narcissism as a distinctly feminine perversion. . . . In *Pink Flamingos,* Divine [becomes] a nineteenth-century sexologist's worst nightmare of the effects of female narcissism.[13]

Studlar recognizes Divine as representing multiple pleasures that patriarchal organizations of eroticism would deem criminal, infantile, and perverse, but ultimately Studlar withholds Divine as an agent capable of upsetting a phallocratic order, for "the antierotic, parodic treatment of Divine guarantees that the position of the heterosexual male viewer will not be made problematic. Just as the homoerotic possibilities of looking are averted, so is the potential for overtly challenging the straight male spectator's sexuality." For Studlar, *Pink Flamingos* defers to the heterosexual male gaze in that it positions Divine as a figure of abjection, through her allegedly stereotypical display of femininity as ugliness, fatness, and infantilization. Barring Studlar's puzzling judgment about Divine's power to dispel homoerotic pleasure, her argument assumes that Divine's iconographic status overwhelms the narrative perversions of Waters's films so that she must eventually be read as a retrograde embodiment of male fear of the female body.

The impulse to read Divine as a conserving emblem of femininity through her parodic status stems in Studlar's argument from the fact that Divine seems so illegible a sign for authorized versions of sex/gender difference. Allowing for the destabilizing effects of Divine's performance around firm demarcations of masculine and feminine erotic pleasures, Studlar situates Divine in the position of the effeminate man:

As a defensive reaction, the patriarchy must censor any male who appears effeminate and chooses to align himself with the "inferior" gender. Any "he" who appears as "she" risks becoming a perverse "feminine body," a soft flowing, multiple-sited morass of dissolute, perverse sexuality that threatens to dismantle the patriarchy's tenuously maintained, phallically centered subjectivity.

In terms of the unhinging of sexual orderings, we might wonder at how such uncooperative images serve to confirm a seemingly irrefutable masculinist and heterosexual ordering. If woman is taken as the threat of castration, a threat that must be warded off within the patriarchal imagination by the imposition of the fetish, then the cinematic status of woman is only ever a sign of the advance of male fear of castration. Paradoxically, the more aggressive such femininity is said to be, the more it purportedly assures the male viewer of his safety from such aggression. Further, any tampering with signs of femininity, vis-à-vis drag, are interpreted as the effeminate male's refusal to confront his masculine cohorts.

In an essay in which they explore the affective coinvestments of fat women and queer men, Eve Sedgwick and Michael Moon offer that their entwined but by no means identical fascinations with the figure of Divine derive from a sense that large women (opera divas in particular) have staged their bodies as a kind of drag, but one shaped on the body as not so much a simplistic taking on of clothing and makeup as a set of gestural and discursive performances that confuse the very notion of sex/gender signification as *either* inherent or constructed. The fat woman inhabits a position alongside conventionally sanctioned notions of desirable femininity that produces a discomfort in her refusal to inhabit her body in the "right" way, in that the fat-phobic imagination can only see her as a disavowal of the labor required to shape herself as a normatively embodied subject. Sedgwick and Moon proffer that this disavowal allows for political alliances between fat women and queer men in that queers endure a similar demand to labor in the reformation of themselves for a heteronormative world. They read Divine in terms of her "fiercely aggressive performances [that] do not conceal or disavow what a dangerous act drag can be." Pointing out that their wish is neither to dismiss drag as a now popular fascination whose thrills have worn off nor to uphold it as a utopian answer to all demands that sex/gender be seen simplistically as "constructed," Moon writes:

Divine's "loud and vulgar" (to use her terms for it) drag style flings the open secrets of drag performance in the faces of her audience: that unsanitized drag disgusts and infuriates many people; and that it is not wearing a wig or skirt or heels that is the primary sign of male drag performance, but rather a way of inhabiting the body with defiant effeminacy; or, the effeminate body itself. And, finally, that is just this conjunction of effeminacy and defiance in male behavior that can make a man the object of furious punitive energies, of gay-bashing threatened or carried out rather than applause.[14]

The homology of the fat drag queen and the fat woman resides in the possibility that the act of dressing up in women's clothing is not the same as wearing one's fat body in a culture so devoted to having continually to remake oneself, as if such efforts could be either entirely volitional or solely ones of pleasurable consumption. The decision not to obey such regimens of bodily apparition comes, as they argue, with all too many costs of verbal and physical harassment, demonstrating that the effort to move through the world without concessions to its antifat or homophobic aggressions is the labor of queer (and here we can include fat) subjects. The labor of Divine's drag, then, is not entirely about the work of putting on one's large-sized dress but about taking on all violences meted out to the subject, male or female, who does so. In *Female Trouble,* Divine is coached in her femininity by the heterosexual couple Donald and Donna Dasher, who team up to help her in her effort to reshape her criminal and abject status into a newfound beauty; Divine discovers that her previously scorned fat femininity might in inverted fashion, through its deliberately excessive display, garner her the attention and applause she has been denied since she escaped the domestic drudgery of her adolescence. *Female Trouble* is organized through a series of alternating demands on her to form her own household, a purported locus of happiness and stability that it never is, and the parade of fashion through the streets and nightclubs of Baltimore, where she finds herself finally recognized, for ill and good effects, as a worthwhile subject of attention. That such attentions at the film's conclusion are manifested by the courts, which finally deny Divine's Dawn Davenport her very life, suggests that such labors are indeed politicized.

Returning to Studlar, the inadequacy of such depictions of femininity as perversion arises from their inability to undermine the family, the central locus of desire and determinations of gender difference.

"One disturbing truth that the midnight movies discussed here generally avoid," according to this logic, is

> the explicit emergence of perversion from within the patriarchal family unit and its conservative function in maintaining rather than exploding that structure. . . . femininity and perversity are bound together in a formula that provides the male with a rationale for denigrating "femininity" and female sexuality. What results, finally, in all these films' contradictions and ambivalences is a masculine vision of the mysteries and pleasure of s/excess.

Yet we might allow for the binding together of femininity and perversion to shatter the family's status in conserving female desire—hence in seeing Divine's performance as newly domesticated.

Divine's performances are problematic in that because of its allegedly "male" position, drag is situated as being unable to disrupt conservatizing sexual orderings; this assumes that an essentialized masculine body arises intact beyond Divine's drag incarnation. In her work on what she identifies as "feminist camp," Pamela Robertson argues that the deployment of comic irony around certain star images, most notably that of Mae West, signals to us that "camp as a structural activity has an affinity with feminist discussions of gender construction, performance and enactment and that, therefore, we can examine camp as a feminist practice."[15] Robertson argues that the power of camp to disrupt gender performance has implications for the reading of female stars like West and their relation to queer male subcultures. The larger point for my discussion is that the treatment of Divine as a retrograde and conservatizing icon is mostly secured through her drag appearance; she is a male female impersonator, as opposed to what Robertson calls West's "female female impersonator." In highly similar ways, Mae West and Divine were "dragging" in order to suggest the complexities of femininity as it is performed for and against a heterosexual male gaze.

There is also a problem in deciding that Divine's performances are identical to the narratives that stage her, and in this regard we discover the camp fascinations of Waters's works as structurally similar to those of other camp texts, between narrative and number, between narrative and spectacle. Waters has commented that cast members and director were asked whether they were the same as the people they portrayed in Dreamland films, suggesting that their performances were somehow expansive on their containment within the diegetic world of the films, and there is a certain fantastic speculation (and either hope or dread) that Divine was the same in everyday "real life" as the figures she enacted. This allows us to understand the films' narratives as enactments of containment of a vivid femininity too large, as it were, to be delimited by film production itself. We thus also need to understand Divine as something other than an autonomous agent within Waters's films, because the films' positioning of her via their narratives is as important for Divine's outrageous status as her iconic and visual scare tactics. The demand that femininity disrupt the familial organization is witnessed by both the family unit's power to instigate perversion (i.e., nongenital, nonreproductive erotic pleasure) and the family's eventual downfall in light of its "monstrous" perverse progeny; this is the narrative of melodrama in its long history.

Perhaps the quarrel that Studlar and others have with the appearance of Divine is that Divine's attempts to evade the outlawing of her pleasure is handled through parodic means: Waters directs comedies, not melodramas. Or more to the point, he directs comedies *about* melodramas. *Female Trouble*—unlike, say, Max Ophuls's 1948 film *Letter from an Unknown Woman* (whose plot parallels *Female Trouble*'s almost uncannily)—aligns perversity with femininity not to justify or offer consolation about the ultimate ascension of patriarchy but to vivify the perverse pleasures that patriarchy ultimately seeks to punish.[16] Waters's insistence that he writes his screenplays with the intent of positioning his viewers to side with the perverse, the criminal, and the outlandish emblematizes the labor to reread these films for their affectively necessary labor as camp's labor.

Trashing Stardom (Part 2): "Stunt Casting"

After Divine's death in 1988 and with the gradual increase in his budgets (primarily from New Line Cinema), Waters's casting has expanded the trash star aesthetic within his subsequent films, pressing his feature films to tamper with the star image in ways perhaps impossible when working with the figures (Divine, Massey, Mueller, etc.) of his earlier efforts. The sense, though, that the figures from "celebrity culture" whom he has showcased (such as Patricia Hearst, Sonny Bono, Deborah Harry, Kathleen Turner, Melanie Griffith) are talent imported to the trash sensibility underestimates the important fact that the institution of stardom signals significant fluctuations in value attribution at any given moment.

If a director such as Waters, working from the "underside" of value, can make Divine a widely known commodity, the camp underpinnings of the trash aesthetic can also resituate popular stars for a debased consumption, from the "top down," so to speak.

Waters's statements about low culture becoming "just plain good" attest to the significant processes at work through which camp becomes, in his estimation, simply "American humor." Most commentators on Waters's work have addressed this through his use of star signification to promote the most likely of nonstars, Divine figuring as the supremely spectacular example of the reinvention of stardom within the trash aesthetic. Waters's stable of stars, christened early in his career the "Dreamland Players," in many ways emulated Andy Warhol's Factory, for the image of eccentrics and drag queens was vital to both. Warhol's stars and those of Waters's films differ, though, in one key way. Warhol and his "superstars" saw themselves as inhabiting an important venue for moving into Hollywood vehicles, whereas the Dreamland Players, with the possible exception of Divine, have maintained lives and jobs outside film production, only returning to the cameras when Waters asked them to.[17] As I have suggested in the previous chapter on Kenneth Anger's *Hollywood Babylon* writings, Hollywood stardom has long been accompanied by its own "suppressed" underside, for scandal and the pursuit of stars' secrets constitute industrially manufactured discourses about stardom; the casting of Waters's earliest films takes this fact in another direction, by seizing on those most marginalized by stardom (its "freakish" fans) and offering them as unique, dynamic screen presences, in short as stars themselves. This effect Waters has called "stunt casting."

The Dreamland Players who have sporadically continued to appear in Waters's films (Mink Stole, Mary Vivian Pearce, and Pat Moran) form only part of Waters's larger project to tamper with the ideal of the star. In a different strategy, Waters casts famous has-beens (Tab Hunter, Joe Dallesandro), stars from other media (Deborah Harry, Ric Ocasek), and people made stars by the media, heiress Patricia Hearst appearing as one of Waters's remarkable coups in situating a popular historical figure within his films. In this respect, Waters draws our attention to the difference between stars as a particular feature of Hollywood narrative film and the more expansive notion that stars are anyone who secures film, TV, and print representation; the distinction becomes more apparent when we contrast Greta Garbo and, say, Connie Chung. Waters draws non-Hollywood figures into his filmmaking enterprises to situate these figures within his narratives, where they offer variable readings of the films around their previous star incarnations.

In addition, they secure for Waters vehicles, in advance, free publicity via their notoriety and fan followings for other reasons. Patricia Hearst's appearances in *Cry Baby, Serial Mom,* and *Cecil B. Demented* remobilize fame from her 1974 trial as a member of the Symbionese Liberation Army and exploit her status as a cult subcultural figure. Hearst's dual appeal, as America's sweetheart and as an emblem of the potential "bad girl" who lurks beneath the exterior of ordinariness, was important within her actual trial, and Waters seizes on her tabloid notoriety (itself a form of trash stardom) for his films' publicity. At the same time, he positions Hearst ironically as bland and unassuming; in *Cry Baby* and *Cecil B. Demented* she plays a middle-aged suburban mother, and in *Serial Mom,* her role as "Juror Number 8" situates her as the white-shoe-wearing object of Beverly Sutphin's rage.[18]

The "stunt" casting of Hearst, along with Harry, Pia Zadora, Ruth Brown, and the female punk rock group L7, in small parts enables Waters to form an ensemble cast that is a mosaic of various subcultural attentions, enfolding within his cinematic output a variety of cultural and economic circuits and their accompanying fascinations with trash aesthetics. In his earlier low-budget efforts, Waters achieved this by casting anomalous figures, who were without such followings but could achieve them within the format of the underground film. Without recourse to the extratextual referencing of figures with greater "name-brand" recognition, Waters's use of outcast figures (like Edith Massey or Cookie Mueller) served to make them stars while seldom giving them access to other venues of the Hollywood film or television. In this respect, their star signature was limited to Dreamland productions. At the same time, there is a question as to whether the appearance of more widely known figures (like Hearst, Harry, or Bono) does limit their appearances elsewhere, and it is striking that these smaller roles have not led to subsequent ones, Bono's later election to the U.S. House of Representatives notwithstanding.

Waters's casting does shift in the course of his movement into making a more recognizably mainstream product, particularly in light of his pursuit of recognizable name talent, but such shifts leave us with the question of what "stunt casting" achieves in both the underground and mainstream moments of his career.[19] I would direct this question toward the fact that, within his films, Waters casts his performers/stars against

Stunt casting: Kathleen Turner in *Serial Mom*.

their type; in the language of commodity culture, he deliberately re-brands them in ways that might endanger the value of their celebrity signature. With regard to such "name-brand" talent, as stars they enact roles in contradistinction to their popular personae, but if they are Waters's local Baltimore talent, he makes a point of transforming them into figures of calculated ugliness. As Waters comments, "beauty is looks you can never forget. A face should jolt, not soothe."[20]

Continually, Waters questions what it means to be a star; as Renée R. Curry suggests, "A Waters film spectacularizes fame and stardom as key issues. What it takes to become a star, and who can become a star are the key interrogatives. Stardom has value. Stardom is costly."[21] Curry reads *Hairspray* as a decisive turn in Waters's career, for there Waters secures a larger budget to make a "slicker," more palatable vehicle for wider consumption. While employing actors whose names contain a particular signifying value certainly entails paying them more, it is not so much that stardom is costly but indeed that stardom can be rendered cheap. Cheap, in that stars such as Pia Zadora or Jerry Stiller (both in *Hairspray*) perhaps take risks with their reputations by appearing in a Waters vehicle, even as they are paid scale wages like those offered elsewhere within the industry. Further, the cheapening of stardom emerges in these films, as Waters has demonstrated from the beginning of his career, by emphasizing that stardom *as notoriety* is secured through advance publicity that guarantees that something "shocking" will occur around a well-known star's image, and this can be done with relatively spartan means.[22] There is a problem, though, in bracketing a vehicle like *Hairspray* apart from Waters's earlier work, for his films have concerned themselves with the question of "what it takes to become a star" even when they did so in comparatively impoverished circumstances.

Pink Flamingos, for example, offers as its central narrative problem the specter of stardom in the everyday, for its characters strive to own the rights to being the "filthiest people alive." Divine and her family compete with their nemeses Connie and Raymond Marble (Mink Stole and David Lochary) to prove themselves more degenerate, more having embraced the pursuit of moral corruption, than anyone else. Having held this trophy, as Waters notes, in the privacy of their own minds, they only "go public" by attempting to exceed any offensive deed that the Marbles might offer. The film plays out the logic of what it takes to become an antistar; rather than serving as examples of the wholesomeness, moral fiber, or appealing sexuality to which Hollywood's own star discourses lay claim, the stars of *Pink Flamingos* stake out a terrain of criminality and perversion that might equally hold the public's imagination.[23]

In this respect, Divine's later struggles with her star image combated a moment most powerfully tied to her notoriety: the closing shot of *Pink Flamingos* in which Divine eats dog feces. Waters insisted that this shot be offered as uninterrupted and has explained at length how the shot was achieved in real time without the use of visual effects; in short, he has showcased the restricted financial circumstances of his productions as a way of disrupting the ordinary circuits of publicity. This moment suggests one of Waters's most consistent practices of finding shock in the most mundane of details, for the moment's capacity to repel derives from the fact of our disgust with our own bodily presences: Pimples get squeezed (*Hairspray*), people sneeze into baby's faces (*Serial Mom*), and these events are disclosed in close-up. These films understand the power of our socialized physical selves as they fail to accede to the demands put on them, but they also understand the complex appeal of stars' physical and gestural embodiments. Thus their camp dimensions are framed by the actors' work-as-play, accompanying their waged labor, to debase the status of the value that might be extracted from their stardom. Although it seems inevitable to ask whether this work does not ultimately serve to expand the market value of such performances in the production of these figures as star commodities, the fact that these films produce a discomfort around the contradictions being staged through camp staging of value's confusions (often expressed in terms of laughter) suggests that they offer a critique of star culture largely unavailable within popular media more generally.

A significant element of this critique is its deliberate confusion of the varying registers of stardom. Kathleen Turner's appearance in *Serial Mom* commanded commentary within the popular press's anticipation of the film's release, the abiding question being one of how a major screen star might appear in a John Waters film. At stake was whether a Hollywood star, by which is meant a commodity associated with the particular habitus associated with consumption of the "mainstream product," could inhabit the ironic valences of stardom that Divine had so violently embodied. Yet the public version of such speculations took the form of whether Turner could in any way supplant Divine's lost potency to shock, and more to the point, the problem of Turner's appearance revolved around the fact that she is perceived, within the ageist logics of the star industries, as a middle-aged star, one perhaps past her prime. The film answered these queries by exploiting Turner's move out of younger roles and fixing her character as a symbol of middle-class niceness as psychosis.[24] The crystalline instance of this combination appears in the film's promotional shot of Turner as Beverly: hair neatly coiffed, dressed in a prim high-collared dress, smiling as she wields a gigantic pair of scissors.

The spectacle of aberrant casting within Waters's films, most notably after the appearance of *Polyester,* stages stardom as a wildly fluctuating commodity within the production of contemporary film, a commodity produced in the camp labor of stars. This arises from the nature of stardom currently, where a host of sources such as pop music, "real-life" courtroom dramas, and tabloid culture are actively fabricating stars of their own. Further, it is worth noting that Waters's impulse to cast out-of-fashion stars has only become more predominant in film and television, as we need only think of the resuscitation of John Travolta's career in Quentin Tarantino's *Pulp Fiction,* the role given to star O.J. witness Kato Kaelin on the syndicated television series *Baywatch,* or the more recent fascination with Richard Hatch, victor of the summer 2000 television success *Survivor.*

Conclusion: Return to Baltimore

This chapter began with one pronouncement from a character in a Waters film, so perhaps a conclusion might also end with one: after her capture by a terrorist film group in Waters's 2000 film release *Cecil B. Demented,* Honey Whitlock (Melanie Griffith) exclaims of her new status as a rogue actress, she is "beyond the critics' reach." We might extend her claim to the sphere of scholars, who have decided not to detect any counterknowledges available in the popular cinema, and one way of knowing such dismissals is the neglect of different social spaces that do differ, not least in their relation to the cultural centers of Los Angeles and New York. The continued insistence on making a place such as Baltimore a site of production becomes important in this theory of camp if it can be noticed to incorporate margins (not the singular "margin" so prized as the conceptual category into which is lumped any social practice that dispels the monopoly of capital on all forms of critical consciousness). If that metaphorical system can be allowed to stand, then it is in a margin that the center can be more clearly ascertained for the domains of production that are not singularly encompassed. Baltimore occupies the cultural imagination of Waters's films as much more than simply a place that is not the capital of either the east or west coasts, and it is in being defined through its negations (not at the center, not identified as the space of innovation) that the ideal of Baltimore becomes most vivid. Baltimore becomes, after its qualifications as everything it is not, a series of substitutions for those very features of contemporary social life that most other kinds of cultural commentary, not least cinema, have chosen to ignore or, when they choose to notice it, chastise.

The antagonism that *Cecil B. Demented* centers on is that between local filmmaking that insists on a camp vision of film as the model of cultural production on which to proceed (characters have the names of Fassbinder, Anger, and William Castle tattooed on them) and the sunny, fatuous local film commission that hopes to jump-start the metropolitan economy by becoming an outpost of Hollywood capital. In one scene, the group takes over a local cineplex and rousts the audience, and in other moments, they enjoin martial arts patrons and pornography aficionados to help them take on, respectively, suburban soccer moms and angry teamsters; and one would be pressed to remember a moment of recent popular film that so vividly showcased such forms of social antagonism. In the specificity of its Baltimore audiences, *Cecil B. Demented* emphasizes that film fandom remains a political commitment, and it is one marked by alliances that fail to be detected in the nomination of the ideological monolith "the audience."

Thus what Baltimore offers in lieu of all that appears as crucial to the epicenters of New York or Los Angeles is the breakdown of our expectations around where a critical stance about contemporary filmmaking might arise. The art critic Adam Gopnik has somewhat cynically, in another context, referred to this as "Sam Shepard Syndrome," where one has "the ability to get all the advantages of an insider while passing (or posing) as an outsider."[25] In part this would seem to situate Waters's capacity to address broader audiences through larger budgets and wider distribution as the most recent answer to a bourgeois audience's immense demand for shock. In this view, the appearance of Waters's vehicles outside urban showcases for independent and art cinema is taken as simply a symptom of Waters's "selling out" to the demands of Hollywood and its cineplex patrons. Darren Tofts comments that Waters himself has contributed to the manufacture of his work as administered culture. Since gaining notoriety with *Pink Flamingos,* he has regularly lectured on his films in American universities and colleges, and has been employed as a teacher in US jails, counselling inmates on the value of displacing criminal desires onto film.[26]

Rather than attending to the particular dynamics of Waters's films in relation to the current film industry, Tofts asserts Waters's figure as one who maintains the currency of an alternative filmmaker while going about the business of a consolidated culture industry. The larger problem for Tofts is that the director's work appears to resist critical analysis, for critical acts endanger potential transgression (not by Waters, but actually by the avant-garde) by becoming "anaesthetized by any number of elegantly turned theories." Such theories present the critic of trash with an either/or proposition:

> One can acknowledge its facticity and the need to address it critically, only to encounter the ideological problems that arise from this procedure; or one can participate in its neo-Dada attack on bourgeois morality and revel in its offensiveness, at the risk of appearing oppressive and apolitical. Trash culture is the most recent manifestation of an aesthetics of silence that baffles and defies the practice of criticism, for apart from the impossibility of describing it without domesticating it, it precludes what Rodolphe Gasche (with Mallarmé in mind) has referred to as the "decidability all criticism presupposes."[27]

For Tofts, the evaluative decisions have already been made in advance: either one recognizes the ideological "facts" of the appeal of Waters's latest films or one rejoins the avant-garde project and risks becoming "apolitical."

The larger, unexplored problem is that there really is no avant-garde cultural production remaining, *as we might wish to recuperate it,* despite the mordant recitations of blockbuster shows at the Museum of Modern Art or Christie's. This does not mean that there are no instances of film production interested in interrogating the claims of reactionary cultural politics or attempting to forge their own aesthetics, but that the model of the avant-garde, in which an autonomous domain of artistic production forges innovations in the name of a left politics, can say much about the fact of current cultural productions as they engage with the dynamics of production and distribution now available. Directors such as Waters (but others, too: Bruce La Bruce, and Chi Chi LaRue) encounter the conditions under which they might make film in a pronouncedly contentious economic sphere, where accusations of failure to approximate the avant-garde, underground, or neodada are of little help.

Waters's current status as a filmmaker is outlined by what Timothy Corrigan has termed the "commerce of auteurism." By recognizing the transformation of Hollywood cinema in light of shifting studio economics, the technologies of VCR and cable, and the sense of fragmentation among audiences, key figures within the American cinema (most prominently for Corrigan, Francis Coppola) have exploited the idea of the authored film in order to address new audience demands; their auteurist status, as a form of product differentiation, is firmly wedded to the marketing of commercial film vehicles.

> The expressionistic privileges of auteurism are directly related to financial actualities of investment and risk: an auteur earns his status by spending himself, and both gestures involve the aggrandizement, demeaning, and "expending" of oneself through a primary identification with the agency and exchange of money.[28]

For Corrigan, the power of the authored film as a marketing tool derives not only from the legacy of auteurism as the touchstone of an art cinema (useful for distinguishing a director such as Francis Coppola's products from other Hollywood fare) but even more significantly because other features for attracting audiences (genre, star iconography, cinema's seeming primacy as a mass medium) have diminished in the postclassical Hollywood, televisual (and now Internet-driven) moment.

Not coincidentally, Waters has allied himself with the very strategies of a commercial auteurism that Corrigan describes, but not always to the same effect; and by way of conclusion, I think it helpful to return to the initial theoretical claims of this book about camp to consider how camp's intellectual strategies redirect critical thought in the moment after the authorial voice has been troubled, on the one hand, by the exertions of poststructuralist theoretical commentary and, on the other, by emerging confusions about the meanings of intellectual property (most handily facilitated by the velocity of information movement on the World Wide Web). In fact, it becomes crucial to understand Waters as a figure for whom the commercially authored film has marked a limit of what audiences are willing to embrace. This can be detected in the fact that Waters's films, even the more widely distributed recent features, have failed to cross over to extensive television markets.[29]

Waters has frequently been named as a symbol of postmodernity, and the increased popularity of his vehicles is taken as proof of the abundance of multiple "alternative" ways of envisioning the world *and* a demonstration of how there seems little opportunity to identify an oppositional politics that circulate through popular media. The effect of postmodern cultural politics is said to be that of the center's feeding from the margins, incorporating a host of styles and sensibilities into the operations of corporatized production. And yet if Waters appears as an heir to Warhol and Anger, he has most clearly been identified not only within idealizations of the center of metropolitan culture (New York, Los Angeles) but also with a margin such as Baltimore.

Let us finish with an exemplary scholarly treatment that decides to read camp as the demise of left politics in the face of apparent corporate appropriations of differing visions. Barbara Klinger writes of the camp embrace of melodrama that "to the potent and pervasive sensibility of mass camp, the products of the Hollywood studio system have become ancient relics whose relevance to culture as anything more than amusing instances of outdated values and conventions has long since passed."[30] Klinger distinguishes between a subcultural camp tied to queer differ- ence and "mass camp," the dispersal of a general postmodern irony where mass culture texts (in the case of her project, the films of the Holly- wood studio films of Douglas Sirk) "could appear rather unintention- ally exaggerated and over-conventionalized," without questioning the potentially disruptive Brechtian features of such a moment of popu- lar production. Though there are shared continuities between the two phenomena, mass camp deflects critical attention away from the con- servative *and* radical meanings of mass cultural production.

This book inverts that reading of camp and wonders about how camp's own schema for examining capital's value codings has eclipsed more customary radical interpretations of cinema to the degree that it is only left critics who might dismiss the cultural politics of camp. I say this for two reasons: first, capital is if nothing else a political economy characterized by its dynamic circulation of commodities, and while we bear witness to its forms of exploitation on a daily basis, we also discover the movement of various enunciations into new sites of production and redissemination in ways that were impossible in the moment of classical Hollywood cinema. These new trajectories are not inherently radical in the orthodox Marxist sense, but neither are they reactionary simply for being imbedded in capital's circuits of exchange; if camp intellectual work accompanies the commodity on its path through the world, it can produce critique in unforeseen quarters. Second, there is now little reason to assume that queer politics are inherently radical in comparison to their nonqueer counterparts, so we are at least at the historical juncture where we need no longer tie camp's critical knowledges to solely one axis of sex/gender difference; here we discover that Waters's films carry less and less any sense of their politics emerging from queer subcultures. (This is not the same as saying, as Sontag does, that camp is "disengaged, depoliticized—or at least apolitical.") While Corrigan's assessment of the traffic in auteurs speaks of a particular register of contemporary film production, he is also describing the conditions under which films are made and marketed, and the situation that camp intellectual work must navigate. Waters has commented that "the only way I could do terrorism at this point in my career would be to make a Hollywood movie that would reach every person—and make them crazy."[31] This, understandably, remains his career's still unrealized project.

AFTERWORD

This book began with the assertion that camp forms a critique of capital's assertions of value, a critique that arises historically in the context of queer male subcultures of the post–World War II metropolitan United States and can be accessed through the examples of cinematic production examined in the foregoing chapters. With the fuller blossoming of gay and lesbian political movements in American social life during the past thirty years, we might now ask whether such critical energies characterize the social consciousness produced by the more publicly articulated forms of identity politics by queer men in the post-Stonewall era. With the ascendancy of visibility as a criteria for the production of such subject identities, it becomes apparent that camp is perhaps less contiguous with such queer subcultural formations than it was at one point. If camp seems less a hallmark of queer consciousness in the present moment, though, it of course should be remembered that camp was never an inevitable set of strategies produced by male same-sex desire but was quite specific to the urban constellation of intellectuals who were responsible for its flourishing. Its languages and fascinations were, like any instance of cultural production, particular to its own historical moment. This book, then, both through its historical attentions and through its theoretical claims, has attempted to give greater specificity to camp as a form of queer intellectual production in the latter half of the twentieth century.

Grounded as most of the claims of this book are in the sense that the political economies and social practices of capital make incommensurate demands on its subjects, felt most acutely in the dual compulsions to labor on value's behalf and to conceal oneself from a larger arena of public signification as queer, to wonder about the current status and future of camp is to consider how the configurations of capital in the present moment are, in the fullest sense of the word, represented. Keeping in mind Marx's frustration in ascertaining that most empty of signs, "value," the era bears witness to a transnational capital predicated on money increasingly as an informational mode of exchange, and the difficulty of "seeing" capital through its variable attributions of value becomes all the more vexing for its subjects. In this regard, camp seems all the more pressing as a manifestation of contrary demands to the sunny prognostications of a cultural life apparently entirely at the behest of the fully saturating market economy. Camp's capacity to produce knowledge of the absurdities of capital's fluctuating designations of value is all the more pressing for those whose livelihoods demand a critique of the political economy that now engulfs us, but the gay male populace may not be intellectuals who need it; Susan Sontag's comment about somebody needing to invent camp if homosexuals had not done so takes on new meanings thirty-five years after her initial assertion. Increasingly it becomes evident that gay male subcultures are not the place to seek such insights, or more generously we might say that they are not the *only* place to discover camp at work now. One measure of the depletion of gay male political culture has emerged in the tendency of same-sex political movements in the past few decades toward an increasingly banal discourse of human property rights, as the relatively affluent gay male (and lesbian) urban sector goes about their business of making or acquiring children, becoming fascinated with the gyrations of property value, and consuming the most sentimental proclamations of celebrity culture seldom without giving a sense of the contradictions at hand. In this light, such political alliances seem unhelpfully to reveal themselves as class formations first and citizens of an impoverished critical capacity second.

Hardly satisfying, though, is a shortsighted decision that such middle-class, mostly white gay men are responsible for an enfeebled critical imagination in the face of capital's reorganized forces, now branded in so much corporatized culture as "globalization" and "interconnectivity." Nor does it help to remark that the expanded public sphere of "sexual politics" means that the conditions for camp intellectual production have changed so profoundly as not to mean that sexual subjects might forge a critical capacity for understanding value's wild career, at least, not in the secretiveness and jeopardy that characterized prior historical moments. Be that as it may, even the social formations that have given rise to the expression of sex/gender difference as so much glossy consumption find themselves reaching a point of exhaustion. And camp so seldom, in what Andrew Ross calls its "creamy wit," seems to be about exhaustion, but is about the renewal of intellectual capacity. Too facile is the insight that the new consumer possibilities of Rainbow Visa cards and the active recruitment of brand-name vodka drinking as an expression of gay "pride" come at the cost of camp's ferocious delights—but only just *a bit* too facile.

It would thus seem to be an even worse act of intellectual bad taste, worse than my initial demand that we take camp seriously, to gesture at this book's conclusion to further intellectual work on the topic by commemorating queer camp's death. Does camp still matter? Perhaps two instances of recent cinema can guide us to an answer here, Derek Jarman's *Blue* (1993) and Sam Mendes's *American Beauty* (1999). The last film of Jarman's career, *Blue* is arguably the campiest film ever made. At once minimal and lavish, *Blue* comprises a solid field of intense blue and a sound track filled with the voice of the ill Jarman, who recounts the struggle to make art in the face of an imminent death. *Blue* is a film about the labor of making film despite the director's loss of energy, an energy he had given so abundantly in such efforts as *Sebastiane, Caravaggio,* and *Queer Edward.* In those films, Jarman extracted the homoerotic underpinnings of each of his subject's lives and grounded them in visual styles gathered from European painting and beefcake physique magazines of the 1950s and 1960s; in *Blue,* by contrast, spectators discover the film frame as an instance of extravagant sparingness in the film's expression of the lush pleasures of the chromatic. As one sits in attendance of Jarman's voice, recording the small and large setbacks of AIDS's attack on his body and consciousness, the point of his decision not to attempt to shape the screen beyond its color saturation drives home the absence of his labor, as a queer man, to go any further with the project of cinema.

I offer Jarman's film to direct the present argument about camp to more recent moments in the production of cinema and to a discussion of film's relation to the current state of gay identity politics. It seems that the function of film as a form of queer labor is altered when, as is the case of the past three decades, the relation of dissident sexualities to the dynamics of profit is changed in light of the claims of gay and lesbian as public nominations of sex/gender difference. The circumstances under which queer male camp arose as a way of producing critical awareness of capital, however, abide to the degree that we discover how both dominant and alternative cinemas are tied to the dissemination of still frequently homogenized forms of film. While the appeal of an independent cinema would seem to showcase how other forms of financing are made possible for the realization of images of gay and lesbian life under modernity by their capacity to mobilize audiences for such nondirectly Hollywood fare, it does not seem that the appearance of queer-themed cinema (in the instances of, for example, *Jeffrey* or *Go Fish*) entirely undoes the historical predications of camp. While conditions of subjectivity and the movement of capital unfortunately do not seem to have abated and indeed have become more intense, the manner in which queer subjectivities articulate themselves can steer us to think of other camps that arise in the face of modernity. I would suggest that camp has not disappeared so much as it has migrated to new venues, and the current state of gay and lesbian identity politics might help to explain why.

The tension between camp as a mode of critical thought and the insistence on a regime of positive, happy images of the "gay lifestyle" adheres to the present moment, with the resulting effect that, if this book's arguments help to understand sexuality in the age of profit, they might be extended to the possibility of camp in other cultural formations such as adolescent 'zine productions or black queer culture. Camp thus might sustain the sense that the domain of cultural production and consumption now more than ever is crosshatched by the conditions of subjectivity as they are informed by not only sexuality but also race and ethnicity, age, gender, and locale. Without queer difference attached to it, camp might also, of course, now take the form of another form of product differentiation, most unnervingly in its appeal to a niche market that wants to claim camp as its own—affluent, urban, mostly white gay men.

Be that as it may, even the productive formations that have given rise to the expression of sex/gender difference as, at least in the *Advocate*'s vision of the world, a vision of upscale consumption (this in the face of AIDS's ongoing grim march through the world) find themselves renewed through camp—only in new and unexpected forms. In *American Beauty,* gay male director Sam Mendes plays out an identifiable set of associations around male homoerotics, where the inability to act on libidinal desire forces into motion the hardly unexpected equation of male same-sex desire with fascism. Neighboring military father Frank Fittes (Chris Cooper) emerges in the film as a customarily closeted homosexual, but not only: his most treasured possession appears to be a piece of Nazi culture, a plate with a swastika embedded in its glaze. Spurned by the protagonist of the film, Lester Burnham (Kevin Spacey), Fittes becomes the film's emblem of unhealthy repression and eventually murders the object of his attraction, fulfilling the liberal sentiment that sexuality must always be expressed, lest it undo familial suburban order. In this regard, *American Beauty* can serve as an instance of the failure of queer male camp to appear in the production of dominant cinema as a product attached to the proper name of an out gay director, and here it should be noted that part of the publicity around the film stemmed from an excitement at the idea that gay men (director Mendes and writer Alan Ball) were largely responsible for crafting such an apparently benevolent vision of the possibilities of straight white suburban life in the United States. If *Blue* demonstrated how camp's critical energies might engage with death, Mendes's film seemed to satisfy audiences who needed to have repressed male homosexuality become, in an astonishing paradoxical fulfillment of Kenneth Anger's vision of American social life, the emblem of death itself, even as gay men were responsible for this articulation. The fact of the cheerful gay male couple (played by Scott Bakula and Sam Robards) who appear momentarily in the film is meant to ward off any condemnation of *American Beauty* as homophobic; this despite the fact that the film finds nothing comic about the gay men's distribution of a hospitality basket to their new Marine-family neighbors, a scene that seems to beg for the directorial hand of John Waters. Nor does the film's status as the product of a gay auteurship help to explain the film's shortcomings in its representation of Lester Burnham's wife, Caroline (Annette Benning), who figures mostly as a shrill, driven harpy responsible for the anger and silence that surround this particular family.

I would argue, though, that *American Beauty* offers a remarkable instance of another kind of camp, beheld not in terms of the film's fascination with male homoeroticism but around the experiences of its adolescent characters. We discover Ricky Fittes (Wes Bentley), son of the aforementioned Marine dad, furtively videotaping the neighborhood's activities and watching these tapes in unapologetically voyeuristic rapture. Ricky's embrace of the new forms of digital visual and acoustic technologies to discover and to produce a videographic vision of the mundane world in which he lives inhabits the camp critical position in ways that seem to respond to Andy Warhol's call to resee through high-tech media the world—of social life, of material things, of boredom, of sexuality in what are to me vitalizing ways. In a key scene, Ricky shows a videotape of "the most beautiful thing I've ever filmed" to his new girlfriend Janie (Thora Burch), and in a piece of videography worthy of Warhol's *Empire,* we watch a disposable plastic supermarket bag as it floats languorously in the wind before an anonymous brick wall. Taping this bag, Ricky tells Janie, allows him to understand that there is an "entire life behind things," a life that allows him to endure the suburban challenges that surround him.

The status of video here in relation to film opens new avenues for considering how dissident subjects find their way into modes of representation that seem prohibited to them, and the use of relatively inexpensive video technology in the domain of Hollywood cinema tells of the possibilities of forms of camp that now find themselves in new social and technological settings. Although it is tempting to see video within the context of *American Beauty* as reenacting some of the more pernicious and rear-guard habits of dominant cinema—such as Ricky's insistence on recording Janie's body in a series of voyeuristic moments— worth remembering too is that Janie videotapes the nude Ricky in his bedroom and makes a visual record of his erotic presence that comes as unexpected within the more habitual embodiment of male subjects in the media of moving imagery. More to the point that this book makes about camp, as an emphasis on the contradictory tendencies toward efficiencies of film production that seldom turn out to be very efficient at all, there is a lingering question about the function of Ricky's videotapes: Adolescents can secret themselves away from profit and familial niceness momentarily, not circulating their productions and enjoying the private spaces of sexuality and representation made in tension with the noise of adult life.

Perhaps, then, camp as a form of knowledge through cinema about capital's strange and unreasonable forms of value no longer applies in the present moment, and the intellectuals whom this book addresses will soon become ciphers of a lost world of urban queer male life that will be unrecognizable, even to gay men who feel some affinity for Vincente Minnelli, Andy Warhol, Kenneth Anger, and John Waters. Such is the effect of history. Nevertheless, we are probably not at so great a distance from the predicaments of these men that we might turn our backs on the lessons they offer through their cinema, not only lessons about the challenges of production in the industrial age and of moving through the social world that has found great energy in condemning queer sexuality, but lessons that give back to us the pleasures of work that the world of capital so insistently forecloses from us in large and small ways each day.

NOTES

Introduction

1 Scholarly and popular treatments of camp have expanded, especially in the past decade, such that the topic now entails discussions of cultural politics; sexuality and gender; feminism; gay, lesbian, and queer studies; subcultures; and film and media studies. The critical literature on the subject (commencing with Susan Sontag's "Notes on 'Camp',", and extending more recently to Andrew Ross's "The Uses of Camp" and the contributors to *The Poetics and Politics of Camp*) treats camp as a form of reception by queer subjects, and in this regard this book extends and inverts their insights to see how, as Marx argued, consumption and production are imbricated and coextensive. In that regard, this book builds on their insights by displacing the critical and theoretical implications of camp to considering, in its many senses, camp's productive possibilities. See Susan Sontag, "Notes on 'Camp,'" *Partisan Review* 31, no. 4 (fall 1964): 530; Andrew Ross, "The Uses of Camp," in *No Respect: Intellectuals and Popular Culture* (London: Routledge, 1989); and Moe Meyer, ed., *The Politics and Poetics of Camp* (London: Routledge, 1994). Fortunately, for the reader eager to see the varieties of commentary sponsored by camp, the subject has blossomed as a site of inquiry to the extent that an anthology might now appear; see Fabio Cleto, ed., *Camp: Queer Aesthetics and the Performing Subject: A Reader* (Edinburgh: Edinburgh University Press, 1999). I would in particular direct the reader to Cleto's introduction, which gives a sufficient overview of the field's dimensions.

2 The quote in the section title is from Timothy Credle, http://www.defycategory.com, an excellent example of camp intellectual work on the World Wide Web.

3 For a splendid account of homophobic historical conditions under which the forms of camp that this book examines appeared, see Robert J. Corber, *Homosexuality in Cold War America: Resistance and the Crisis of Masculinity* (Durham, N.C.: Duke University Press, 1997).

4 Karl Marx, *The Grundrisse,* ed. and trans. David McLellan (New York: Harper and Row, 1972), 35.

5 Karl Marx, *Capital,* Vol. 1, trans. Ben Fowkes (London: Penguin, 1976) p. 106.

6   Marx, *Capital,* vol. 1, p. 171.

7   For example, see the elegant work of Andreas Huyssen in *After the Great Divide: Modernism, Mass Culture, Postmodernism* (Bloomington: Indiana University Press, 1986); and Peter Bürger, *Theory of the Avant-Garde,* trans. Michael Shaw (Minneapolis: University of Minnesota Press, 1984).

8   Marx, *The Grundrisse,* 104.

9   Hannah Arendt, *The Human Condition* (Chicago: University of Chicago Press, 1958), 128.

10   Max Horkheimer and Theodor W. Adorno, *Dialectic of Enlightenment* (New York: Continuum Publishing, 1972), 131.

11   Horkheimer and Adorno, 135.

12   Horkheimer and Adorno, 131.

13   Clement Greenberg, "Avant-Garde and Kitsch," in *Mass Culture: The Popular Arts in America,* ed. Bernard Rosenberg and Daniel Manning White (New York: Free Press, 1957), 102.

14   See Pierre Bourdieu, *Distinction: A Social Critique of the Judgement of Taste* (London: Routledge, 1979); and Herbert J. Gans, *Popular Culture and High Culture: An Analysis and Evaluation of Taste* (New York: Basic Books, 1974).

15   The work of Stanley Fish on interpretive communities, or Hans Robert Jauss's conception of the viewer's "horizon of interpretation," and also the bulk of feminist psychoanalytic treatment of cinema take as their starting point the problem of *not* being synthesized by the address of the text. See Stanley Fish, *Is There a Text in This Class? The Authority of Interpretive Communities* (Cambridge: Harvard University Press, 1980); and Hans Robert Jauss, *Toward an Aesthetic of Reception,* trans. Timothy Bahti (Minneapolis: University of Minnesota Press, 1982).

16   Clement Greenberg, "Avant-Garde and Kitsch," in *Art and Culture: Critical Essays* (Boston: Beacon Press, 1989), 3.

17   Several commentators have noticed that homosexuality has frequently within Sontag's work become the symptom, but not the determination, of several features of modernity. D. A. Miller critiques Sontag's *AIDS and Its Metaphors* for rendering gay men as coincidental to the health crisis, for gays become simply another metaphor for the disease's effects. Marcie Frank reads Sontag's essay "Fascinating Fascism" as an exercise that repeats the rhetorical strategy of "Notes on 'Camp'" by eventually treating the stylistics of homosexuality as the ultimate expression of certain cultural tendencies, in this case the fetishization of Nazi paraphernalia in gay s/m. For both Miller and Frank, Sontag's writing preserves her critical stance by sanctioning a distance from the very objects of her analysis, gay men and same-sex subcultures. See D. A. Miller, "Sontag's Urbanity," *October* 49 (1989): 91–101; and Marcie Frank, "The Critic as Performance Artist: Susan Sontag's Writing and Gay Cultures," in *Camp Grounds: Style and Homosexuality,* ed. David Bergman (Amherst: University of Massachusetts Press, 1993), 173–84.

18   Sontag, "Notes on 'Camp,'" 118.

19 Vivian Gornick, "It's a Queer Hand That Stokes the Campfire," *Village Voice,* 7 April 1966, 1.

20 Sontag, "Notes on 'Camp,'" 530.

21 Paula Graham, "Girl's Camp? The Politics of Parody," in *Immortal, Invisible: Lesbians and the Moving Image,* ed. Tamsin Wilton (London: Routledge, 1995), 163.

22 See, for example, Linda Mizejewski, "Camp among the Swastikas: Isherwood, Sally Bowles, and 'Good Heter Stuff,'" in Cleto, *Camp;* and Pamela Robertson, *Guilty Pleasures: Feminist Camp from Mae West to Madonna* (Durham, N.C.: Duke University Press, 1996).

23 John Chase, *Exterior Decoration: Hollywood's Inside-Out Houses* (Los Angeles: Hennessey and Ingalls, 1982).

24 These conversions from modest bungalow to suburban Petit Trianon and culvert-side Roman villa were so often achieved with the use of unconventional materials—a lot of less-than-durable styrofoam and plasterboard was wielded, the California climate being more forgiving than the weather in most other places. Chase's account suggests that postmodernity in domestic architecture was born not in the stylings of Charles Jencks or Michael Graves three decades later but by these largely anonymous do-it-yourself home renovators.

25 Karl Marx, "Economic and Philosophic Manuscripts of 1844," in *The Marx-Engels Reader,* ed. Robert C. Tucker (New York: W. W. Norton, 1978), 114.

26 Gayatri Chakravorty Spivak, "Scattered Speculations on the Question of Value," in *In Other Worlds: Essays on Cultural Politics* (New York: Routledge, 1988), 160.

ONE *Working like a Homosexual: Vincente Minnelli
in the Metro-Goldwyn-Mayer Freed Unit*

1 Interviews with Lela Simone (the source of the chapter epigraph) conducted by Rudy Behlmer for the Academy of Motion Picture Arts and Sciences Oral History Project. These conversations took place by phone over a period of several months during 1990 and 1991 and were taped by Behlmer and transcribed by Barbara Hall, the Academy's oral historian.

2 See Judith Mayne, *Directed by Dorothy Arzner* (Bloomington: Indiana University Press, 1994), for a theoretical treatment of lesbian auterism and Patrick McGilligan, *George Cukor: A Double Life* (New York: St. Martin's Press, 1991), for a more popular account of a queer male director's labor within studio production. We should note that important work in the field of queer studies has emphasized the processes of reception by queers; the emphasis in Mayne and McGilligan is on the dynamics of production and the role that queers have played within that domain of commodity culture. Further, despite our best intentions, we might remember that, as Marx argues, every moment of production is simultaneously one of consumption, and attempts to exclude one from the other are frequently simplifications of the workings of commodity circulation. I argue, indeed, that the importing of a camp sensibility by queer

laborers to Hollywood figures as one of those nexus moments of which Marx speaks. See Karl Marx, "Production Is at the Same Time Also Consumption," in *The Grundrisse,* trans. David McLellan (New York: Harper and Row, 1961), 23.

3 This does not mean that the conditions under which the employees in the Freed unit operated were exempt from the customary divisions of labor, but that among them queer workers managed to produce the films with a camp dimension to their visual and acoustic elements. For an account of the ways that the studios organized their labor pools in this period and the corresponding labor cultures, see Danae Clark, *Negotiating Hollywood: The Cultural Politics of Actors' Labor* (Minneapolis: University of Minnesota Press, 1995).

4 Thomas Schatz, *The Genius of the System: Hollywood Filmmaking in the Studio Era* (New York: Pantheon Books, 1988), 440–62.

5 Hugh Fordin, *The Movies' Greatest Musicals: Produced in Hollywood USA by the Freed Unit* (New York: Frederick Ungar, 1975), 3. Worth noting is that Freed befriended Roger Edens at MGM early in the 1930s, both men playing roles in the development of Judy Garland's stardom. Freed at that time was a lyricist, and Edens was a piano accompanist and vocal arranger.

6 For an expansive history of the Hollywood film musical form that offers a context for understanding Freed's career in the industry, see *Lullabies of Hollywood: Movie Music and the Movie Musical, 1915–1992* (New York: McFarland, 1993). A treatment of the relation of queer men to the production of the Broadway musical of the 1930s can be found in Leonard Leff, " 'Come On Home with Me': 42nd Street and the Gay Male World 1930s," *Cinema Journal* 39, no. 1 (fall 1999): 3–22.

7 Joseph Andrew Caspar, *Stanley Donen* (Metuchen, N.J.: Scarecrow Press, 1983), 47.

8 Quoted in Fordin, *The Movies' Greatest Musicals,* 119.

9 Janet Staiger, "The Package-Unit System: Unit Management after 1955," in *The Classical Hollywood Cinema: Film Style and Mode of Production to 1960,* by David Bordwell, Janet Staiger, and Kristin Thompson (New York: Columbia University Press, 1985), 330.

10 Jane Feuer, *The Hollywood Musical,* 2d ed. (London: BFI Books, 1993), 141.

11 A fascinating document through which Metro's finances can partially be traced is a ledger commissioned by E. G. Mannix in the early 1960s that shows, from the studio's earliest years, the breakdown of each film's cost, domestic and international grosses, and final profit. The ledger is subdivided by year, so one can chronologically trace the studio's investments, and each year through the mid-1950s, the costs for the Freed-produced films far exceed those of other Metro-Goldwyn-Mayer films, usually by a factor of at least two. This continues to be true through the L. B. Mayer–Dory Schary transition.

12 James Naremore, *The Films of Vincente Minnelli* (Cambridge: Cambridge University Press, 1993), 3.

13 Naremore, 149.

14 It is also worth noting that Minnelli would claim in 1974, well after Susan Son-

tag's comments about the matter, that *The Pirate* "was great camp, an element that hadn't been intentionally used in films." See Vincente Minnelli and Hector Acre, *I Remember It Well* (Garden City, N.Y.: Doubleday, 1974), 164.

15 For a glimpse of the more private dimensions of these men's lives in Hollywood, see Jean Howard, *Hollywood: A Photo Memoir* (New York: Harry N. Abrams, 1989). Howard, the wife of agent Charles K. Feldman, was a highly accomplished amateur photographer who documented Hollywood's parties in the 1940s and 1950s, and large parts of her book form a kind of "family album" of the Freed unit's talent, portraying Minnelli, Garland, Edens, and Porter at play.

16 George Feltenstein, senior vice president and general manager of Metro Goldwyn Mayer/United Artists Home Video, interview by the author, 12 October 1993. Feltenstein was one of the producers of Metro-Goldwyn-Mayer's 1994 release *That's Entertainment III* and had interviewed for that film most of the still-living Metro-Goldwyn-Mayer Freed talent. I am grateful to him for his time, insights, and humor on the subject of Freed's queer talent during the period I am discussing.

17 However, it was something of a boost to my energies to have the queer dimensions of these figures affirmed by no less than a vice president of Metro-Goldwyn-Mayer himself.

18 Indeed, the decision to isolate a given figure as an auteur within the studio mode of production is itself problematic, as such a move can almost entirely disallow for collaborative labor among all laborers.

19 Karl Marx, *Capital,* vol. 1, trans. Ben Fowkes (London: Penguin, 1976), 72.

20 Eve Kosofsky Sedgwick, *The Epistemology of the Closet* (Berkeley: University of California Press, 1990), 154.

21 Of course, Marx was being somewhat coy in asserting that the commodity is "a very queer thing, abounding in metaphysical subtleties and theological niceties." For Marx, the task of critique is to strip the commodity of its queerness and its spiritual pretensions to understand its material fixedness. See *Capital,* vol. 1, p. 76.

22 No small paradox that some municipalities in Australia and Europe now seek to capture the earnings of queer subjects in so-called pink-money neighborhoods, where queers are encouraged to buy houses and settle. The labor of queers in domesticity is now acknowledged to be vital for the expansion of property value.

23 Susan Sontag, "On Style," in *A Susan Sontag Reader* (New York: Viking, 1983), 141.

24 David Shipman, *Judy Garland* (London: Fourth Estate Press, 1992). Shipman comments in the introduction: "The most contentious matters in most biographies are the sexual ones, and I can only say that of all the people I spoke to who knew Garland and Vincente Minnelli only one did not take it for granted that I already knew of Minnelli's homosexuality" (xi).

25 For example, classical Hollywood film melodramas deserve much greater critical treatment in terms of the roles of different forms of femininity in the ideological networks of domesticity; African American femininity, for example,

functions as a form of affective labor in domesticity and child rearing and as such enables white working-class and bourgeois femininity. An important contribution to this question is Lauren Berlant's "National Brands/National Body: *Imitation of Life*," in *Comparative American Identities: Race, Sex, and Nationality in the Modern Text*, ed. Hortense Spillers (New York: Routledge, 1991).

26 Richard Dyer, "Entertainment and Utopia," in *The Cultural Studies Reader*, ed. Simon During, 2d ed. (London: Routledge, 1999), 381.

27 Audience preview cards from screening held at Academy Theater in Pasadena, California, on 10 October 1947. Although these cards record the number of viewers whose opinions were solicited (in this case, 150), they do not convey whether this is the entire audience, or the conditions under which audience responses were solicited, such as whether there were two screenings, trailers, cartoons, and so forth. In most cases the responses were typed in all capital letters and mimeographed for studio executives. Audience preview cards in the Arthur Freed files on *The Pirate* at the University of Southern California Metro-Goldwyn-Mayer archives.

28 Rick Altman, *The American Film Musical* (Bloomington: Indiana University Press, 1987), 5.

29 In his account of the films of Busby Berkeley, Martin Rubin argues that the narrative-number tension cannot be resolved, even through what seems a high degree of integration, inasmuch as the tension defines the musical form. Rubin comments that "nonintegration—a built-in and formalized resistance to the ultimate homogeneity or hierarchy of discourse—is essential to the musical genre, which is based precisely on a shifting and volatile dialectic between integrative and nonintegrative elements. Viewed in this way, the history of the musical becomes not so much a relentless, uni-directional drive toward effacing the last stubborn remnants of nonintegration, but a succession of different ways of articulating the tension between integrative (largely narrative) and non-integrative (chiefly spectacle) elements." See Martin Rubin, *Showstoppers: Busby Berkeley and the Tradition of the Spectacle* (New York: Columbia University Press, 1993), 12.

30 It is striking that the MPAA censoring of the Freed productions occurred in terms of innuendo around the heterosexual narrative while the camp visual codes went unnoticed. The MPAA files on Freed films reveal the gaze of the Breen office to have been keen to the games that Cole Porter, Betty Comden, and Adolph Green played with their song lyrics and scripts around male-female bonding. In excess of what MPAA readers could detect as licentious were the visual codes of art direction, where at the level of content there seems little room to note the presence of queer production. In this context, Minnelli's history in Hollywood is striking, given his reputation as a director who devoted much of his energy to art direction and the mise-en-scène. See MPAA files on *The Pirate* at the Academy of Motion Picture Arts and Sciences Margaret Herrick Library, Los Angeles, Calif.

31 Naremore, 28.

32 *Film Quarterly* 12, no. 2 (winter 1958): 21.

33 Stephen Harvey, *Directed by Vincent Minnelli* (New York: Harper and Row, 1989), 57.

34 MGM was capitalizing on the fact that it owned the cinematic use of the name of Ziegfeld and had already successfully cast Powell as Ziegfeld in its 1936 biopic *The Great Ziegfeld.*

35 According to Hugh Fordin, *Ziegfeld Follies* was conceived at the outset as a showcase for Metro talent and a commemorative film for the studio's twentieth anniversary in 1944. Holdups in the production and the deletion and addition of various numbers held up the film's release until 1946. See Fordin, 140.

36 The emergence of marginal identities and sensibilities within the wartime revue musical can be witnessed elsewhere in *Star Spangled Rhythm* (1942) and *Stage Door Canteen* (1943).

37 Garson's position as a target for Minnelli's mockery was no accident: the number was originally conceived as a way for audiences to see Garson, the star of numerous somber biopics and melodramas, as having a lighter, playful side. When courted to do the number by Freed and Minnelli, Garson displayed a marked humorlessness and abruptly refused. It was then offered to Garland, who apparently took relish in lampooning her primary rival as the studio's most important female star. See Hugh Fordin's account of the production of *Ziegfeld Follies.*

38 Garland's relation to queers would continue until her death. Although the labor of documenting and analyzing queer fan relations to Garland has shed light on the fascination of queer fans with the Garland star persona, little work has been devoted to the depiction of her with the men who surround her, a relation that begins with Ray Bolger, Jack Haley, and Bert Lahr in *The Wizard of Oz* (1939). For example, one of Garland's signature numbers, "Get Happy," from *Summer Stock* (1950), dresses her in suit jacket and fedora, hair tugged cleanly up into a butch chignon. There she temporarily becomes one of the "boys in the band," while simultaneously maintaining herself as a figure of feminine seduction for the audience through the emphasis on her high heels and bared legs. Even in *A Star Is Born* (1954) Garland is staged as most "naturally" herself when relaxing with the men in the musical combo in the "Man That Got Away" sequence.

39 Harvey, 62.

40 Peter N. Chumo reads Kelly's performance in the subsequent setting of *Singin' in the Rain* as a venue where "dance and physical flexibility become metaphors for generic flexibility, [and] the ability to move along different forms of entertainment and survive Hollywood's transition to talkies." We might read Astaire's and Kelly's performance in "The Babbitt and the Bromide" as exerting a similar flexibility to import queer signification to the form. See Peter N. Chumo II, "Dance, Flexibility, and the Renewal of Genre in Singin' in the Rain." *Cinema Journal* 36, no. 1, (fall 1996): 39–54.

41 Ed Lowry, "Cinema Texas Program Notes: *Yolanda and the Thief,*" 12, no. 4 (1978): 64.

42 Here camp takes up one of its more pernicious forms, trafficking in the stereotypical and racist imagery of the period.

43 Lowry, "Cinema Texas Program Notes," 64.

44 Interestingly, this ensemble was noted within popular critical appraisal of the film's fashions: "Astaire's most attractive outfit was a pair of eggshell pajamas with oversized collar and huge frogs," claims the reviewer in a column titled "New Astaire Film Introduces Unusual Styles by Yolanda." Unfortunately, the source for the article, other than a byline for a Harriet Wilbur, is not included in Freed's files, although the notation that the clipping comes from "Irene Scrapbook" suggests that *Yolanda and the Thief*'s costumer is the source for circulating the review within the studio.

45 Steven Cohan, " 'Feminizing' the Song-and-Dance Man," in *Screening the Male: Exploring Masculinities in Hollywood Cinema,* ed. Steven Cohan and Ina Rae Hark (New York: Routledge, 1993), 47.

46 The problem of how we describe Astaire's apparent femininity, what might more usually be termed effeminacy, within the heterosexual narrative stems from the codes of effeminacy as being connotative, not denotative, of male homosexuality. Like camp, effeminacy serves as a baffle or barrier to locating any "real" or "actual" homosexual while also offering to others within queer subcultures the opportunity to wonder about a "fellow traveler." See Alan Sinfield, *The Wilde Century: Effeminacy, Oscar Wilde, and the Queer Moment* (New York: Columbia University Press, 1994), for a discussion of the history whereby the connotative codes of effeminacy came to signify queerness in urban subcultures.

47 See, for example, Christopher Finch, *Rainbow: The Stormy Life of Judy Garland* (New York: Grosset and Dunlap, 1975).

48 Vincente Minnelli, with Hector Acre, *I Remember It Well,* (Garden City, N.Y.: Doubleday, 1974), 164.

49 Naremore, 44.

50 Harvey, 91.

51 Cole Porter's songs for the film were full of camp sexual innuendo in their initial versions and had to be rewritten to meet the demands of the Breen office, as can be witnessed in lyrics for "Mack the Black":

> Mococo the Pirate / The fierce and the irate
> He knows his worthy men / He pays them with glamor
> And leaves them their grammar / The why's and whatfor's and when's
> He keeps them in humor / And feeds them with rumor
> Mococo loves his men!

Contained in studio correspondence dated 2 April 1947, MGM files, USC.

52 Richard Dyer, *Heavenly Bodies: Film Stars and Society* (New York: St. Martin's Press: 1986), 185–86.

53 *Yolanda and the Thief* cost $2,444,000 and lost $1,644,000; *Ziegfeld Follies* was more lucrative for the studio, budgeting out at $3,403,000 and only losing

$269,000. All figures from the E. J. Mannix ledger at the Academy of Motion Picture Arts and Sciences Margaret Herrick Library.

TWO *Andy Warhol and the Crises of Value's Appearances*

1   J. Hoberman has perhaps said this more succinctly: "[Warhol] made movies that didn't have to be seen to make themselves felt." See J. Hoberman, "Bon Voyeur: Andy Warhol's Silver Screen," in *Vulgar Modernism: Writing on Movies and Other Media* (Philadelphia, P.A.: Temple University Press, 1991), 180.

2   The bulk of Warhol's experiments in moving images was in film, but he also turned his attentions to the nascent form of consumer video. Here I attend to the films largely because they coincide with the moment of camp's migration from queer subcultures to the larger landscape of mass-cultural forms. Another important project remains in the trajectory of video in Warhol's oeuvre in the 1970s and 1980s.

3   David James, "The Producer as Author," in *Andy Warhol: Film Factory* (London: BFI, 1990), 136.

4   Hans Magnus Enzensberger, "Constituents of a Theory of Media," in *Electronic Culture: Technology and Visual Representation,* ed. Timothy Druckrey (New York: Aperture Foundation Books, 1996), 64.

5   Thomas Waugh, "Cockteaser," in *Pop Out: Queer Warhol* (Durham, N.C.: Duke University Press, 1996), 52.

6   It should be clear that this treatment of Warhol's cinema cannot claim to be an exhaustive one, and anyone familiar with his films will immediately be disappointed that several key texts are not treated here, most obviously *Chelsea Girls, The Loves of Ondine,* and *I, a Man.*

7   Even as his films grew longer and achieved greater narrative sophistication, Warhol was dedicated to the power of the aleatory. Despite the use of scripts by Ron Tavel for projects such as *Kitchen,* he insisted on keeping "bad" takes in the finished project—the first reel of *Poor Little Rich Girl,* for example, is severely (and by all accounts, inadvertently) unfocused, and the blurred image of Edie Sedgwick and accompanying sound of her going about talking on the phone and putting on her makeup heightens the appeal of finally registering, in the second reel, a clearer visual icon of what has just previously been prohibited from sight. I have tried to discover a word that names the importance of the coincidence in Warhol's work, and offer the neologism "aleation."

8   *Tape Recording* 12, no. 5 (September–October 1965): 19. Warhol's interest in video expanded later in his life in the 1970s and 1980s with his work in TV; his interest in video in the 1960s was probably limited by the inability to reach the audience that underground film was then garnering. The limitations of video as a vehicle for dissemination were no doubt felt as an effect of video's narrow access and comparative expense— the home video recorder was another two decades away.

9   The amateur status of his films abides as a fixture of the question of his long-

term artistic worth, as the legal cases surrounding the monetary value of the portion of Warhol's nonpersonal effects (i.e., his artwork) was centered on the question of how to appraise his photographs. The Warhol Foundation, the inheriting legal body on which was bestowed the artist's personal holdings of his own art, sought to have Warhol's 66,000 photographs deemed as archival materials, and thereby holding no particular value, whereas the opposing parties of Frederick W. Hughes and Edward W. Hayes, who stood to garner 2 percent of the value of the estate, sought to have them established as works of art, a difference between the estate being valued at $95 million by the foundation and $708 million by Hughes and Hayes, the latter party ultimately winning. See Paul Alexander, "The Question of Warhol's Photographs," *ARTnews*, February 1995, 100–103; and *Death and Disaster* (New York: Villard Books, 1994). The importance of this question of evaluation, and the entwined workings of monetary and artistic value, holds special prominence for the films. Are Warhol's films works of art, documents, mass-media texts? As the films will not be widely disseminated in the foreseeable future by the foundation, that question will have to be postponed.

10 As a child, Warhol played with paper dolls of stars and sent letters to Shirley Temple. David Bourdon reports that a long-standing household icon during Warhol's childhood was a signed glossy of Temple that was displayed on the living-room mantel, and he was an avid filmgoer as a child and teenager. See David Bourdon, *Warhol* (New York: Harry N. Abrams, 1989), 17.

11 Two accounts resituate Warhol's life in 1950s New York and its influence on his 1960s aesthetic, *Success Is a Job in New York* and *Pre-Pop Warhol,* both of which underscore Warhol as a member of urban gay life in the period, schooled in its playful (and often secretive) habits of reception and production.

12 Tally Brown, interview by Patrick S. Smith, *Andy Warhol's Art and Films* (Ann Arbor, Mich.: UMI Research Press, 1981), 239.

13 Camp fascination with glamour takes off from a perception of star imagery similar to that of Laura Mulvey in "Visual Pleasure and Narrative Cinema." Mulvey described the tendency of the female star to arrest, however temporarily, the narrative momentum of a Hollywood film, and her primary interest was to theorize the dynamics of patriarchal pleasure, that is, how heterosexual male spectators were positioned to gaze on the sight of the star. Interestingly, Mulvey's subsequent addendum to her essay addressed *female* (both heterosexual and lesbian) spectatorial pleasure but did not provide an account of how the male homosexual might respond to the same image. See Mulvey, "Visual Pleasure and Narrative Cinema," *Screen* 16, no. 3 (autumn 1975), and "Afterthoughts on 'Visual Pleasure and Narrative Cinema' Inspired by *Duel in the Sun,"* *Framework* 6, nos. 15–17 (1981).

14 Richard Dyer, "Charisma," in *Stars: Industry of Desire,* ed. Christine Gledhill (London: Routledge, 1991), 59.

15 The work demanded to achieve glamour, we should remember, is highly regimented and coordinated, and frequently in Hollywood performed by women.

Although some of this labor is rendered glamorous in itself (as in accounts of Cecil Beaton's work, for example), more often it has taken the form of sweatshop labor. See Elizabeth Nielsen, "Handmaidens of the Glamour Culture: Costumers in the Hollywood Studio System," in *Fabrications: Costume and the Female Body*, ed. Jane Gaines and Charlotte Herzog (New York: Routledge, 1990), 160–79.

16 Callie Angell, *The Films of Andy Warhol, Part 2* (New York: Whitney Museum of American Art, 1994), 16.

17 The final portions of Warhol's *POPism: The Warhol Sixties* on the years of 1968 and 1969 report the failed efforts of Factory figures such as Candy Darling and Jackie Curtis to make Hollywood careers for themselves. Not so clear are Warhol's own desires in fact to make studio pictures—while the wish is recorded, the effort does not to appear to have been substantial. This, of course, is the period in which he was shot and hospitalized, and his convalescence put him at a substantial remove from the Factory for a period in which the talents involved dispersed to a multitude of other projects.

18 A portion of *POPism* in which Warhol describes Truman Capote's legendary 1966 Black and White Ball, given in honor of *Washington Post* publisher Katherine Graham at the Plaza Hotel, describes a different relation to celebrity than one customarily discovers in accounts of the period. Here Warhol tells of attending the party with art curator Henry Geldzahler and of being so intimidated by the mass of political, artistic, and "social" talent in attendance that he could only stand back and disappear: "It was so strange, I thought: you get to the point in life where you're actually invited to the party of parties—the one people all over the world were trying desperately to get invited to—and it *still* didn't guarantee that you wouldn't feel like a complete dud! I wondered if anybody ever achieves an attitude where nothing and nobody can ever intimidate them." See *POPism*, 196.

19 Patrick S. Smith, *Andy Warhol's Art and Films* (Ann Arbor, Mich.: UMI Research Press, 1986), 140.

20 Quoted in Smith, 141.

21 I am grateful to Callie Angell of the Warhol Film Project for making me aware of *Paul Swan*.

22 Because different films bearing the title *Haircut* have emerged, the Andy Warhol Film Project has numbered them, beginning with the version that most critics seem to have seen, *Haircut (No. 1)*. There is some disagreement about the actors who appear in this vehicle; Ron Tavel suggests that a young actor named Philip Fagan seems to have been involved, but Callie Angell identifies the men as Freddy Herko, Billy Name, John Daley, and James Waring. The difference, of course, might be explained by the different versions that seem to have been shot. Here, though, I am discussing what is now agreed on as *Haircut (No. 1)*. For Tavel's oral history of the Factory, see Smith, 480–84.

23 Freddy Herko, one of the stars of *Haircut (No. 1)* was an important figure for Warhol in his transition to the underground scene in New York; Herko brought

many of the "A-men" (amphetamine users) to the early Factory and put Warhol in touch with many of the figures who would populate the Factory. Warhol later wrote, "The people I loved were the ones like Freddy, the leftovers of show business, turned down at auditions all over town. They couldn't do something more than once, but their one time was better than anyone else's. They had star quality, but no star ego—they didn't know how to push themselves. They were too gifted to lead 'regular lives,' but they were also too unsure of themselves to ever become real professionals" (Warhol, *POPism,* 56.)

24 Koch, 57.

25 Gregory Battcock, "Four Films by Andy Warhol," in *Andy Warhol: Film Factory,* ed. Michael O'Pray (London: BFI Publishing, 1989), 42.

26 Warhol, 34.

27 See, for example, Mark Francis, "The Democracy of Beauty: An Introduction to the Collections of the Andy Warhol Museum," in *The Andy Warhol Museum* (New York: Distributed Art Publishers, 1994), 93–114. Francis suggests that "Andy Warhol's work was about beauty. As a young man, he captured the lineaments of beauty in drawings of boys, feet, flowers, and shoes. He recognized a permanent beauty in the iconic images of modern life," thus universalizing Warhol into the largely undifferentiated canon of Great Art.

28 Richard Dyer, *Now You See It: Studies on Lesbian and Gay Film* (London: Routledge, 1990), 154.

29 Interview with Tally Brown, in Smith, 235.

30 David James, in *Andy Warhol: Film Factory,* 138.

31 Although numerous male homoerotic forms of representation had emerged, most notably the work of physique photographers such as Bruce of Los Angeles and the Athletic Model Guild, and the sadomasochistic drawings of Tom of Finland, cinematic renderings of the male body had not kept pace, and understandably so when we remember the larger expense and coordination involved in producing and exhibiting films.

32 Parker Tyler comments about *My Hustler* that it demonstrates how "Warhol has a most economical way with technique"; its acoustic components, according to Tyler, offer the bulk of the film's narrative information (mostly through the propositions offered to Paul), leaving the film's visual field to long periods of erotic contemplation of his body. Tyler is one of the most significant contemporaneous proponents of Warhol's cinema, and his book *Screening the Sexes* appears, in a moment of historical paradox, in 1972, soon after Warhol has ceased the labor-intensive hands-on making of film. This seems to me no small thing, because the kind of film aesthetic Tyler advocated might have shaped a different context for the reception of Warhol's films in the post-Stonewall decade, but the films by that point were seldom exhibited. See Tyler, *Screening the Sexes: Homosexuality in the Movies* (New York: Anchor, 1972), 55.

33 Dyer, *Now Your See It,* 159.

34 Koch, 84.

35 Corey K. Creekmur, "Acting like a Man: Masculine Performance in *My Darling*

Clementine," in *Out in Culture: Gay, Lesbian, and Queer Essays on Popular Culture,*
ed. Corey K. Creekmur and Alexander Doty (Durham, N.C.: Duke University
Press, 1995), 167–82.

36   Gidal, 126.

37   Dyer, *Now You See It,* 161.

38   During Warhol's lifetime, Stephen Koch and Peter Gidal offered the narrative of Warhol's failure after the late 1960s to critique popular representation,
both writing in the early 1970s. More recent accounts reiterate the claim, most
notably those of Bob Colacello and John Giorno. See Peter Gidal, *Andy Warhol, Films and Paintings: The Factory Years* (New York: Da Capo Press, 1971); Bob
Colacello, *Holy Terror: Andy Warhol Close Up* (New York: HarperCollins, 1990);
and John Giorno, *You Got to Burn to Shine* (New York: High Risk Books, 1994).

39   I am not disregarding the fact that there were numerous radical critiques of
the imbrication of conforming sexualities and capitalism in both scholarly and
activist dimensions but instead am indicating that such critiques have not flourished in the face of "rainbow" Visa cards and the forms of consumption that
one discovers at the heart of the unsatisfying articulation "gay and lesbian community."

40   Since 1982 it has been the task of the Andy Warhol Film Project to find and restore Warhol's films, many of which were lost, impounded, and censored. This
project, headed by Callie Angell of the Whitney Museum of American Art,
continues, as many of the films are unaccounted for and have not been screened
since their initial production.

41   Warhol himself understood this: the release of John Schlesinger's *Midnight Cow-
boy* in 1969 was heralded by many in the Factory as an affirmation by Hollywood
that the image of the urban hustler had percolated through to nonunderground
filmmaking. Warhol: "We were thrilled to have the attention of Hollywood—
now it was only a matter of time, we felt, before 'somebody out there' would
want to finance some of our breakthroughs instead of just sitting back and
commenting on them. I mean, we'd done *My Hustler* back in '65, and now here
Hollywood was in '67 just getting ready to shoot a movie called *Midnight Cow-
boy* . . . Paul and I read *Variety* all the time, really feeling that at last we were
part of the commercial movie business" (Warhol, *POPism,* 204.

42   Andrew Britton, *Katharine Hepburn: The Thirties and After* (London: Tyneside
Cinema, 1984), 40.

43   This continues to be a hot political issue within gay and lesbian communities.
1993's "March on Washington" and the 1994 "Stonewall 25" celebration in New
York were marked by the recurring debate about whether drag queens should
be allowed to march, portraying as they do for some voices an unseemly image
of the gay and lesbian community.

44   Andrew Britton, "FOR Interpretation: Notes against Camp," *Gay Left* (London), no. 7 (1978): 14.

45   One reads with a certain poignancy the tales of failure that dominate the lives
of old Factory regulars: Holly Woodlawn's is perhaps the most compelling ac-

count of a Factory star whose fame brought her no tangible successes after *Trash.* See Holly Woodlawn and Jeff Copeland, *A Low Life in High Heels: The Holly Woodlawn Story* (New York: St. Martin's Press, 1991).

46   Warhol, *POPism,* 44.

THREE   *"A Physical Relation between Physical Things": The World of Commodity according to Kenneth Anger*

1   In the case of Jack Smith's films, Marc Siegel has demonstrated that Smith's *Flaming Creatures* poses a challenge if read as a form of documentary about "gay" desire; Siegel argues that the polymorphous eroticism offered in Smith's cinema cannot accord with normative forms of same-sex erotic representation and in so doing was even more antagonistic to notions of propriety and normalcy. Similar to Siegel's reading of Smith's work, I want to underscore in Anger's productions how much they fail to inhabit most aesthetic or political categories, either in their moment of production or in their current critical assessments. See Marc Siegel, "Documentary That Dare/Not Speak Its Name: Jack Smith's *Flaming Creatures,"* in *Between the Sheets, in the Streets: Queer, Lesbian, Gay Documentary,* ed. Chris Holmlund and Cynthia Fuchs (Minneapolis: University of Minnesota Press, 1997).

2   Anger's fascinations bear in some measures a striking similarity to those of Andy Warhol, and the two can be apprehended as forming an important counterpairing in the history of camp filmmaking; despite their continual linkage in histories of the avant-garde and experimental forms, though, they diverged notably in the features of American film culture that they sought to make visible through their different intellectual projects. If Warhol's films focused on glamour and stardom as studio products, Kenneth Anger brings our attention to the fetishistic and often uncomfortable truths of lending the erotic imagination to the powers of mass production.

3   Emily Apter, introduction to *Fetishism as Cultural Discourse,* ed. Emily Apter and William Pietz (Ithaca: Cornell University Press, 1993), 3.

4   P. Adams Sitney, *Visionary Film: The American Avant-Garde,* 2d ed. (New York: Oxford University Press, 1979), 100.

5   Dyer, *Now Your See It,* 118.

6   I am indebted to Ryan Cook for pointing out the slowed-down motion of *Puce Moment,* making it possible that Anger undercranked the camera to achieve a langorous, dreamy quality for the film.

7   The impulse to skew the sense of proportions in *Eaux d'Artifice* is demonstrated by Anger's use of a circus dwarf to play the courtesan, the human proportions becoming even more attenuated in contrast to those of the monumental gardens. See Sitney, 103.

8   Quoted in Sitney, 125.

9   See Dick Hebdige, *Subculture: The Meaning of Style* (London: Methuen, 1979);

and Angela McRobbie, ed, *Zoot Suits and Second-Hand Dresses: An Anthology of Fashion and Music* (Boston: Unwin Hyman, 1988).

10 Anger's films have typically met with the frustrations of finding funding for alternative cinemas. The lengthy gaps of time between his films are partly explained by his attempts to finance them. *Kustom Kar Kommandos* was produced with a grant from the Ford Foundation, a source that dried up, preventing Anger from realizing the full project.

11 Hoberman, 175.

12 Indeed, the appropriation of popular music for his sound tracks would mark the film as underground in the sense of *illegal* cinema. Although Anger does not seem to have encountered any legal trouble for uncredited use of hit music, subsequent uses of music suffered at the hands of copyright law. The most recent incident would be that of Todd Haines's *Superstar,* whose use of Carpenters' music (and, to be fair, Mattel's Barbie figures) would lead to the film's withdrawal from any further public screenings.

13 Philip Core, *Camp: The Lie That Tells the Truth* (New York: Delilah Books, 1984), 18.

14 Originally published in *Film Culture,* cited in J. Hoberman and J. Rosenbaum, *Midnight Movies* (New York: Harper and Row, 1983), 58.

15 Indeed, a more succinct literary formulation of the relation between the forms of masculinity and the varying degrees of homoeroticism therein would have to wait another thirty years, in Eve Sedgwick's description of homosociality. While we might see *Scorpio Rising* as a camp gay treatment of a hyper-masculine (but not necessarily gay) subculture, this partition too easily ignores the pleasure of the film's participants in their own sexualized images. By homosociality, Sedgwick (albeit in a very different context) sought to elucidate the forms of homoeroticism that do not endanger patriarchal operations. This has made many readers, gay and nongay alike, uncomfortable. See Eve Kosofsky Sedgwick, *Between Men: Male Homosocial Desire and Literature* (New York: Columbia University Press, 1986).

16 Dyer, *Now You See It,* 128.

17 Andrew Hewitt, *Political Inversions: Homosexuality, Fascism, and the Modernist Imaginary* (Stanford, Calif.: Stanford University Press, 1996), 7.

18 Hewitt, 207.

19 Sitney, 97.

20 Anger in fact returns etymologically to the roots of glamour, writing as he does of the casting of a "glamor" in one of his films. Glamour comes to its current meanings through the idea of being a magical spell that renders its beholders helpless in the face of beauty.

21 Indeed, I would hazard that Anger's own version of black magic takes as many pages out of film history as it does from Aleister Crowley's volumes on occult lore. The character of Cesare from *The Cabinet of Dr. Caligari,* for example, figures in *Inauguration of the Pleasure Dome* alongside those of Hecate, Kali, and Pan.

22 Chauncey cites a medical researcher of 1930s gay life who quotes several gay men on the importance of the party: "Homosexuals are more interested in cocktail parties than other men [are]," and "homosexuals have an exaggerated sense about these parties. . . . They're on the go all the time." The "exaggerated sense" no doubt derived from the fact that such celebrations were among the few opportunities for gays to congregate, share their own languages, and demonstrate physical pleasure. One is reminded of Andy Warhol's comment "I have a social disease. I have to go out every night." See George Chauncey, *Gay New York: Gender, Urban Culture, and the Making of the Gay Male World, 1890–1940* (New York: Basic Books, 1994), 278–80.

23 At the "Sacred Mushroom" screening of Anger's films in New York in 1966, filmgoers were directed by the film's printed program to ingest their "magic sugar-cubes" at key moments during the screenings: the hallucinatory effect of Anger's multiple montages was to be felt not only from the film screen's array of images.

24 Dyer, *Now Your See It*, 128–29.

25 Ed Lowry, "The Appropriation of Signs in *Scorpio Rising*," *Velvet Light Trap* (summer 1983): 41.

26 Anger seems to be addressing the popular journalistic account of Hollywood, witnessed in the pages of *Photoplay, Confidential*, and other fan mags; more contemporary versions can be found in the pages of *People* and *Entertainment Weekly* (the upscale publishing venues), as well as the *Globe, Sun, Enquirer*, and *Weekly World News*.

27 Fiske's and Radway's immensely important contributions to the discussion of fandom demonstrate that fans actively shape the meanings that they derive from the objects of their fan devotions (Madonna fans, in the case of Fiske's studies, for example, and popular romance readers in the case of Radway's work) even as they encourage discursive and material limits to their participation in the creation of popular culture. But the fans whom Fiske and Radway describe are seldom called on to conceal the particular concerns that fandom allows them to express, in the way that camp allows gays to comment on mass culture without being named as perverse or dissident subjects. Nevertheless it seems to me that Fiske and Radway offer what are the sustaining questions for current work on fan culture; Fiske's analysis of the coterminous economies of fandom to those of the industry and Radway's ideological critique of the complexities of fan affective investments have suggested a variety of avenues for subsequent work on fan culture. For other readings on this topic, see Jane Feuer, *Seeing Through the Eighties: Television and Reaganism* (Durham, N.C.: Duke University Press, 1995); Henry Jenkins, *Textual Poachers: Television Fans and Participatory Culture* (New York: Routledge, 1992); and Jackie Stacey, *Star Gazing: Hollywood Cinema and Female Spectatorship* (London: Routledge, 1994).

28 Judith Mayne, *Cinema and Spectatorship* (London: Routledge, 1993), 84.

29 Mayne, 86.

30 Miriam Hansen, *Babel and Babylon: Cinema and Spectatorship* (London: Routledge, 1993), 84.

31 Although she does not expand on this insight, Hansen does offer that Valentino seems to have had a gay following, her primary form of evidence residing in Anger's tribute to the star in *Hollywood Babylon*. The citation of Anger does not so much demonstrate that a significant gay cult of Valentino existed during the star's ascendancy as much as it forms a moment through which Anger is typically referenced as an ethnographic resource. Nevertheless Hansen implies an important affinity between gay camp fandom and female fans' culting of Valentino, inasmuch as they offer readings of a star contrary to what might be expected.

32 Mayne, 166.

33 The question of gay discourses as having only inhabited the margins of representation, that is, the question of the metaphors of invisibility, becomes increasingly important for gay theory and history. Robert C. Corber, in fact, argues that invisibility was not the problem for gay writers such as Gore Vidal, Tennessee Williams, and James Baldwin, but that their writings failed to coincide and indeed antagonized all varieties of orthodox politics—left and right—of the fifties. See Robert C. Corber, *Homosexuality in Cold War America: Resistance and the Crisis of Masculinity* (Durham, N.C.: Duke University Press, 1997).

34 Kenneth Anger, *Hollywood Babylone* (Paris: J. J. Pauvert, 1959), 8; translation mine.

35 Kenneth Anger, *Hollywood Babylon* (New York: Bell Publishing, 1975), 266.

36 Gossip forms an important part of the experience of alterity; yet gossip in its relations to everyday life, popular culture, and representation has been little theorized or historicized. Despite the obvious intractability of the topic in its capacity to be verified—it is hard to "prove" gossip, and that's indeed the point—the subject deserves greater attention. For two considerably different feminist treatments of the subject, see Patricia Mellencamp, *High Anxiety: Catastrophe, Scandal, Age, and Comedy* (Bloomington: Indiana University Press, 1990); and Patricia Meyer Spacks, *Gossip* (Chicago: University of Chicago Press, 1985).

37 The publishing history of the *Hollywood Babylon* volumes is as labyrinthine as anything described in their own pages. The first edition appeared in France in 1959, and an English version appeared in 1965. By the mid-1960s, some of the recent events to which Anger had drawn his readers' attention in the first edition had lost their immediacy and were deleted. Further, Anger revised the volume extensively in each of its subsequent printings, and although the tone and argument of the book remain largely intact, many of the illustrations that contained graphic nudity were omitted for the American edition, which was issued in softcover. When *Hollywood Babylon II* was published in 1984, it contained several portions from the first French edition that American readers had never seen before in combination with new materials. As with his film work, Anger's projects can seldom be said to be completed, returning as he does to

rework older materials. A photo of Marlon Brando in *Hollywood Babylon II* is captioned "Why is he laughing? He knows that I can't print the indiscreet photo of *him*" (284–85), suggesting the promise of perhaps a third volume.

38 Anger, *Hollywood Babylone,* 10.

39 The similarity between Anger's use of photographs and illustrations to abet the reader's critical powers and those offered by way of leftist critique is striking. John Berger, for example, structures *Ways of Seeing* as a pedagogical exercise in which the reader is invited to analyze uncaptioned reproductions of Western figure painting through critical terms of property, class, and gender difference, forging a dialectic of interpretation through written text and photoreproduction. Similarly, Anger provides his reader with star photographs whose meanings become unstable when analyzed in the spirit of his commentary, for we can consider how even Hollywood's own official discourses host a variety of interpretations and responses. See John Berger, *Ways of Seeing* (London: British Broadcasting Corporation/Penguin Books, 1977).

40 For a compendium of Hollywood gossip whose legitimacy is authorized by the author's claim to gay identity, see Boze Hadleigh's *Hollywood Babble-On,* which sustains long-standing gossip about stars. Indeed, the volume's punning title signals its debt to Anger as integral to gay commentary on Hollywood. Hadleigh's book purports simply to be quoting stars as they gossip about each other, thus attempting to validate the authenticity of the material and claiming truth value because such gossip is said to have its origins within Hollywood. See Hadleigh, *Hollywood Babble-On: Stars Gossip about Other Stars* (New York: Birch Lane Press, 1994). Steven Cohan's work on Judy Garland listservs and Web sites suggests in fact that fans do not necessarily seek adjudication from Hollywood for what can deemed proper and improper gossip; rather, fans negotiate the truth value of every claim about a star in relation to the body of gossip *and* official discourses, sometimes preferring alternate readings of a star over the available official ones. See Steven Cohan, "The Judy Thing Revisited: Garland Fandom on the Web," in *Key Frames: Popular Cinema and Cultural Studies,* ed. Matthew Tinkcom and Amy Villarejo (London: Routledge, 2001).

41 Kenneth Anger, *Hollywood Babylon* (Phoenix, Ariz.: Associated Professional Services, 1965), 21.

42 I call attention to the effects of labeling such subjects as "marginal" (that is, not central to Hollywood production) because gay viewers may not have been explicitly addressed as the industry's intended audience, but through gossip and anecdotal history insert themselves into the circulation of star imagery.

43 I am here momentarily cleaving sexuality from other illicit practices, such as bootleg alcohol and suicides, although virtually every "forbidden" subject intersects with another at some moment in *Babylon;* alcoholics have affairs, stars emerge from unhappy alliances to take their lives, and so forth.

44 *Hollywood Babylon* (1965), 217. For an account of West's fascination as sexualized female star icon and her status as a camp feminist emblem, see Pamela Robert-

son, *Guilty Pleasures: Feminist Camp from Mae West to Madonna* (Durham, N.C.: Duke University Press, 1996).

FOUR *"Beyond the Critics' Reach": John Waters and the Trash Aesthetic*

1 This tendency situates Waters's works in relation to feminist film criticism on the Hollywood melodrama and to the functions of what critic Pamela Robertson has identified as "feminist camp," a phenomenon quite distinct from queer male camp, but related to it through the excessive performative aspects of the female film star.

2 While the nomination of "trash aesthetics" seems hardly to be of Waters's invention, recent scholarly work on the topic has largely neglected his contributions to the topic. *Trash Aesthetics: Popular Culture and Its Audience,* eds. Deborah Cartmell, I.Q. Hunter, Heidi Kaye, and Imelda Whelehan (London: Pluto Press, 1997), focuses on the variety of subcultural embrace around nonmainstream popular forms but neglects Waters as a central intellectual figure in the dissemination of trash.

3 The epigraphs following the section title are quoted from John Waters, *Shock Value* (New York: Dell, 1981), 214; and Eddie Dean, "Tits a Living," *Washington City Paper,* 7 April 1995, 34.

4 Allison Graham, "Journey to the Center of the Fifties: The Cult of Banality," in *The Cult Film Experience: Beyond All Reason,* ed. J. P. Telotte (Austin: University of Texas Press, 1991).

5 Bruce Kawin, "After Midnight," in *The Cult Film Experience: Beyond All Reason,* ed. J. P. Telote (Austin: University of Texas Press, 1991), 25.

6 A. Graham, 117.

7 This is achieved by a feat of gender mobility: in a scene after Dawn's escape from the parental household, Dawn is raped and impregnated. Divine plays both Dawn and the man who attacks her, leading to Divine's later claims that she was "the only star who ever fucked herself." See Bernard Jay, *Not Simply Divine: Beneath the Makeup, above the Heels, and behind the Scenes with a Cult Superstar* (New York: Fireside Books, 1993), 35.

8 At least, the earliest of his films available. *Hag in a Black Leather Jacket* (1964), *Roman Candles* (1966), and *Eat Your Makeup* (1967) have never been made available by the director. Even so, descriptions of them suggest their narrative structures. For a Waters filmography, see John G. Ives, *John Waters* (New York: Thunder's Mouth Press, 1992).

9 Jacqueline Rose, *Sexuality in the Field of Vision* (London: Verso Books, 1986), 208.

10 *Polyester* was Waters's first attempt at a more mainstream vehicle, having been underwritten by New Line Cinema with a budget of $300,000 and shot in 35 mm, as opposed to Waters's smaller-budgeted efforts executed in the 16-mm format.

11 Waters enforced the film's olfactory obsession through the use of scratch-and-

sniff cards distributed to audience members before the screening; this feature allowed the film to be offered as part of the innovation "Odorama." Signaled at various moments by the appearance of flashing numbers in the frame, viewers then scraped their card to reveal particular smells. Part of the shock of this gimmick was Waters's use of off-screen space to situate both Francine and the audience to smell before they gazed, leading to the substitution of more agreeable smells (roses, perfume) with vile ones: old tennis shoes, gasoline, flatulence. Yet another instance of Waters's ability to exploit cheap media, in this case a marketing tactic like those of William Castle, to garner his films' distinction from other cinematic fare.

12 Ives, 170.

13 Gaylyn Studlar, "Midnight S/Excess: Cult Configurations of 'Femininity' and the Perverse," in *The Cult Film Experience: Beyond All Reason* (Austin: University of Texas Press, 1991), 145.

14 Eve Kosofsky Sedgwick and Michael Moon, "Divinity: A Dossier, a Performance Piece, a Little-Understood Emotion," in *Tendencies* (Durham, N.C.: Duke University Press, 1993), 220.

15 Pamela Robertson, " 'The Kinda Comedy That Imitates Me': Mae West's Identification with the Feminist Camp," in *Camp Grounds: Style and Homosexuality,* ed. David Bergman (Amherst: University of Massachusetts Press, 1993), 156.

16 Consider: in Ophul's *Letter from an Unknown Woman,* the female protagonist is exiled from her bourgeois Viennese family because of her desire for the exotic pianist, Stefan. She bears a child out of wedlock and attempts to restore herself to the phallic economy of the family by marrying another man, eventually discovering that the perverse desire for Stefan, encoded through aural pleasure, cannot be subsumed to her loveless marriage. Finally, she is punished through both the loss of her child and her own eventual death. Equally, Dawn Davenport eventually succumbs to the law of the father (in this case, embodied in the state) for her aggressive femininity, figured in the nightclub act where she leaps onto a trampoline and fires a gun into the crowd.

17 Divine's attempts to secure parts in non-Waters vehicles came with the insight that she would have to prove herself capable of other roles; she needed to insist that Divine, the heroine of Waters's films, should be distinguished from Divine, the star. Before her death on 7 March 1988, Bernard Jay records Divine as having commented on the complexity of her star image as a problem for casting: "Do you mean the character Divine or the person Divine? There's the Divine you're talking to now and there's the character Divine, which is just something I do to make my living. She doesn't really exist at all." Protests that Divine was a fictional invention notwithstanding, Harris Glenn Milstead (Divine's birth name) understood all too well that Divine had become a star, one whose power he struggled against to win other roles, such as the bit part in the 1985 Alan Rudolph film *Trouble in Mind.* See Jay, 3.

18 Sutphin (Turner) attacks Hearst's character for a violation of taste codes in which she has worn white shoes out of season.

19   Waters suggests that the stars with whom he is most interested in working are Hollywood's best-known figures, such as Meryl Streep and Jodie Foster. Interestingly, he mentions none of the most successful male box office stars, and I would take this to indicate his recurrent fascination with the hallmarks of female stardom and femininity. Further, he does not record the fact that his later films have become platforms for younger talent to augment their careers, Ricki Lake and Johnny Depp figuring as two marketable talents whose careers were enhanced by their appearances in Waters films. See Ann Magnuson, "Moveable Bloodfeast: An Interview with John Waters," *Paper Magazine* June 1994, 32–36, for Waters discussing the casting of his future projects.

20   Waters, *Shock Valve,* 128. And if the particular face at hand is not striking enough, Waters mandates his chief makeup artist, Van Smith, to apply a variety of bad hair, blemishes, scars, and prosthetic devices in order to render it so. Here the extra-added labors of camp work at odds with the inventions of Hollywood glamour production.

21   Renée R. Curry, "To Star Is to Mean: The Casting of John Waters's *Hairspray,*" in *Cultural Power, Cultural Literacy: Selected Papers from the 14th Florida State University Conference on Literature and Film,* ed Bonnie Braendlin (Tallahassee: Florida State University Press, 1991), 168.

22   1950s scare impresario William Castle, innovator of such technologies as "the Tingler" and given to stationing women dressed as nurses outside his cinemas, as "insurance against patrons dying of fright," has been an important influence on Waters's sense of cheap publicity. For example, Waters suggests that young directors might "try variations of the movie-star look-alike contests, but instead of intimidating audiences by forcing them to imitate such impossible classics as Marilyn Monroe or James Dean, pick someone as unremarkable as Jill Clayburgh and let everybody win. Go for community support!" See John Waters, "Whatever Happened to Showmanship?" in *American Film: Magazine of the Film and Television Arts* 9, no. 3 (1983): 58.

23   In this, Waters anticipated the proliferation of tabloid culture as a domain for reporting on criminality as stardom. Compare, for example, the long-standing fascination with outlaws to be found in *Mondo Trasho, Pink Flamingos,* and *Serial Mom* with Oliver Stone's 1994 release *Natural Born Killers.* Where Waters depicts a comic and pleasurable lawlessness within the everyday (which takes numerous forms, from outrageous makeup to cannibalism), Stone panics that the soul of American culture has been corrupted by *Hard Copy* and *Current Affair.* The difference between the two framings of criminality suggests an interest in shocking a viewer with the knowledge that outlaws already inhabit the social (Waters) as opposed to proposing an extension of the "lock 'em up" ethos that pervades current political commentary (Stone).

24   Read across her star performances, though, Turner's status as a murdering woman was in some ways already allowed for in her first and arguably her most celebrated performance, that of the femme fatale in Lawrence Kasdan's 1981 retro-noir vehicle *Body Heat.*

25 Adam Gopnik, "The Nauman Principle: A Provocateur's Body of Work at MOMA," *New Yorker,* 27 March 1995, 103. Gopnik reviews the work of contemporary artist Bruce Nauman, one of the most prominent heirs to pop art; Nauman lives and works in New Mexico, prompting Gopnik's comments about Nauman's status inside and outside of the New York art world.

26 Darren Tofts, "The Terrain of the Unspeakable: *Pink Flamingos* and the Culture of Trash," *Meanjin* 51, no. 4 (summer 1992): 816.

27 Tofts, 817.

28 Timothy Corrigan, *A Cinema without Walls: Movies and Culture after Vietnam* (New Brunswick, N.J.: Rutgers University Press, 1991), 110.

29 As Waters himself notes, *Hairspray* was not allowed to be shown on commercial airline flights, perhaps the most tamed of screening venues for contemporary film.

30 Barbara Klinger, "Mass Camp and the Old Hollywood Melodrama Today," in *Melodrama and Meaning: History, Culture, and the Films of Douglas Sirk* (Bloomington: Indiana University Press, 1994), 154.

31 Quoted in Ives, 74.

BIBLIOGRAPHY

Alexander, Paul. *Death and Disaster*. New York: Villard Books, 1994.

——. "The Question of Warhol's Photographs." *ARTnews,* February 1995, 100–103.

Altman, Rick. *The American Film Musical*. Bloomington: Indiana University Press, 1987.

Angell, Callie. *The Films of Andy Warhol, Part 2*. New York: Whitney Museum of American Art, 1994.

Anger, Kenneth. *Hollywood Babylone*. Paris: J. J. Pauvert, 1959.

——. *Hollywood Babylon*. Phoenix, Ariz.: Associated Professional Services, 1965.

——. *Hollywood Babylon*. New York: Bell Publishing, 1975.

——. *Hollywood Babylon II*. New York: Dutton, 1984. N.Y.

Apter, Emily, and William Pietz, eds. *Fetishism as Cultural Discourse*. Ithaca, N.Y.: Cornell University Press, 1993.

Arendt, Hannah. *The Human Condition*. Chicago: University of Chicago Press, 1958.

Battcock, Gregory. "Four Films by Andy Warhol." In *Andy Warhol: Film Factory,* ed. Michael O'Pray. London: BFI Publishing, 1989.

Berger, John. *Ways of Seeing*. London: British Broadcasting Corporation/Penguin Books, 1977.

Berlant, Lauren. "National Brands/National Body: *Imitation of Life*." In *Comparative American Identities: Race, Sex, and Nationality in the Modern Text,* ed. Hortense Spillers. New York: Routledge, 1991.

Bordwell, David, Janet Staiger, and Kristin Thompson. *The Classical Hollywood Cinema: Film Style and Mode of Production to 1960*. New York: Columbia University Press, 1985.

Bourdieu, Pierre. *Distinction: A Social Critique of the Judgement of Taste*. London: Routledge, 1979.

Bourdon, David. *Warhol*. New York: Harry N. Abrams, 1989.

Britton, Andrew. "FOR Interpretation: Notes against Camp." *Gay Left* (London), no. 7 (1978).

——. *Katharine Hepburn: The Thirties and After*. London: Tyneside Cinema, 1984.

Bürger, Peter. *Theory of the Avant-Garde*. Trans. Michael Shaw. Minneapolis: University of Minnesota Press, 1984.

Cartmel, Deborah, I. Q. Hunter, Heidi Kaye, and Imelda Whelehan, eds. *Trash Aesthetics: Popular Culture and Its Audience*. London: Pluto Press, 1997.

Caspar, Joseph Andrew. *Stanley Donen*. Metuchen, N.J.: Scarecrow Press, 1983.

Chase, John. *Exterior Decoration: Hollywood's Inside-Out Houses*. Los Angeles: Hennessey and Ingalls, 1982.

Chauncey, George. *Gay New York: Gender, Urban Culture, and the Making of the Gay Male World, 1890–1940*. New York: Basic Books, 1994.

Chumo, Peter N., II. "Dance, Flexibility, and the Renewal of Genre in *Singin' in the Rain*." *Cinema Journal* 36, no. 1, (fall 1996): 39–54.

Clark, Danae. *Negotiating Hollywood: The Cultural Politics of Actors' Labor*. Minneapolis: University of Minnesota Press, 1995.

Cleto, Fabio, ed. *Camp: Queer Aesthetics and the Performing Subject: A Reader*. Edinburgh: Edinburgh University Press, 1999.

Cohan, Steven. "'Feminizing' the Song-and-Dance Man." In *Screening the Male: Exploring Masculinities in Hollywood Cinema*, ed. Steven Cohan and Ina Rae Hark. New York: Routledge, 1993.

———. "The Judy Thing Revisited: Garland Fandom on the Web." In *Key Frames: Popular Cinema and Cultural Studies*, ed. Matthew Tinkcom and Amy Villarejo. London: Routledge, 2001.

Colacello, Bob. *Holy Terror: Andy Warhol Close Up*. New York: HarperCollins, 1990.

Corber, Robert J. *Homosexuality in Cold War America: Resistance and the Crisis of Masculinity*. Durham, N.C.: Duke University Press, 1997.

Core, Philip. *Camp: The Lie That Tells the Truth*. New York: Delilah Books, 1984.

Corrigan, Timothy. *A Cinema without Walls: Movies and Culture after Vietnam*. New Brunswick, N.J.: Rutgers University Press, 1991.

Creekmur, Corey K. "Acting like a Man: Masculine Performance in *My Darling Clementine*." In *Out in Culture: Gay, Lesbian, and Queer Essays on Popular Culture*, ed. Corey K. Creekmur and Alexander Doty. Durham, N.C.: Duke University Press, 1995.

Curry, Renée R. "To Star Is to Mean: The Casting of John Waters's *Hairspray*." In *Cultural Power, Cultural Literacy: Selected Papers from the 14th Florida State University Conference on Literature and Film*, ed. Bonnie Braendlin. Tallahassee: Florida State University Press, 1991.

Dean, Eddie. "Tits a Living." *Washington City Paper*, 7 April 1995, 34.

DeSalvo, Donna M. *"Success Is a Job in New York": The Early Art and Business of Andy Warhol*. Pittsburgh, Pa.: Carnegie Museum of Art, 1989.

Dyer, Richard. *Heavenly Bodies: Film Stars and Society*. New York: St. Martin's Press, 1986.

———. *Now You See It: Studies on Lesbian and Gay Film*. London: Routledge, 1990.

———. *Stars: Industry of Desire*. Ed. Christine Gledhill. London: Routledge, 1991.

———. "Entertainment and Utopia." In *The Cultural Studies Reader*, ed. Simon During. 2d ed. London: Routledge, 1999.

Enzensberger, Hans Magnus. "Constituents of a Theory of Media." In *Electronic Culture: Technology and Visual Representation,* ed. Timothy Druckrey. New York: Aperture Foundation Books, 1996 .

Fehr, Richard, and Frederick G. Vogel. *Lullabies of Hollywood: Movie Music and the Movie Musical, 1915–1992.* Jefferson, N.C.: McFarland, 1993.

Feuer, Jane. *The Hollywood Musical.* 2d ed. London: BFI Books, 1993.

———. *Seeing Through the Eighties: Television and Reaganism.* Durham, N.C.: Duke University Press, 1995.

Finch, Christopher. *Rainbow: The Stormy Life of Judy Garland.* New York: Grosset and Dunlap, 1975.

Fish, Stanley. *Is There a Text in This Class? The Authority of Interpretive Communities.* Cambridge: Harvard University Press, 1980.

Fiske, John. *Media Matters: Everyday Culture and Political Change.* Minneapolis: University of Minnesota Press, 1996.

Fordin, Hugh. *The Movies' Greatest Musicals: Produced in Hollywood USA by the Freed Unit.* New York: Frederick Ungar, 1975.

Francis, Mark. "The Democracy of Beauty: An Introduction to the Collections of the Andy Warhol Museum." In *The Andy Warhol Museum.* New York: Distributed Art Publishers, 1994.

Frank, Marcie."The Critic as Performance Artist: Susan Sontag's Writing and Gay Cultures." In *Camp Grounds: Style and Homosexuality,* ed. David Bergman. Amherst: University of Massachusetts Press, 1993.

Gans, Herbert J. *Popular Culture and High Culture: An Analysis and Evaluation of Taste.* New York: Basic Books, 1974.

Gidal, Peter. *Andy Warhol, Films and Paintings: The Factory Years.* New York: Da Capo Press, 1971.

Giorno, John. *You Got to Burn to Shine.* New York: High Risk Books, 1994.

Gopnik, Adam. "The Nauman Principle: A Provocateur's Body of Work at MOMA." *New Yorker,* 27 March 1995.

Gornick, Vivian. "It's a Queer Hand That Stokes the Campfire." *Village Voice,* 7 April 1966.

Graham, Allison. "Journey to the Center of the Fifties: The Cult of Banality." In *The Cult Film Experience: Beyond All Reason,* ed. J. P. Telotte. Austin: University of Texas Press, 1991.

Graham, Paula. "Girl's Camp? The Politics of Parody." In *Immortal, Invisible: Lesbians and the Moving Image,* ed. Tamsin Wilton. London: Routledge, 1995.

Greenberg, Clement. *Art and Culture: Critical Essays.* Boston: Unwin Hyman, 1973.

Hansen, Miriam. *Babel and Babylon: Cinema and Spectatorship.* London: Routledge, 1993.

Harvey, Stephen. *Directed by Vincente Minnelli.* New York: Harper and Row, 1989.

Hebdige, Dick. *Subculture: The Meaning of Style.* London: Methuen, 1979.

Hewitt, Andrew. *Political Inversions: Homosexuality, Fascism, and the Modernist Imaginary.* Palo Alto, Calif.: Stanford University Press, 1996.

Hoberman, J. *Vulgar Modernism: Writing on Movies and Other Media.* Philadelphia, Pa.: Temple University Press, 1991.

Hoberman, J., and J. Rosenbaum. *Midnight Movies.* New York: Harper and Row, 1983.

Horkheimer, Max, and Theodor W. Adorno. *Dialectic of Enlightenment.* New York: Continuum Publishing, 1972.

Howard, Jean. *Hollywood: A Photo Memoir.* New York: Harry N. Abrams, 1989.

Huyssen, Andreas. *After the Great Divide: Modernism, Mass Culture, Postmodernism.* Bloomington: Indiana University Press, 1986.

Ives, John G. *John Waters.* New York: Thunder's Mouth Press, 1992.

James, David. "The Producer as Author." In *Andy Warhol: Film Factory.* London, BFI, 1990.

Jauss, Hans Robert. *Toward an Aesthetic of Reception.* Trans. Timothy Bahti. Minneapolis: University of Minnesota Press, 1982.

Jay, Bernard. *Not Simply Divine: Beneath the Makeup, above the Heels, and behind the Scenes with a Cult Superstar.* New York: Fireside Books, 1993.

Jenkins, Henry. *Textual Poachers: Television Fans and Participatory Culture.* New York: Routledge, 1992.

Kawin, Bruce. "After Midnight." In *The Cult Film Experience: Beyond All Reason,* ed. J. P. Telotte. Austin: University of Texas Press, 1991.

Klinger, Barbara. *Melodrama and Meaning: History, Culture, and the Films of Douglas Sirk.* Bloomington: Indiana University Press, 1994.

Koch, Stephen. *Stargazer: Andy Warhol's World and His Films.* New York: Praeger, 1973.

Kornbluth, Jesse. *Pre-Pop Warhol.* New York: Random House, 1988.

Leff, Leonard. "'Come On Home with Me': 42nd Street and the Gay Male World 1930s." *Cinema Journal* 39, no. 1 (fall 1999): 3–22.

Lowry, Ed. "Cinema Texas Program Notes: *Yolanda and the Thief.*" *Cinema Texas Program Notes* 12, no. 4 (1978): 64.

——. "The Appropriation of Signs in *Scorpio Rising.*" *Velvet Light Trap* (summer 1983).

Magnuson, Ann. "Moveable Bloodfeast: An Interview with John Waters." *Paper Magazine,* June 1994.

Marx, Karl. *The Grundrisse.* Ed. and trans. David McLellan. New York: Harper and Row, 1972.

——. *Capital.* Vol. 1. Trans. Ben Fowkes. London: Penguin, 1976.

——. "Economic and Philosophic Manuscripts of 1844." In *A Marx-Engels Reader,* ed. Robert C. Tucker. New York: W. W. Norton, 1978.

Mayne, Judith. *Cinema and Spectatorship.* London: Routledge, 1993.

——. *Directed by Dorothy Arzner.* Bloomington: Indiana University Press, 1994.

McRobbie, Angela, ed. *Zoot Suits and Second-Hand Dresses: An Anthology of Fashion and Music.* Boston: Unwin Hyman, 1988.

Mellencamp, Patricia. *High Anxiety: Catastrophe, Scandal, Age, and Comedy.* Bloomington: Indiana University Press, 1990.

Meyer, Moe, ed. *The Politics and Poetics of Camp.* London: Routledge, 1994.

Miller, D. A. "Sontag's Urbanity." *October* 49 (1989).

Minnelli, Vincente. "Vincente Minnelli on Vincente Minnelli." *Film Quarterly* 12, no. 2 (winter 1958).

Minnelli, Vincente, and Hector Acre. *I Remember It Well*. Garden City, N.Y.: Doubleday, 1974.

Mulvey, Laura. "Visual Pleasure and Narrative Cinema." *Screen* 16, no. 3 (autumn 1975).

———. "Afterthoughts on 'Visual Pleasure and Narrative Cinema' Inspired by *Duel in the Sun.*" *Framework* 6, nos. 15–17 (1981).

Naremore, James. *The Films of Vincente Minnelli*. Cambridge: Cambridge University Press, 1993.

Nielsen, Elizabeth. "Handmaidens of the Glamour Culture: Costumers in the Hollywood Studio System." In *Fabrications: Costume and the Female Body*, ed. Jane Gaines and Charlotte Herzog. New York: Routledge, 1990.

Radway, Janice A. *Reading the Romance: Women, Patriarchy, and Popular Literature*. Chapel Hill: University of North Carolina Press, 1991.

Robertson, Pamela. *Guilty Pleasures: Feminist Camp from Mae West to Madonna*. Durham, N.C.: Duke University Press, 1996.

Rose, Jacqueline. *Sexuality in the Field of Vision*. London: Verso Books, 1986.

Ross, Andrew. *No Respect: Intellectuals and Popular Culture*. London: Routledge, 1989.

Rubin, Martin. *Showstoppers: Busby Berkeley and the Tradition of the Spectacle*. New York: Columbia University Press, 1993.

Schatz, Thomas. *The Genius of the System: Hollywood Filmmaking in the Studio Era*. New York: Pantheon Books, 1988.

Sedgwick, Eve Kosofsky. *Between Men: Male Homosocial Desire and Literature*. New York: Columbia University Press, 1986.

———. *The Epistemology of the Closet*. Berkeley: University of California Press, 1990.

Sedgwick, Eve Kosofsky, and Michael Moon, "Divinity: A Dossier, a Performance Piece, a Little-Understood Emotion." In *Tendencies*. Durham, N.C.: Duke University Press, 1993.

Shipman, David. *Judy Garland*. London: Fourth Estate Press, 1992.

Siegel, Marc. "Documentary That Dare/Not Speak Its Name: Jack Smith's *Flaming Creatures.*" In *Between the Sheets, in the Streets: Queer, Lesbian, Gay Documentary*, ed. Chris Holmlund and Cynthia Fuchs. Minneapolis: University of Minnesota Press, 1997.

Sinfield, Alan. *The Wilde Century: Effeminacy, Oscar Wilde, and the Queer Moment*. New York: Columbia University Press, 1994.

Sitney, P. Adams. *Visionary Film: The American Avant-Garde*. 2d ed. New York: Oxford University Press, 1979.

Smith, Patrick S. *Andy Warhol's Art and Films*. Ann Arbor, Mich.: UMI Research Press, 1981.

Sontag, Susan. *A Susan Sontag Reader*. New York: Viking, 1983.

Spacks, Patricia Meyer. *Gossip*. Chicago: University of Chicago Press, 1985.

Spivak, Gayatri Chakravorty. *In Other Worlds: Essays on Cultural Politics*. New York: Routledge, 1988.

Stacey, Jackie. *Star Gazing: Hollywood Cinema and Female Spectatorship.* London: Routledge, 1994.

Studlar, Gaylyn. "Midnight S/Excess: Cult Configurations of 'Femininity' and the Perverse." In *The Cult Film Experience: Beyond All Reason.* Austin: University of Texas Press, 1991.

Tape Recording 12, no. 5 (September–October 1965).

Tofts, Darren. "The Terrain of the Unspeakable: *Pink Flamingos* and the Culture of Trash." *Meanjin* 51, no. 4 (1992): 314–22.

Tyler, Parker. *Screening the Sexes: Homosexuality in the Movies.* New York: Anchor, 1972.

Warhol, Andy. *The Philosophy of Andy Warhol: From A to B and Back Again.* New York: Harcourt Brace Jovanovich, 1975.

Warhol, Andy, and Pat Hacket. *POPism: The Warhol '60s.* New York: Harcourt Brace Jovanovich, 1980.

Waters, John. "Whatever Happened to Showmanship?" *American Film: Magazine of the Film and Television Arts* 9, no. 3 (1983): 58–60.

———. *Shock Value.* New York: Dell, 1981.

Waugh, Thomas. "Cockteaser." In *Pop Out: Queer Warhol,* ed. Jennifer Doyle, Jonathan Flatley, and José Esteban Muñoz. Durham, N.C.: Duke University Press, 1996.

Woodlawn, Holly, and Jeff Copeland. *A Low Life in High Heels: The Holly Woodlawn Story.* New York: St. Martin's Press, 1991.

INDEX

MATTHEW TINKCOM is Assistant Professor of English and
Communication, Culture, and Technology at
Georgetown University.

Library of Congress Cataloging-in-Publication Data
Tinkcom, Matthew.
Working like a homosexual : camp, capital,
cinema / Matthew Tinkcom.
p. cm. — (Series Q)
Includes bibliographical references and index.
ISBN 0-8223-2862-3 (cloth : alk. paper)
ISBN 0-8223-2889-5 (pbk. : alk. paper)
1. Homosexuality and motion pictures.
2. Gay motion picture producers and directors—
United States—Biography.   I. Title.   II. Series.
PN1995.9.H55 T56   2002
791.43′653—dc21   2001054302